This book may be kept
        FOURTEEN DAY
A fine of TWO CEN

# CHRISTIAN THEOLOGY

## An Ecumenical Approach

*By the Same Author*

THE PHILOSOPHY OF THE ABBÉ BAUTAIN

THEISM AND THE MODERN MOOD

A PSYCHOLOGICAL APPROACH TO THEOLOGY

THEISM AND THE SCIENTIFIC SPIRIT

REALISTIC THEOLOGY

GOD (HAZEN BOOK)

CONTEMPORARY ENGLISH THEOLOGY

CONTEMPORARY CONTINENTAL THEOLOGY

THE GROWTH OF RELIGION (*with Henry Nelson Wieman*)

CAN CHRISTIANITY SAVE CIVILIZATION?

OUR ETERNAL CONTEMPORARY

OUR CHRISTIAN FAITH

TOWARD A REBORN CHURCH

# CHRISTIAN THEOLOGY

## An Ecumenical Approach

BY 08695

## WALTER MARSHALL HORTON

REVISED AND ENLARGED EDITION

*BT*
*75*
*.H82*

HARPER & ROW, PUBLISHERS

NEW YORK AND EVANSTON

*Gratefully dedicated to*
*The Faculty of Protestant Theology*
*The Faculty of Catholic Theology*
*The Faculty of Letters*
*at the*
*University of Strasbourg*
*(Alsace, France)*

# Contents

vii

# Contents

viii

## Preface to the First Edition

I HAVE been convinced for most of my life that sectarian theology is something just as absurd as the "Baptist astronomy" which a devout Baptist trustee of the University of Chicago wanted to have taught there in the early days. That is why I went to Union Theological Seminary instead of to some denominational school; that is why I have been happy to spend my life in another interdenominational school of theology, at Oberlin; that is why I have given so much of my time to the Ecumenical Movement in the last twenty years.

Increasingly in recent years, I have been guiding my theological students toward a more ecumenical position by comparing the agreements and differences in the tentative statements prepared every two weeks by the class, with the agreements and differences that have emerged at Lausanne, Edinburgh, Madras, Amsterdam and other ecumenical conferences. The Ecumenical Movement has come to a common mind (or to put it the other way, met with serious obstacles to agreement) much more clearly on some theological topics than on others; but enough has become clear to make it possible for beginners in theology to sharpen their personal convictions on the whetstone of world opinion. Where ecumenical pronouncements are lacking, comparison of contemporary theologies coming from different churches, different countries, different schools of thought can help to fill the gap.

Hence, the method of this book. My primary conviction that theology is one since God is one, dictates the question asked in the first main section of each chapter: *What is the universal* (*"ecumenical"*) *human problem which underlies this topic in theology?* I take it to be a sound assumption that a universal problem, posed by the One God to the whole human race, underlies every major doctrine of the Christian faith; and I advise teachers to debate this problem freely with their classes (perhaps with the aid of the questions and references appended to each chapter) before proceeding to the second section, where the next point is raised: *What is the universal (*"ecumenical"*) Christian answer to this problem, so far as the Christian churches and schools of thought are now agreed?* If the student finds he is at odds with this ecumenical consensus, he must decide whether he is thinking superficially and provincially, or whether the Flock of Christ in this generation is crowding sheeplike into some broad trail that leads to destruction. Finally, each chapter closes with a section where a third point is raised: *What are the principal disagreements and conflicts which obscure the clarity of the Christian answer to this particular problem?* The attempt is made in each of these last sections to see the conflict in perspective and point a way out, if possible; but it must be said in advance that the ecumenical approach to theology does not promise to reduce Christian doctrine to flat uniformity, by eliminating every last shade of difference. What the Roman Catholic Church has not done, nor even tried to do, with all its powerful machinery, must not be aimed at nor wished for by the Ecumenical Movement. Honest dissent is the spice of life and the seed of progress, in theology as in politics.

In the introductory chapter, the method just described is explained and applied to the question that precedes all specific Christian doctrines: *What is Christianity?* Then the same method is applied to seven cardinal Christian doctrines: the Knowledge of God, the Nature of God, God and the World, God and Man,

## Preface to the First Edition

Christ the Savior, the Church and the Means of Grace, and the Christian Hope. Obviously, this book is meant for use in theological classes, either as a textbook or as collateral reading; but it is short enough and clear enough, I hope, to be interesting and helpful to any Christian minister or layman who wants to clarify his own faith in the light of current ecumenical thinking.

This essay in ecumenical theology is primarily addressed to Americans, and more especially to the Protestants who form the majority group in American church life. For reasons that will appear in the Introduction, I do not find it feasible at the present time to try to write for all geographical areas and all denominations at the same time, without addressing any special constituency. I hope, however, that I have written for American Protestants, *not* as though they were the whole Church Universal by themselves, but as though they were responsible members of the Ecumenical Movement, eager to shape and reshape their convictions in conversation with Christians from other areas and other church traditions.

A rather detailed outline of the book was drafted while I was some distance away from America, as Fulbright Visiting Lecturer at the University of Strasbourg during the second half of the academic year 1951–52. The outline was discussed with several of my colleagues there, both Protestant and Catholic— to whom in gratitude I am now dedicating the finished product— and it got a careful going-over from a group of Benedictine monks who invited me to talk with them about my ecumenical project. None of my European friends (particularly not the Catholics) must be held responsible for the views here expressed; but I feel they have helped me to write a more-than-American book for Americans, and a more-than-Protestant book for Protestants.

## Preface to the First Edition

While writing for American Protestants, I am very eager to serve the ecumenical cause in a more extensive way if possible. I am therefore sending copies of this first edition, through the good offices of the Study Division of the World Council of Churches, to theologians of various denominations in all parts of the world, asking them to tell me candidly what amendments and additions would be needed in a second edition, to make it more useful in their locality, and more adequately ecumenical from their point of view. I hope that this may stimulate others to make essays in ecumenical theology, perhaps on quite different plans. If meanwhile this small book (perhaps with amended lists of references and added notes) could be useful in the British Commonwealth, or on the Continent of Europe, or in Japan or the Philippines, as well as in America, I should of course be very happy.

In addition to my friends at Strasbourg and my kind Benedictine critics, I have to express my thanks to my wife for prolonged exertions over the typing of this manuscript, in all sorts of odd places and times during the past three years; to the staff of the World Council of Churches for permission to quote from Faith and Order pamphlets and other ecumenical documents; to the students in my theological classes at Oberlin and to my auditors at Anderson College, at Boston University, and at the Western Pastors' School, La Forêt, Colorado, for stimulating comments on parts of the manuscript which I have read to them. My hope is to be able to thank many correspondents, in many parts of the world, for critical comments leading to changes in the next edition.

WALTER MARSHALL HORTON

*Oberlin, Ohio*
January 10, 1955

# Preface to the Revised and Enlarged Edition

CORRESPONDENTS in many parts of the world, and reviewers in many periodicals, have generously answered my invitation, issued in the Preface to the first edition, "to tell me candidly what amendments and additions would be needed in a second edition." Some of the suggestions for amendments and additions would require a complete recasting of the plan of this book, or its expansion to much greater length. Balancing these radical proposals against a considerable mass of evidence that the book in its original form and size has proved useful to an even wider group of readers than I first had in view—laymen and undergraduate students as well as ministers and theological students—I have decided that a more conservative type of revision is what is indicated at the present early date: (1) Correction of some inaccuracies. (2) Rewording of some unfair or misleading statements. (3) Addition of some new references. (4) An appendix on "Christianity and Other Living Faiths," to make the book more useful in mission fields. (5) The clarification in a new preface of *the basic concern of an ecumenical approach to theology*, as I now see it in the light of much searching criticism.

It will be noted that the book is not entitled *"Ecumenical Theology."* No such thing exists as an ecumenical theology, in the sense of an official doctrine taught by the Ecumenical Movement. No complete system of theology could be based upon the findings of ecumenical conferences as, for example, a complete system of Roman Catholic theology could be based upon the authoritative documents compiled in Denzinger's *Enchiridion.* What exists is a process of ecumenical *conversation* between hitherto divided churches and schools of thought within Christendom, which permits one to make an approach to the ecumenical theology of the future by studying the agreements and differences that have emerged in the course of this conversation.

What is the *basic concern* of the ecumenical theology that is gradually emerging from this process of conversation? It is a fair assumption that it relates closely to the basic concern of the whole Ecumenical Movement. Only one aspect of that movement (Faith and Order) is explicitly theological, but all aspects of the movement are dominated by a concern expressed in a biblical motto from John 17:21: "That they all may be one . . . . that the world may believe." In this motto, a concern for the unity of the Church is indissolubly connected with a missionary concern for the world. Christ prays for the unity of his disciples, not for their own sake, but for the sake of the world into which he was sent by his Father, and into which he sends them as his ambassadors. Disunity in the Christian movement is disastrous above all because it hurts the Christian mission, and makes it hard for the world to accept Christ as the world's Savior. It is a matter of history that the Ecumenical Movement began with a missionary concern, expressed in many co-operative missionary ventures throughout the nineteenth century, and culminating in the World Missionary Conference at Edinburgh in 1910. Only *after* the foundations for world missionary co-operation were laid (now embodied in the International Missionary Council) was it time to start those more direct movements for Church Unity (Life and Work, Faith and Order) which are now combined in the World Council of Churches. It is axiomatic, then, that a truly ecumenical theology must be first of all a *missionary* theology.

Let us try next to define the nature of the *unity* sought by the

Ecumenical Movement. This is a controversial question, which neither the Oberlin conference on "The Nature of the Unity We Seek" nor other similar regional discussions can quickly resolve; but some general principles can be derived from the previous development of the Ecumenical Movement. The *first* of these has already been suggested: *no conception of Church Unity is acceptable which is divorced from missionary concern.* A *second* observation grows out of the first: *no conception of Church Unity is acceptable which is not truly world-wide in scope.* If we are be united for the sake of the world, it must be nothing less than the *whole inhabited world* that is in view. Social or national unity at the expense of world unity would place an intolerable limitation on the scope of the Christian mission, which is a mission to "all the world" and "every creature." The words "catholic" and "ecumenical," which appear together in the Greek phrase *kath' holēn tēn oikoumenēn,* both originally had this meaning. The modern distinction between these two words suggests a *third* observation: *no conception of Church Unity is acceptable which does not somehow combine "catholic" unanimity with "protestant" liberty and variety.* In the Early Church, this ideal combination was so nearly realized (though of course never perfectly) that the words "catholic" and "ecumenical" could be used interchangeably. Today the word "catholic" has acquired a meaning opposed to the words "protestant" or "evangelical," so that it is necessary to bring the old word "ecumenical" to life again, and use it to express the deep longing of our divided churches for a Christianity at once evangelical and catholic. Unless this longing for evangelical catholicity is measurably realized, the Ecumenical Movement will be a failure. The mere fact that Protestant churches of many different types are now fellow members of the World Council of Churches with Anglo-Catholics, Old Catholics, and Eastern Orthodox, is enough to support this judgment.

Combining these three observations about unity with the priority of the missionary motive, we arrive at the following general definition of the basic concern of ecumenical theology: *a truly ecumenical theology would be one in which various schools of catholic and protestant theology would confront each other sympathetically, and strive toward an ultimate reconciliation, in view of their common concern to interpret the same Christian faith to "all the world" and "every creature."*

Two possible misunderstandings of this definition need to be cleared away:

(1) An ecumenical theology, while of course opposed to any *merely* denominational, confessional, or provincial type of theology, would not destroy all loyalty to particular churches, nor exclude the cultivation of special schools and traditions of Christian thought. It is a matter of experience that the first effect of joining the Ecumenical Movement is to make everyone *more*, not *less*, conscious of his own special loyalties and traditions. This is quite natural and proper; ecumenical theology is neither *un*confessional nor *anti*-confessional, but *inter*-confessional. As an American free churchman, I am even convinced that it is the duty of free churchmen to defend the distinctive marks of their tradition far more sharply and polemically than they have yet done in ecumenical conferences. Efforts at restatement of one's own tradition need to alternate with efforts to interpret the common consensus. It is hard to do both at the same moment.

(2) The ideal of evangelical catholicity is not to be defined simply by noting the doctrinal agreements that underlie the historic differences between Roman Catholicism and the Protestant churches. Those agreements are far-reaching, as Melanchthon

xvi

was one of the first to observe, but they still leave differences of fundamental principle unresolved. On the other hand, it is futile to attempt to isolate the catholic principle completely from the protestant principle; every such attempt which I have studied amounts to no more than a characteristic difference of emphasis between rival interpretations of the same Christian faith.[1] In spite of these ambiguities and perplexities, the ideal of evangelical catholicity keeps reasserting itself. Among those who have held it may be mentioned John Frederick Oberlin, Archbishop Söderblom, Friedrich Heiler, and the members of the Communauté de Taizé in France, a Protestant monastic order. What these "Catholic Protestants" have in common with one another, and with the "Protestant Catholics" who are their "opposite numbers," is not so much one common theological position as one basic concern of the sort we have seen to underlie the whole Ecumenical Movement—a concern for a Christianity big enough and various enough to fulfill its God-given mission to the whole world. What precisely is meant by evangelical catholicity will have to be defined progressively as men of this disposition continue to confront one another and the world in faith, hope and love.

Turning now from the *definition* of the basic concern of an ecumenical theology to the *methods* by which it may be applied to the writing of theological books, let me say at once that there is no need to abandon all traditional methods in order to write an ecumenical theology. The examination of Biblical texts relating to a doctrine, the study of the main stages in its historical development, the unfolding of its implications, the discussion of problems arising from its apparent contradiction of other doctrines and other forms of truth, are all as appropriate methods to employ in writing ecumenical theology as in writing confessional

---

[1] See the discussion of this point, *infra*, pp. 221–29.

theology. The most obvious difference will be that, in addition to these traditional methods, an ecumenical theologian will spend a good deal of his space examining the reports of ecumenical conferences for evidence of important agreements and disagreements between different church traditions. In my own book, so as not to make it too long, I have given major attention to this sort of material, and reduced the Biblical, historical and analytical methods to a minimum. This means (as many of my critics have noted) that I have not given a well-rounded treatment but a highly specialized treatment of Christian theology, so that when I use my book as a textbook in my own theological courses, I must supplement it with other books whose method is more comprehensive. This is not a *necessary* method for books of ecumenical theology, but only a *convenient* method for a first book in the field, concentrating attention on what is new and different. Ultimately, the ecumenical might appear as just one determinative factor in a theological system as vast as Aquinas' or Barth's.

More fundamental than the use or abandonment of traditional theological methods is the question how such books could meet the requirement implied in the first basic concern of ecumenical theology: the requirement that it be a *missionary* theology. One obvious answer has been suggested to me by a Japanese critic of my book: that at least for use in mission fields, there should be a chapter on "Christianity and Other Living Faiths." I am adding such a chapter as an appendix to this revised edition; but what I felt necessary in the first edition was a missionary factor in *every* chapter. I found what I sought in Paul Tillich's principle of "correlation," whereby everything in the Christian revelation appears as the divine "answer" to some persistent, inescapable human "question," given in the conditions of existence that

xviii

all men share. Because Tillich's *Systematic Theology* uses this method of correlation throughout, it is always an "apologetic" theology (i.e., a missionary theology, addressed to men in the world, answering their questions) and never merely a "kerygmatic" theology like Barth's or Aulén's, concerned only that the Christian message should be true to its revealed sources and consistent with itself. I cannot believe that a merely kerygmatic theology adequately fulfills the first basic concern of ecumenical theology; therefore I begin every one of my chapters with a statement of the universal human needs, questions and problems to which Christian faith gives the answer. My statement is less formal and systematic than Tillich's; it draws largely upon my experience in teaching courses on religion to undergraduate students, untrained in theology. The descriptions of human needs, questions and problems which I now have incorporated in my ecumenical theology are those which I have found comprehensible to such secular-minded undergraduates.

No other aspect of my book has aroused so much controversy as this. Soon after it was published a group of our theological students spent an evening discussing it with me, and most of their questions had to do with this aspect. For example, they asked whether I thought that the correlation between human questions and Christian answers was such a close, hand-and-glove correlation that it proved the universal validity of the Christian answers and the falseness of other answers. I replied that I made no claim to be able to prove the truth of the Christian faith so simply as this. The correlation of the Christian answers with universal human questions proves only their relevance, and their possible missionary appeal, when other answers turn out to be self-defeating; but it is always possible for several different gloves to fit the same hand. I do not believe that man's soul is *naturaliter christiana,* but only that it is *naturaliter religiosa,* so that it must find *some* ultimate object of trust and devotion, *some* ultimate goal of hope and endeavor, and *some* way of salvation to connect the two, or else remain restless and dissatisfied with life. There are some important *reasons* to prefer the Christian answer to its logical alternatives—especially the more extreme alternatives—but finally it must be accepted as an act of faith based upon witness rather than upon coercive proof. Neither coercive argument nor blind faith is the basis of Christian commitment, but faith seeking rational verification (*fides quaerens intellectum*).

I have not tried to harmonize the answers with the questions too closely, for I am convinced that the answers both fulfill and transcend the questions, requiring a conversion of the questioner before he can accept an answer which at first disappointed him. As in the special case of the Law and the Gospel, the Christian answer is no simple fulfillment of pre-existing hopes and assumptions; it is at once good news and bad news to the natural man. Since in any event I am not trying to prove the *truth* of the Christian answers by correlating them thus with human questions, but only their *missionary relevance,* the admitted complexity of the relation between questions and answers presents no serious objection to the method.

How is it now with the other aspect of Ecumenical Theology's basic concern, as we have previously defined it—its desire to realize step by step the ideal of evangelical catholicity? This ideal was never absent from my thoughts when I was planning and writing the book. It governed the selection of theological authors upon whose works I have commented in every chapter, especially the chapter on the Church. These authors include not only the main church traditions represented in the World Council of Churches, but some other traditions as well (notably the Roman Catholic) whose exclusion would seriously hurt the evangelical catholicity of the book. I have tried to show the catholicity of protestantism, both in its classical Lutheran and Calvinist forms and in its free church forms; and I have also quoted from Catholic theologians such as Père Congar who make room in their conception of catholicity for evangelical liberty and the need of reform.

The unresolved issues which I analyze in the last section of every chapter should make it clear that the ecumenical consensus stated in each middle section is not by itself the whole of ecumenical theology. If it were the whole, then Protestants in the Ecumenical Movement might well fear that a new authoritarian dogmatism was likely to crush out protesting dissent. Actually, however, the freedom to dissent is carefully guarded in the movement, and all agreements are subject to revision in the light of further study and discussion. For this reason, the anxiety expressed by one of my American critics, lest the statement of an ecumenical consensus on every Christian doctrine should discourage further thought and shut off free discussion, is groundless. I can testify that in my own theological classes, where much time has always been given to discussion, the use of this new book has *not* prevented my students from freely expressing their views.

My method of pursuing the ideal of evangelical catholicity by successively stating the consensus and the dissent, the universal agreements and the unresolved issues on every Christian doctrine, is of course not the only possible method to use in writing an ecumenical theology. It is an adaptation of the method which was dominant in the Faith and Order branch of the Ecumenical Movement, down to the Lund Conference in 1952. At Lund it was called "the method of comparative ecclesiology," and most of the leading speakers concurred in the judgment that it had now made its contributions, revealed its limitations, and needed to be supplanted or supplemented by new methods. My own term for this method would be "comparative theology," since it is applicable to all topics in theology, as well as to ecclesiology, and can be used to discover consensus and dissent among theologians as well as churches. I agree that the method has severe limitations, and needs to be supplemented by new methods; but since these new methods have not yet been tried out adequately and have not yielded any very well-defined results, it seemed best to me to confine myself to the time-honored method whose results had been registered in a great abundance of ecumenical documents.

Future writers on ecumenical theology will certainly need to supplement the comparative method by other methods suggested at Lund, and now being tried out in some Faith and Order commissions. The purpose of these new methods is to resolve stubborn theological disagreements which are only accentuated by the comparative method. The tactics proposed are to turn aside temporarily from the controversial doctrine, begin again with some related doctrine on which there is wide agreement, and then build a bridge, slowly and carefully, between the area of agreement and the area of disagreement. So, for example, the controversial doctrine of the Church is now being reconsidered by Faith and Order commissions, on both sides of the Atlantic, in the light of the doctrines of Christ and the Holy Spirit, on which there has been wide agreement since the Councils of Nicaea and Chalcedon.

It is certainly a paradoxical fact, which my own studies have tended to throw into bold relief, that on the early topics of

Christian Theology—God and the World, Man and Sin, Christ and Redemption—there is deep agreement between most Christian churches, except for "school" differences cutting across denominational lines; whereas on the later topics, especially the Church, Ministry and Sacraments, there are stubborn disagreements which still hold churches apart.

Disagreements of this magnitude will not yield easily, even to these new methods. A great variety of methods, derived from Life and Work as well as from Faith and Order, will need to be employed. Hendrik Kraemer, one of the first to send me a critical comment upon my book, remarked that some of the best contributions to ecumenical theology had been made by Life and Work conferences, in the context of Christian Ethics. In the field of Ethics, of Church Government, and in many other fields with which the Ecumenical Movement is concerned, there are social and cultural factors which powerfully affect theology. *Essays* in ecumenical theology should take account of these factors as fully as possible, though they are hard to deal with in textbooks like mine, without destroying the order and balance of the topics. Finally, of course, it is only the Providence and Grace of God that can achieve the missionary reactivation and evangelical catholicity of the Church, which are the twin concerns of ecumenical theology. Formal theology can at best clarify issues and clear away needless intellectual obstacles which impede the divine work; but if pursued with this end in view, theology may be used of God to create a new situation in the next generation. With the prayer that this may be so, I send out this revised edition.

Walter Marshall Horton

*Oberlin, Ohio*
*January, 1958*

# CHRISTIAN THEOLOGY

## An Ecumenical Approach

# I

# INTRODUCTION

## SECTION 1. "ECUMENICAL" THEOLOGY

THE idea of an "ecumenical" theology is not new. Catholic theology, Orthodox theology, and Anglican theology have always been guided by the findings of the Seven Ecumenical Councils of the ancient "undivided" Church—especially the Council of Nicaea (325) and the Council of Chalcedon (451). The Protestant Reformers likewise had great respect for the general Christian consensus worked out at these councils; and it was never their intention to replace the universal Christian message, preachable *kath'holēn tēn oikoumenēn*,[1] by any narrowly sectarian theology. They wanted to purify the common faith, not to dissolve it into a congeries of competing faiths. The modern Ecumenical Movement arose, naturally enough, on Protes-

[1] *Kath'holēn tēn oikoumenēn*, "throughout the whole inhabited earth." (A phrase which occurs frequently in the Greek Fathers.) The word *oikoumenēn*, "inhabited," modifies the word *gēn*, "earth." It will be noted that the Greek roots for our words "catholic" and "ecumenical" occur together in this phrase. Both mean "universal." For both ancient and modern use of the term "ecumenical" see the pamphlet by Dr. W. A. Visser 't Hooft on *The Meaning of Ecumenical*. Increasingly, the term is used to imply a universality that is more than geographical: "that the Church of Christ is world-wide, supra-national, supraracial . . . essentially one," but "contains a variety of gifts," so that a "spiritual traffic" is needed to draw the various denominations "out of their isolation and into a fellowship of conversation, mutual enrichment, common witness and common action." (Pp. 27, 28.)

tant soil, where the evils of sectarian division were most acutely felt; but it has had the constant collaboration of Anglicans and Orthodox, and attracted the sympathetic interest of many Roman Catholics, because it represents the revival of an ideal common to all the divided branches of Christendom: "that they all may be one" (John 17:21). The main difference between the ancient and modern ecumenical councils is political: Nicaea and Chalcedon had the sometimes embarrassing sponsorship of the Roman Emperors, who used all the machinery of a half-heathen secular government to support the theological views they preferred, and suppress dissent from these views; whereas the Christian unity that emerged at Edinburgh (1910, 1937), Lausanne (1927), and Amsterdam (1948) was the result of a genuinely *free* consensus, binding only those who were glad and willing to be bound by it. The modern Ecumenical Movement thus unites the Catholic ideal of Christian unity with the Protestant ideal of Christian liberty, and promises to break the tragic deadlock between these opposite but equally essential trends in Christian life and thought.

At the turn of the present century, when optimistic forecasts of all sorts were being made—many of them destined to be rudely disappointed—a prophetic voice declared that the only theology worthy of the twentieth century would be a theology produced by "the ecumenical reason and conscience, enlightened by the Holy Spirit." [2] This prophecy at least does not sound off-key, since the mid-point in a very disillusioning century has been passed; and in some measure it has been realized. Short statements of the Christian message were adopted at Lausanne (1927) and Jerusalem (1928), and a fuller statement of faith

[2] G. M. Grant, "The Outlook of the Twentieth Century in Theology," *American Journal of Theology*, VI (1902).

at Madras (1938) which furnished a framework or outline for modern ecumenical theology such as the Apostles' and Nicene Creeds (on which they are modeled) gave to ancient ecumenical theology. At Edinburgh (1937) the delegates dared to advance beyond a general confession of faith to a confrontation of specific theological problems on which the churches have in the past been sharply divided—the Church and the Word of God, Grace and Free-Will, etc.—and at point after point the solemn verdict was: *many problems still unsolved, but no adequate reason here for continuing our unhappy divisions.*[3] These findings enable us to discriminate much more sharply than hitherto between the elements in various theologies which represent the common Christian faith and those which represent a special denominational heritage or a special school of thought.

Among textbooks of Christian theology which have been widely used in the twentieth century, two at least have had an unmistakably "ecumenical" quality: William Adams Brown's *Christian Theology in Outline* (1906) and Gustaf Aulén's *The Faith of the Christian Church* (English translation 1948). Both Brown and Aulén have been active leaders in the Ecumenical Movement; so it is no accident if their textbooks bear the stamp of a Christianity more universal than the liberal American Presbyterianism and the neo-orthodox Swedish Lutheranism which are the immediate background of their authors' thought. The ecumenical quality of Brown's *Outline* is to be seen in the wide catholicity of the bibliography, the fairness of the historical surveys with which each doctrine is introduced, and the search for "main elements" or "permanent elements" in the Christian

---

[3] See the Report of the Edinburgh Faith and Order Conference, as printed in Bell's *Documents on Christian Unity: Third Series, 1930-1948.* The verdict referred to appears, for example, on pp. 250, 251, 252 in this sourcebook (chap. on "The Grace of our Lord Jesus Christ").

view of each doctrine, underlying all the divisions of the sects and schools. For example, three such "permanent elements" are found in the Christian view of the world: "(1) real existence, (2) dependence, and (3) adaptation to the Christian end." [4] All this, before the Ecumenical Movement had even officially begun!

In the case of Aulén's book, a full generation of ecumenical achievement had preceded it, and its consciously ecumenical character is correspondingly more marked: (1) In the original Swedish edition, the *title* is *Den allmänneliga kristna tron,* which may be translated *"The Universal (Catholic, Ecumenical) Christian Faith."* (2) In the Preface to the English edition, Aulén says explicitly that "theology must firmly adhere to the ecumenical perspective," meaning that it must be more than "the private confession of a theologian" and broader than any "narrow and self-satisfied confessionalism." (3) In many passages (e.g., pp. 57, 152, 394–99) he proves the sincerity of his ecumenical convictions by transcending the old disputes between Lutherans and Calvinists, and defining a more universal Christian position which includes both parties. (4) In searching out the essentials of the universal Christian faith, he uses the Lundensian method of "motive-investigation," which "does not stop with the external formulas, but penetrates to the ideas and purposes which these formulas are intended to express" (p. 94). Aulén's "principal ideas or themes" (p. 6, note) are so similar to Brown's "main or permanent elements" that our two authors may fairly be said to use the same method of liberating the common Christian faith from the sectarian and scholastic particularities in which it is entangled.

It may be asked what need there is for another textbook of ecumenical theology to supplement Brown's and Aulén's. The

[4] *Outline,* p. 198.

4

answer, in the case of the American theologian, is simply that time has passed on. *Any* book written before the First World War broke out, before the name of Karl Barth was heard of, must fail to orient theological students to the prevailing thought currents and burning issues of the second half of the twentieth century, as a good textbook should do. Brown's great text belongs to history, although some of his later work is still contemporary.

With Aulén's, the situation is of course quite different. Despite the time lag in translation—his book had already reached its fourth edition in Swedish—no better orientation in present theological issues could be given. Aulén understands Barth and Brunner better than they understand him, and presents the neo-orthodox critique of liberalism in constant balance with an equally acute critique of the old scholastic orthodoxy—a balance not always so well maintained by the Swiss theologians. But at one crucial point of theological method he agrees entirely with Karl Barth—and thereby seriously limits the helpfulness of his textbook. The point is that Christian theology, for Barth and Aulén, is exclusively based upon faith in divinely given revelation, which is to be understood and expounded, but under no circumstances to be rationally argued for or defended, lest we commit the blasphemy of measuring God by human standards. This cuts off theology from contemporary philosophy, absolutely: "no combination of the theses of faith and metaphysics can be allowed" (p. 95). I am not now concerned to examine the validity of this concept of a purely revelational, strictly nonphilosophical theology; I am only concerned to point out its practical effect upon students who have come to their theological course with an accumulation of intellectual problems gathered in their liberal arts course. When such students find that Bishop Aulén consistently refuses to deal with their difficulties, except by telling them what Christian faith says, they feel disappointed and irritated; and the fiftieth or hundredth time they are told what "faith" affirms, denies or requires, they are tempted to rebel openly, and declare themselves unbelievers! At this stage they may protest the choice of a textbook and ask for a book that will really speak to their condition.

The condition of perplexed belief, or believing unbelief, is so widespread in our time that Christian theology has a solemn obligation to confront it. Convinced of this after years of teaching (both undergraduate courses in religion, and graduate courses in theology) I am really distressed by the apparent implication of Aulén's method, that to reason about the Christian faith with perplexed inquirers is to commit high treason against the faith. Both in Europe and America, there are multitudes of faith-hungry people who envy and respect their Christian friends, but who shrug their shoulders and pass on sadly when simply confronted by an unsupported affirmation of faith. "Evidently," they say, "you either have faith, or you don't; and if you don't, there's nothing to be done about it."

In Paul Tillich, I find a contemporary theologian just as ecumenical as Aulén, but using in his *Systematic Theology* a method which brings out the "correlation" at every point between modern man's philosophical "questions" and the Christian faith's "answers" to those very questions. While not prepared to accept all the implications of Tillich's system, I rejoice in the way it breaks through the particular *impasse* just described. Significantly enough, Tillich fully agrees with Barth and Aulén concerning the danger of idolatry and blasphemy when ordinary rational categories are applied to God—treating the Unconditioned Ground of Being as though He were a mere finite *thing*.

6

But Tillich does not conclude from this that theology should give up the apologetic and philosophical task of relating Christian faith to modern perplexities and modern secular knowledge, confining itself (with Barth and Aulén) to the purely "kerygmatic" task of clarifying the Christian message. He holds that philosophic and kerygmatic theology when rightly correlated do not contradict each other, but supplement and illuminate each other.

In this I heartily agree with Tillich; and I propose to follow a method roughly analogous to his. Not as an instrument of system building, but as an instrument of orientation for perplexed believers and interested unbelievers, I propose to open each principal topic of theology with a statement of the question at issue as *all* men have to face it in our age, not as Christians or Buddhists or Communists but simply as human beings. This I take to be one essential element in the ecumenical approach to theology: the clear recognition that despite Iron Curtains and fiercely disputing ideologies we belong to one human race, wherever we happen to live in the "inhabited world." Only after thus opening up *the universal human question* will it be time to give *the universal Christian answer*, so far as a generally agreed answer has emerged in the Ecumenical Movement; and only after the generally agreed answer has been stated and interpreted will it be time to raise certain *unresolved issues* with which Christian theology must busy itself in our age. The Ecumenical Movement has helped us not only to recognize our existing unity in Christ, but also to define our differences more accurately, so that they can be dealt with more hopefully.

Two possible ambiguities in the meaning of the word "ecumenical" need to be cleared up before we can proceed:

1. *Does "ecumenical" imply a literally world-wide perspec-*

*tive on the theological thought currents of our age?* Must European and American trends be carefully checked with trends in India and Japan before any assertion about "ecumenical consensus" is risked? Eventually, but not yet. Delegates from the "Younger Churches" have contributed essential insights to the findings of recent ecumenical conferences; but it will be at least another generation before their formal treatises on theology will begin to influence the thought of Christendom at large. In the interim, three principal geographic areas needing to be canvassed in search of a Christian consensus are Continental Europe, the British Commonwealth, and America. Even here, the ecumenical issues differ so much between areas that a book written primarily for Americans cannot be equally useful to Europeans, and vice versa.

Generally speaking, the fault of perspective most needing correction is the ignorance of the older portions of Christendom concerning developments in the newer portions. Great Britain (especially Scotland) knows more about the Continent than the Continent knows about Britain; America knows more about Britain and the Continent than they know about America; New Zealand and Australia know more about America, Britain and the Continent than they know about anything "down under"; and the still newer Christendom of the mission fields is of course the least understood of all. In some respects the most ecumenically-minded Christian theologian I have met was the late Principal John Dickie of Knox College, Dunedin, New Zealand, the "senior theologian of the Southern Hemisphere," whose excellent textbook, *The Organism of Christian Truth*[5] combines influences emanating from America (Shedd, Brown, Royce), Britain (Forsyth, Flint, W. P. Paterson) and the Continent

[5] London, Clarke, 1931.

(Haering, Harnack, Rudolf Otto) in a far more cosmopolitan perspective than most Europeans would be capable of. Such a perspective as Dickie's, corrected by criticisms from still younger and newer Christian lands—criticisms which are hereby earnestly solicited—represents the presently achievable ideal of geographic ecumenicity toward which this book aspires.[6]

2. *Does "ecumenical" imply a literally universal perspective on all denominations claiming to be Christian?* Must a formula be found for including Roman Catholics, Unitarians and Jehovah's Witnesses, before we can talk about an "ecumenical consensus"? The answer is again that complete world-wide inclusion is an ideal to be approached only by stages. At the present stage of the Ecumenical Movement, none of the three denominations just mentioned is an active member of the World Council of Churches, so on a strictly parliamentary definition of ecumenicity, all could be ignored.

Wholly to ignore these and other nonparticipant bodies would, however, be most unrealistic. To treat the largest and most powerful of all Christian bodies as a negligible factor in contemporary Christian theology would bring a well-deserved protest from many active participants in the Ecumenical Movement, such as the Anglicans and the French Protestants. To pass over the Unitarian objections when discussing the doctrine of the Trinity and the Incarnation, would be to put the whole discussion out of focus. To describe the "Christian" faith without any reference to the radical new movements that are claiming the name "Christian," would unduly encourage complacency in

[6] The insufficiency of Dickie's textbook for present use is somewhat similar to that of Brown's, though of lesser degree. When I visited Dunedin in 1938 I found Dickie discussing Brunner's *Divine Imperative;* but Barth and Brunner had not come clearly over the horizon of the Southern Hemisphere when *The Organism of Christian Truth* was published. Since 1931 the theological picture has changed more than it changed between 1906 and 1931.

a revolutionary epoch. It is necessary, therefore, to interpret the term "ecumenical" in a somewhat prophetic way, standing upon the achieved unity of the World Council of Churches but reaching out to a more inclusive unity wherever a possible basis for it can be detected.

Since the Amsterdam Assembly has defined the "deepest difference" running through the member churches as the "catholic-protestant" difference, it is particularly important to reach out for a formula including the Roman Catholics, wherever such inclusion seems honestly possible. At this point Paul Tillich's theology again becomes significant, for he defines ideal Christianity not simply in Protestant terms, but as a vital union between the Catholic sacramental principle and the Protestant prophetic principle. If this conciliation in principle could be extended to moot issues, the word "ecumenical" would take on a larger meaning than it actually has at the present day.

## SECTION 2. UNIVERSAL NECESSITY OF RELIGION

The problem of religion is not well put in terms of belief *vs.* unbelief, or religion *vs.* irreligion. Where Christianity or some other form of religious faith has been well established, any departure from it appears as "unbelief" or "irreligion"; but mere negation is never the final outcome of religious revolt. Sooner or later, antireligious movements that begin with an act of rejection take the form of a positive substitute for the rejected religion. So Auguste Comte, after rejecting all theology in his earlier works as unscientific superstition, formulates a Religion of Humanity in his later works, complete with a substitute deity, a substitute church, and even a new catechism and calendar of saints—"Catholicism minus Christianity," as Huxley called it. Karl Marx, after defining religion as the "opiate of the people," cannot consistently formulate a new "religion"; but the subsequent history of Marxian Communism shows *Das Kapital* becoming a new Koran, Marx becoming a new Mohammed, and "deviations" from the Marx-Lenin-Stalin party line, as defined in Moscow, being punished just as rigidly as dogmatic religions punish heresy. Hitler and Rosenberg were simply more traditional in their vocabulary than their temporary allies in Moscow, when they recognized that they were offering the German people a new religious "myth," composed in part of ancient "Aryan" materials, to serve them in the next thousand years as Christianity served them (or misserved them) in the last thousand.

Let us not quarrel over mere words. Communism will never admit that it is a "religion," and it claims to be "scientific"—not a matter of "faith"—but any fair-minded observer can perceive that Communism spreads because it creates confidence outrunning its actual achievements, offers a comprehensive pattern for living as the great faiths have done, and answers to human needs similar to those which the historic religions have satisfied. If it also disappoints the faith it kindles, through callous disregard for human needs and brutal use of power, that has happened in the case of other militant religions and quasi-religions. Religion in *some form* (good or bad) and by *some name* (traditional or newly invented) is not an optional factor in human life; it is a universal "must."

What are the human needs which historic faiths have satisfied, and which modern substitutes for religion are meeting in new ways—often without being aware that they are doing so? They are mainly three: *the need for an ultimate object of trust and de-*

11

*votion; the need for a final goal of hope and endeavor; the need for a concrete connection between trust and hope, devotion and endeavor, whereby power from above ("saving grace") is released into the stream of daily life, and man moves toward his goal with the aid of his God.* These three needs can be diagrammed as a right-angle triangle, its upper angle reaching vertically toward heaven, its lower right-hand angle reaching horizontally toward the goal of life, and its lower left-hand corner representing the point of intersection where the divine presence and power become "a very present help" to troubled mortals. The two principal lines of this triangle are the vertical and hori-

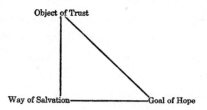

zontal; but the diagonal line connecting the upper angle with the lower right-hand angle reminds us that there is connection and coherence in all great religions between the object of trust and the goal of hope—or in Christian terms, between God and the Kingdom of God.

The three human needs just described are universal and ineradicable human needs, which must be met if man is to go on living at all; above all, if he is to find durable satisfaction in living. The first springs from the situation of a finite mortal creature in a vast, mysterious universe, where he is simply lost and helpless unless he allies his puny strength with something greater and more enduring than himself. The third springs from the multiplicity of human desires, which reduces human life to meaningless confusion unless some goal of hope and endeavor, some "chief end of man" generates a scale of values in terms of which particular choices can be made. The second springs from the necessity of inspiration from the depths and heights of Being, if man is to move toward his ideal goal without succumbing to weariness or despair.

Ground of trust, way of salvation, goal of hope—these three elements can be recognized, always present though with differing degrees of proportionate emphasis, in all historic religions. Schleiermacher emphasized the first when he defined religion as "the feeling of absolute dependence"; Ritschl emphasized the third when he saw religion driving toward the goal of "victory over the world"; both implied a relationship between the two such as our "point of connection" indicates. John Dickie says that

> In every religion there are three elements which constitute its essential content, and by means of which religions may be compared . . . the idea of a religious blessing which the believer regards as supremely valuable and which he believes that he can secure by the help of the divine power [chief end or goal] . . . some sort of conviction as to the nature and character of this divine power [object of trust and devotion] . . . certain requirements [way of salvation] which the divine power lays down as the condition of the bestowal of the religious blessing on those who wish to secure it.[7]

Philosophers of religion who disagree on many other points agree substantially in recognizing something like this threefold structure and function running through all religions. Henry Nelson Wieman speaks of (1) the human ("created") good, (2) the divine ("creative") Source of human good, and (3) various ways and means by which religion cures ills and secures goods.[8] The outline of Paul Tillich's *Systematic Theology* pre-

[7] Dickie, *op. cit.*, p. 15. (Bracketed notes are mine.)
[8] Wieman, *The Source of Human Good*, Chaps. III and X.

sents a fivefold division presupposing a threefold analysis of the universal situation: (1) man's outreach toward the Ground of "Being"; (2) his search for deliverance from the ills with which "Existence" and "Life" are beset; (3) his hope for some meaningful issue of human endeavor, in or beyond "History." [9]

If we are correct in our conviction that the three main human needs expressed in historic religion are "universal and ineradicable," we must expect to find them expressed (perhaps in truncated form) in the lives of allegedly "nonreligious" people, and in the organization of "secular" societies and civilizations. As we noted in the case of Communism, Nazism and the Religion of Humanity, the negative phase of antireligious reaction tends to exhaust itself pretty rapidly; and when the exigencies of life are seriously faced, something like a new religion emerges with a new deity, a new way of salvation, and a new goal of hope. Communism resembles original Buddhism in having a very truncated theology and a violent antipathy to theology; but one ventures to predict that if Communism lasts as long as Buddhism (which is unlikely), its empty heavens will be as thickly repopulated with gods and demigods as they become in later Buddhist art. It will be piquant to see Marx, Lenin and Stalin reclining on celestial cloudbanks, along with Amitabha and Kwan Yin! Their colossal pictures, held aloft in Communist parades and meetings, represent already the first stage in their ascension to heaven.

The helplessness and disorientation of the detached, irreligious individual are so terrible that he can seldom resist for long the tendency to make of his family life, his business, his lodge, his

---

[9] See *Systematic Theology*, I, pp. 66–68, for the outline. The second of the three points above yields two divisions ("Existence and the Christ," "Life and the Spirit") while a fifth division, "Reason and Revelation," introduces the whole system.

college, his military corps or his nation something like a substitute religion. The need for religious support, orientation, inspiration, is less manifest in the case of societies and cultures than in the case of individuals; yet they, too, are finite entities, needing a frame of reference to relate them to the world beyond themselves.

If we take the triangle of personal need and make it rotate on its vertical axis, it will give us a cone that roughly symbolizes the need of religion in societies and cultures. Great civilizations have generally been based upon some sort of religious faith, represented primarily by the vertical axis. The upper end of this

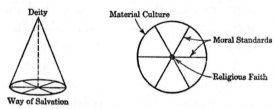

axis, at the top of the cone, stands for the supreme deity recognized in this society. The point where it impinges on the horizontal, at the center of the lower circle, stands for the way of salvation. Taking a cross section of the cone near the base, it appears like a wheel, with hub, spokes and rim. The rim is the material culture, composed of the various ways and means by which this social order solves the problems of feeding, housing, transportation, etc., set by its physical environment. The spokes are the moral standards or *mores*, the spiritual ends and meanings served by these material ways and means, and controlled in their turn by the religious hub or center, through some dominating concept of the "chief end of man."

Societies do not have to be quite so integrated as individuals, and can tolerate a fairly high degree of inconsistency between their elements; but when the unifying force exerted by a common religious faith is reduced below a certain minimum, the society moves toward anarchy. When religious trust and inspiration disappear, moral values and standards become more and more relativistic, till they are no longer capable of controlling the ways and means of living in the interest of any inherently meaningful ends. About this time, social confusion gets so unbearable that people will gladly extend a welcome to some dictator who will impose a new system of social order, no matter what. Ancient society and medieval society—down to and including the regimes with state churches established in many Protestant countries after the Reformation—had such a vivid sense of the social necessity of a common religious faith that they were "closed societies," punishing religious heresy as a crime. Since that time experiments with "open societies" have been tried, most notably in the United States, and it has been proved that large religious tolerance and wide religious diversity are compatible with social strength and cohesion. It has not yet been proved, however, that *absolute* toleration of all convictions, however violently antithetic to one another, can escape the nemesis of social anarchy—and the tyranny that follows hard upon its heels. The real issue before our free democratic societies today is not whether they can continue to drift forever toward complete religious indifferentism. That is not a possible alternative. The real alternatives are *either* to discover some new "common core" of religious unity, on a basis of free consent and continued toleration; *or*, failing that, to relapse into the old closed society, with some new compulsory religion imposed on everyone by the state—probably a bad religion cruelly imposed by a dictatorial regime. Total religious conformity is not necessary to social well-being; but no society can cohere without a minimum core of religious agreement. Socially as well as individually, at least this much religion is a universal human necessity.

## SECTION 3. ESSENTIAL CHRISTIANITY ECUMENICALLY DEFINED

What may be called the *shape* of a creed—triangular or conical in our symbolic diagrams—is determined by the universal human need of a ground of trust, a way of salvation, and a goal of hope; but the *content* of the creed is distinctive in each historic religion and each modern substitute for religion. Momentous consequences hang on these distinctions. A religion may drive a whole nation to destruction and involve the whole world in tragedy, as we saw happen in the case of German Nazism; or it may offer real deliverance and positive blessing to all who genuinely meet its conditions. What is the distinctive or essential content of the Christian faith, as generally understood by Christians? —that is the first and most fundamental question of Christian theology.

It was Schleiermacher who first gave a central position in theology to this question of the essence of Christianity; and the answer he gave to it still remains classic, in spite of the recent wave of revulsion which has swept away much of his work: "Christianity is a monotheistic faith belonging to the teleological type of religion, and is essentially distinguished from other similar faiths in that everything in it is related to the redemption accomplished in Jesus of Nazareth." [10] Whatever one may think of the idealistic philosophy underlying so much of Schleiermacher's system, one must admit that he here speaks as an accu-

[10] Schleiermacher, *The Christian Faith*, Edinburgh: Clark, 1928. Introduction, sec. 11.

rate student of comparative religion, and as a fair interpreter of the ecumenical Christian consciousness.

As a student of comparative religion, Schleiermacher places Christianity in the right *genus*, along with Judaism, as one of those ethical or prophetic faiths which not only derive all reality from one God (monotheism) but also see history driving toward one divine *telos* or goal that gives it meaning (the Kingdom of God), in sharp contrast to certain purely mystical or "aesthetic" faiths which find no ethical goal in history and define salvation as escape from the wheel of temporal existence. As an interpreter of the ecumenical Christian consciousness, he rightly differentiates Christianity from Judaism and Mohammedanism by the unique position and character of its Founder, who is not simply a Teacher like Moses or Mohammed, but the world's divine-human Redeemer. This positive conception of essential Christianity is negatively confirmed by a list of four "natural heresies" that fundamentally subvert the Christian faith: the *Docetic*, by denying Christ's humanity; the *Ebionite*, by denying his deity; the *Manichaean*, by denying that mortal man can be redeemed; the *Pelagian*, by denying that he needs a Redeemer.[11] If no other heresies endanger the Christian faith quite so much as these, the concept of the divine-human Redeemer must be the distinguishing mark of the Christian faith.

A century of criticism and amendment has neither greatly upset nor greatly improved this classic definition. Ritschl and Harnack found fault with Schleiermacher's one-sided emphasis upon Christ as Redeemer, and presented Christianity as an "ellipse with two foci," the new focus being the ethical-social ideal of the Kingdom of God, equated with the universal reign of love. However, Schleiermacher had already included the King-

[11] *Ibid.,* sec. 22.

dom of God in his definition of Christianity as a form of "teleological monotheism"—the *telos* toward which Christianity actively strives being expressly called the Kingdom of God [12]—while he had not come so close as his Ritschlian critics to identifying the Christian religion with modern liberal humanitarianism. Harnack's well-known summary of the Christian Gospel in his *What is Christianity?* sounds bare and strange today—"the higher righteousness and the commandment of love . . . the Kingdom of God and its coming . . . God the Father and the infinite value of the human soul"—but Schleiermacher's definition of essential Christianity and his four "natural heresies" still have an authentically ecumenical sound. William Adams Brown, who critically reviews all modern definitions of Christianity, offers nothing better.[13] Aulén, who contrasts his theological position at all important points with Schleiermacher's, is in substantial agreement with him concerning essential Christianity: "The essence of Christianity is characterized by the fact that everything in Christianity is related to and determined by the act of God in Christ" [14]—which is later described as "a work of redemption," [15] or "that act of divine love through which God establishes the reconciliation between himself and the world." [16] Aulén detects excessive "evolutionary optimism" in Schleiermacher's account of how the Holy Spirit, communicating Christ's redemption to mankind and the world "permeates the whole more and more perfectly";[17] but even this disagreement

[12] *Ibid.*, sec. 9, par. 2: "In Christianity all sorrow and all joy are religious only in so far as they are related to activity in the Kingdom of God." (A passage which should satisfy even an American activist!)

[13] "The religion of divine sonship and human brotherhood, revealed and realized by Jesus Christ." (*Outline*, p. 41; cf. his *Essence of Christianity*, Scribner, 1902, p. 309.)

[14] Aulén, *The Faith of the Christian Church*, p. 66.

[15] *Ibid.*, p. 207.      [16] *Ibid*, p. 223.      [17] *Ibid.*, p. 69.

cannot conceal the agreement of these otherwise sharply opposed theologians concerning the central position of Christ's redeeming act in the whole structure of the Christian faith.

This consensus between Schleiermacher and Aulén is confirmed by ecumenical Christian statements, both ancient and modern. The earliest Christian confession, "Jesus is Lord," pointed to God's conquest of the world in Jesus as the decisive element in the Christian Gospel. The "fish" acrostic, used by the early Christians as a password in time of persecution, conveys the same message in slightly expanded form: "Jesus the Christ, God's Son, Savior." The Apostles' Creed and the Nicene Creed have three main articles, reflecting the inevitable "triangular shape" of all developed religious creeds; but their decisive and distinctive article is the second, in which God's redemptive act in Jesus Christ is set forth. From here on down to the Lausanne and Jerusalem confessions of 1927 and 1928, the *articulus stantis aut cadentis ecclesiae* has always been faith in Jesus Christ as the divine-human Redeemer of the world, while at the same time all attempts to cut this faith from its roots in Jewish ethical monotheism have been stoutly and stubbornly resisted. The Jerusalem statement puts the ecumenical faith of Christendom simply and beautifully, when it says, "Our message is Jesus Christ. He is the revelation of what God is and what man through him may become." More than this is not absolutely essential for Christian faith to affirm; less than this is not Christianity at all. This is the rock on which the modern Ecumenical Movement is built: the confession that Jesus Christ is "God and Savior." [18]

When the distinctive Christian faith in Jesus as "the Christ,

---

[18] On this somewhat unusual form of words and its meaning, see my analysis in *Toward a Reborn Church*, Harper, 1949, pp. 62, 63; cf. also Chap. VI, sec. 2, *infra*.

the Son of God, the Savior" takes the threefold shape to be seen in all worked-out creeds, it appears as faith in (1) the "God and Father of our Lord Jesus Christ"; (2) the incarnation of this God in Jesus the Christ, and his victory on Easter over the powers of sin and death who apparently overcame him on Good Friday; (3) the persistent working of the risen and glorified Christ through the Holy Spirit in the Church, until the world for which he lived and died is finally reconciled to the Father who sent him. The Christian God, the Christian way of salvation, the Christian goal are thus concretely expressible in terms of the person of the Founder himself; or if the spirit of the Founder be abstractly described as the spirit of redemptive, self-giving love (*agapé*) embodied in his life, teaching and Cross, then Christianity affirms (1) that "God is love"; (2) that the love of God in Christ "constrains" us by dying for us; and (3) that such love is the greatest of all goods (I Cor. 13) and its triumph is the goal toward which the whole creation presses. Combining the concrete and abstract, we may say that the Christian answer to the three great human needs is all contained in the love of Christ. Here is what men may finally trust, here is the highest goal to which they may aspire, here is the power that will actually move them toward their goal.

It is evident that Christianity is by definition a religion that ardently claims to be true—not excluding all truth from other faiths, but testifying that here, in the reconciling love of Christ, the answer to the world's problems has been found, needing only to be applied and implemented to bring the whole world to its true destiny. John Dickie presents this truth claim of Christianity in the following words:

Christianity is true provided that the Christian religious blessing, the God who bestows that blessing, and the terms of its bestowal, are as Christianity represents them. The Christian religious blessing is salvation, or reconciliation with God; the God who bestows that blessing is the God and Father of the Lord Jesus Christ; and the sole condition of its bestowal according to our Protestant or Evangelical Christianity, is faith in Jesus Christ, the Son of God, our Lord and Saviour. . . . Christianity is God's own gift to sinful man of reconciliation with Himself through Jesus Christ, and the only true and absolute religion.[19]

The truth claim of Christianity will be considered in subsequent chapters (especially in the next chapter on "The Knowledge of God"). At this point, we simply note the fact that Christianity makes a *relevant response* to all of the universal religious needs of mankind. It presents the God and Father of Jesus Christ as the Ground of trust, his everlasting Kingdom as the Goal of hope, and Christ himself as "the Way, the Truth and the Life."

### SECTION 4. UNRESOLVED ISSUES CONCERNING ESSENTIAL CHRISTIANITY

While there exists a practically complete consensus concerning the centrality of Christ in Christianity, there has always been much honest division of opinion among Christians as to *what else* is essential to Christianity; i.e., *how* Christ's centrality is to be maintained in the life of the Christian fellowship.

Every important issue on which the early Christians were divided is in the last analysis a dispute about the essence of Christianity. Paul's dispute with the "Judaizers," hotly debated at the

---

[19] Dickie, *op. cit.*, p. 15. This statement would need but little change to be acceptable to Catholics.

Council of Jerusalem, involved the question whether Christianity was a sect of Judaism, requiring obedience to all the national particularities of Jewish Torah, or whether it was a strictly universal religion, open to Jews and Gentiles on equal terms. Irenaeus' dispute with the Christian Gnostics, which forms part of the background of our Apostles' Creed, raised the issue whether Christianity was a Greco-Oriental mystery cult, providing a way of escape from this evil, material, temporal world, or whether the Jewish faith in God's good creation, and the Jewish faith in God's special activity in a particular sequence of material, temporal events, were still essential parts of the Christian faith. The Councils of Nicaea and Chalcedon wrestled with the problem whether Christ's admitted centrality in Christianity, as Savior, can be maintained if he is only the incarnation of a created being, however exalted (Arius), or if his humanity is dissolved in his deity (Eutyches), or if his humanity is too widely separated from his deity (view attributed to Nestorius).

The medieval and modern divisions of the Church are of the same sort. The schism between the Eastern Orthodox Churches and the Roman Catholic Church was not so much over the famous *filioque* as over the question whether Romanism confirms or corrupts essential Christianity—whether the Roman system of centralized government, with the Bishop of Rome in Caesar's place, helps to maintain the centrality and headship of Christ through this his earthly Vicar, or tends to secularize and de-Christianize Christianity. The Protestant Reformation in its "material principle" (justification solely by faith) gave a new simple definition of essential Christianity, while in its "formal principle" (*sola Scriptura*) it offered a criterion for distinguishing between essential Christianity and its medieval corruptions. Each new Protestant sect began with an earnest attempt to protect essential Christianity against some threatening danger, and re-establish its vital connection with its Head and Founder. Quite recently, the controversies between fundamentalism and modernism, and between liberalism and neo-orthodoxy, have been controversies over the essence of Christianity: Are the plenary, verbal inspiration of the Scripture, and the literal veracity of the miracles recounted in Scripture, essential parts of the Christian message, or can essential Christianity be disentangled from these doctrines without any such fatal impairment of its purity as took place (according to all conservatives) in most modern liberal versions of the Gospel?

Not all historic issues that have divided Christians are still burning issues. It is fortunate that this is so; for if all divisions remained permanently outstanding, all problems unresolved, there could be no ecumenical Christian theology at all, but only the separate theologies of separate sects, each claiming to contain the whole essence of Christianity and all together destroying Christianity's claim to be the one true religion for all mankind. There are still some sects (mostly very new ones, like Jehovah's Witnesses) which claim a monopoly of Christian truth and un-church all others as apostate; but the Ecumenical Movement has proved again and again that time has resolved the greater part of the issues that have historically divided Christian churches and parties; and the present leaders of divided churches and parties are not actually so far apart as time-honored slogans and popular stereotypes would lead one to suppose. The best example of this is the discussion of the "Theology of Grace" before and during the Edinburgh Faith and Order Conference of 1937. Concerning "grace, free-will, foreknowledge absolute," and the allied questions of human merit and divine predestination, the Protestants have fought the Catholics, the Jesuits have fought the

Dominicans, the Calvinists have fought the Arminians, and it has sometimes seemed impossible even to touch such questions without flying apart. Yet in 1931, six years before the Edinburgh Conference, the theological committee appointed to make an advance study of these thorny issues reported as follows:

> As to the relation of men and God's Grace, we all agree, simply upon the basis of the New Testament and Christian experience, that the sovereignty of God, in fulfilling His purpose for the individual and with mankind, is supreme, and that we men owe our whole salvation to His gracious Will, but, on the other hand, that God's action in Grace needs to be actively appropriated by man's personal will, and for this decision man remains responsible.
>
> Many theological attempts have been made on philosophical lines, to reconcile the apparent antithesis of God's sovereignty and man's responsibility, emphasizing too exclusively one side or the other, thus causing much strife among Christians. But these speculations are not a necessary part of the Christian Faith. . . . Provided the different Churches agree in holding the essentials of the Christian faith, such differences would form no barrier to union between them.[20]

If it may fairly be affirmed, on the basis of this declaration—as I think it may—that a large part of the theological issues historically dividing Protestants into Lutherans, Calvinists and Arminians, and even a considerable part of the issues dividing Protestants from Catholics, have now become dead issues, what then are the living issues which still divide us, and demand careful definition? There is danger of personal and denominational

---

[20] Faith and Order Pamphlet No. 66, *The Theology of Grace*, pp. 25, 26, 28. This report is signed by Greek Orthodox, Presbyterians, Lutherans, Anglicans, and representatives of other denominations whose spiritual ancestors were at swords' points on these issues. Cf. the almost identical statement which was incorporated in the Report of the Edinburgh Conference in 1937 (Bishop G. K. A. Bell, *Documents on Christian Unity*, Third Series, pp. 250-51) on "The Sovereignty of God and Man's Purpose."

prejudice in every precise answer to this question; but unless a judicious selection of living issues is made, we shall be lost in a morass of trivialities and irrelevancies. The selection here made has been subjected to ecumenical criticism, but inevitably represents the author's best judgment—subject to further criticism and correction from the readers of this book. On each special topic of theology there are specially vital issues which will be indicated in the proper place; but at this point it is necessary only to note differences of such magnitude and such fundamental importance that they divide contemporary Christians into major types of faith and order, distinguished by characteristic conceptions of essential Christianity. These major types, all divisible into subtypes, are the following:

|     |     |     |
|-----|-----|-----|
| I. | *Catholic:* | Roman and non-Roman. |
| II. | *Conservative Protestant:* | Scholastic and Fundamentalist. |
| III. | *Liberal Protestant:* | Idealistic and Realistic. |
| IV. | *Radical Protestant:* | Humanistic and Naturalistic. |
| V. | *Neo-Orthodox:* | Swiss, Swedish and American subtypes. |
| VI. | *Anglican:* | High (Catholic), Low (Evangelical), Broad (Liberal) and Central. |

The consideration of subtypes is best deferred to the next chapter, since the doctrine of the Knowledge of God is perhaps the most delicately critical issue on which the schools divide; but the six main types of contemporary Christianity may at once be seen to diverge from one another on two basic issues: the catholic-protestant issue and the conservative-liberal issue. The first of these issues divides the Catholics from all four types of Protestants, and runs straight through the Anglican communion; the second divides the Protestants into four types, and again divides the Anglicans. (It also divides the Catholics along parallel lines, but less clearly and dramatically.) Neither of these two basic issues is exactly what it was at the time of the Reformation, or even in the first half of the twentieth century. In both cases, it is important to define differences freshly, as they actually stand in the second half of the century.

Schleiermacher's famous antithesis between Protestantism and Catholicism—"the former makes the individual's relation to the church dependent on his relation to Christ, while the latter, contrariwise, makes the individual's relation to Christ dependent on his relation to the church" [21]—cannot be regarded as a correct definition of the present issue between the two great wings of Christendom. As Aulén rightly points out, this conception of Protestantism represents an extreme individualism which is untrue to Luther's conception of the Church as "the mother who bears and fosters every Christian," and is even inconsistent with Schleiermacher's own teaching in other parts of his system. Brown's definition of Protestantism in terms of "direct access to God," "freedom and individualism," and "the principle of private judgment," shares the one-sidedness of Schleiermacher's at this point, and needs to be revised.[22]

Yet Schleiermacher was on the right trail when he sought the clue to the distinction between the Catholic and Protestant types of Christianity somewhere in the complex and mysterious interrelationships between Christ, the Church and the individual. Recent ecumenical discussion has returned to this trail and found

[21] Schleiermacher, *op. cit.*, sec. 24, quoted and discussed in Aulén, *op. cit.*, pp. 347–50.
[22] Brown, *Outline*, pp. 63–64.

some new clues. Both at Edinburgh (1937) and Amsterdam (1948), it was found that particular differences between churches were largely reducible to a "deepest difference" dividing the more "catholic" from the more "protestant" churches. While no fully satisfactory formula has yet been found for defining this difference, a very helpful distinction was made by the late Dr. C. T. Craig, chairman of the theological commission which prepared for this particular discussion at Amsterdam: between a "horizontal" and a "vertical" conception of the relationship of Christ to the Church.[23] Those who stress the "horizontal" relationship of Christ to the Church attach the greatest importance to unbroken *institutional continuity* between the historic Founder and the modern Church, maintained through "Apostolic Succession" and the Sacraments; those who stress the "vertical" relationship attach the greatest importance to *spiritual continuity*, maintained through the preaching of the Word and the immediate guidance of the Holy Spirit. It is clear that "horizontalism" tends to exalt the authority of the Church over its members, while "verticalism" tends to assert the prophetic right of the individual to correct and reform the Church—a right asserted by Amos against Amaziah, and Paul against the "Judaizers," as well as by Luther against the Papacy. To this extent, Schleiermacher's emphasis on direct relationship between Christ and the Christian individual is not misplaced.

What recent discussion has made clearer than ever before is *the consistency in principle between the more "catholic" and the more "protestant" conceptions of Christianity, and the impossibility of defining either position without some reference to the*

---

[23] *Official Report of the Amsterdam Assembly*, Harper, 1949, pp. 33, 34. See also my article on "Progress in Christian Unity from Edinburgh to Amsterdam," in *Religion and Life*, Vol. XIX (Summer, 1950), pp. 400-407.

*other*. In a symposium on this subject in the *Ecumenical Review*,[24] two "catholic" and two "protestant" writers were in substantial agreement that both "horizontal" and vertical" relationships between Christ and the Church are necessary, and that neither "institutional" nor "spiritual" continuity can be wholly broken without destroying Christianity altogether. The difference between Catholicism and Protestantism thus reduces itself to a difference of emphasis between two equally essential Christian principles. Where Catholic emphasis on the continuity of a priestly, sacramental, institutional church is exaggerated, there is danger, as Paul Tillich points out, of the "heteronomy" of a "self-absolutizing and, consequently, demonically distorted church." [25] Where the Protestant emphasis on the right and duty of prophetic protest is exaggerated, there is danger of destructive "autonomy." A truly "theonomous" Christianity would equally emphasize the dependence of the individual Christian on churchly tradition, and his duty to criticize the Church in Christ's name. While it is a long way from this reconciliation of the Catholic and Protestant principles to the actual reconciliation of the Catholic and Protestant churches, theology can already declare that to labor for such a consummation is not to labor foolishly for a sheer impossibility.

The issue between conservative and liberal Protestantism (and Catholicism) is not so sharply drawn as it was at the height of the fundamentalist-modernist controversy, between 1920 and 1925. Pius X in the *Encyclical Pascendi* (1907) had described Catholic modernism as "the synthesis of all heresies"; so Protestant fundamentalists, a little later, described liberal, modernistic

[24] Vol. I (1949), pp. 361–98. Cf. the discussion of this same issue in Chap. VII, sec. 3, *infra*.
[25] Tillich, *op. cit.*, I, p. 227.

29

Protestantism as a great apostasy from the New Testament faith. J. G. Machen put the issue clearly in the polemical title of his sharp little book, *Christianity and Liberalism* (1923). Liberals and modernists reciprocated by describing the fundamentalists as "obscurantistic," "pre-scientific" and generally unprogressive in their mental outlook. Moreover, they denied that "the Fundamentals" were really part of essential Christianity. Harry Emerson Fosdick, in his sermon, "Shall the Fundamentalists Win?" complained that these heresy hunters busied themselves with "tiddledy-winks and peccadilloes" while the great problems of the modern age remained unfaced and unsolved. A British visitor to the United States about this time observed that theological extremes were alarmingly strong in America, and the theological center was very weak by comparison.

Since that time, more moderate forms of conservatism and liberalism have emerged, which have considerably strengthened the center against the extremes, both in America and in other parts of Christendom. In the United States, the shift was stimulated by the crisis of the early years of the great economic depression (1930–35), when religious humanists continued to teach man's ability to save himself through applied science and cooperative social action, while the whole course of events appeared to most people to teach man's tragic inability to extricate himself from the trap which his own folly and wickedness had laid for his unwary feet. Under these circumstances, even radical Protestants reacted against a purely man-centered interpretation of Christianity, and took up Henry Nelson Wieman's "naturalistic theism," stressing man's absolute dependence upon a super-human God as much as Schleiermacher had done, while finding this God manifested in the integrative, value-making processes that run through all nature and history, rather than in any special, supernatural events. Liberal Protestants at the same time became increasingly self-critical, ceased to call themselves "modernists," and generally agreed with Fosdick's sermon, "Beyond Modernism," which urged that it was the duty of Christians to correct and judge the modern age, rather than to conform uncritically to its prevailing ways.

The newest factor in the new situation, however, was the sudden increase of interest in the "new orthodoxy," a movement which had appeared ten years earlier in Continental Europe, in the dialectical theology of Barth and Brunner, but which now found powerful American allies in Reinhold Niebuhr, Paul Tillich, John Mackay, G. W. Richards, Edwin Lewis, and many others. So aggressive has neo-orthodoxy become throughout the Protestant world, so prominent in the leadership of the Ecumenical Movement, that all other theological trends have been forced to renovate themselves in order to meet the neo-orthodox challenge. Liberalism today is a chastened liberalism, less idealistic and more realistic than in 1920. Even fundamentalistic conservatism is not simply repeating old shibboleths, but studying the neo-orthodox position critically and defining its own position in relation to it.[26]

A definition of present issues between conservatives and liberals must therefore center in a definition of neo-orthodoxy. We shall be defining it more precisely in the next chapter, where we shall consider the neo-orthodox position on the knowledge of God; but broadly and provisionally, neo-orthodoxy may

[26] Cf. W. Van Til, *New Modernism*, Presbyterian Reformed Pub. Co., 1946, and E. J. Carnell, *Theology of Reinhold Niebuhr*, Eerdmans, 1950. For the trend of liberal theology, see Arnold Nash (ed.), *Protestant Thought in the Twentieth Century*, Macmillan, 1951, Chap. V, "Liberalism Chastened by Tragedy." Cf. the account of the same transition by a conservative evangelical, Carl F. H. Henry, in his *Fifty Years of Protestant Theology*, Wilde, 1950.

be defined as a revival of the main emphases of Luther and Calvin, of St. Augustine and St. Paul, on the insufficiency of human reason, the depravity of human nature, the inexorability of divine judgment, and the absolute need of divine grace if man is to be saved—all without slavish attachment to the details of traditional orthodox systems, and with a clear sense of the difference between the Word of God speaking *in and through* Scripture and the literal *words* of Scripture. It is a reaffirmation of the "evangelical" type of Christianity, in contrast to the "humanism" of Pelagius, Erasmus and Harnack. Neo-orthodoxy differs from scholastic and fundamentalistic conservatism in its free and symbolic use of the Bible, and its impressionistic interpretation of orthodox doctrines; from radical Protestantism in its profound distrust of natural science and natural theology as possible paths to deliverance; from liberal Protestantism, in its sharp opposition to every theology based on human experience, even if the experience be "religious" and "Christian."

Despite these differences, neo-orthodoxy has done much to bridge the gulf between liberals and conservatives, and show that both liberalism and conservatism have a necessary place in essential Christianity. By its sharp polemic against liberal and radical Protestantism, it has shown the peril of a theology so enamored of "relevance" that it copies its cultural environment and loses its own independent message. At the same time, it has shown by example—even if its theory fails to satisfy its critics—how a theology anchored in the unchanging Word of God may speak to the condition of twentieth-century man as though it were a letter addressed to him personally. As Paul Tillich appreciatively says of Barth's practice—in the very midst of an attack upon his theory—"Barth's greatness is that he corrects himself again and again in the light of the 'situation' and that he strenuously tries not to become his own follower." [27] Thus it is being proved in practice that the alternative between a faithfully Scriptural but hopelessly archaic theology and one that is modern but unbiblical is an unreal alternative. Conservative attachment to the eternal Gospel and liberal adaptation to modern needs and problems are not mutually inconsistent but equally necessary concerns. Without the first, Christianity becomes lost in its environment; without the second, its message does not reach the world for which Christ died, and into which he sent and sends his apostles. Only a reactionary conservatism or a reckless radicalism wholly lacking in one or the other of these concerns can be declared unchristian; essential Christianity keeps both concerns in fruitful tension and commerce with each other.

### SECTION 5. PROPOSED OUTLINE OF TOPICS

This is a textbook of Systematic Theology. In the theological curriculum, as traditionally organized, Systematic Theology follows Exegetical Theology (Old and New Testaments) and Historical Theology (Church History, History of Doctrine), and precedes Practical Theology (Homiletics, Pastoral Theology, Christian Education, etc.). From the other theological disciplines it derives its knowledge of the classic documents, historic development and present situation of the Christian Religion; to the other disciplines it gives an orderly, systematic account of the chief Christian convictions, their connections with one another and their relations with other faiths. As William Adams Brown

[27] Tillich, *op. cit.*, I, p. 5.

points out, it is "like philosophy in the curriculum of the university . . . midway between the sciences and the arts." [28]

There are three main branches of Systematic Theology, whose time-honored titles are Apologetics, Dogmatics, and Christian Ethics; or, as many schools now call them, Philosophy of Religion, Systematic Theology proper, and Christian Ethics. Apologetics or Philosophy of Religion compares the Christian faith with other faiths and thought systems, defines the nature of religion and of Christianity, discusses the most basic religious ideas, and defends the essential truth of Christianity without entering much into particulars. Dogmatics or Systematic Theology presents the Christian faith as an orderly, consistent system of doctrine. Christian Ethics does the same for the Christian moral ideal. Our concern in this textbook is with Systematic Theology proper; but as already said, we shall not abstain from apologetical or ethical questions so rigidly as some theologians. The line between the three neighboring branches of Systematic Theology is in our conception an arbitrary line, drawn only for convenience in the division of labor. When introducing each topic in Systematic Theology, we shall view it from the universal human perspective, as the Philosophy of Religion views it; before concluding the topic we shall try to show how the Christian faith gives a unique answer to the universal human question posed at the beginning. Ethical problems will be treated only in connection with the main divisions of the Christian faith.

What are these main divisions? Three have already been indicated, in our longer definition of essential Christianity: Theology proper (doctrine of God), Christology (doctrine of Christ the Savior), and Eschatology (doctrine of final destiny). These three divisions, corresponding as they do to the three articles of

[28] Brown, *Outline*, p. 5.

34

the Apostles' and Nicene Creeds, have been considered sufficient by some theologians; for example, by John Dickie, who names his third division "The Doctrine of the Holy Spirit," and Aulén, who names it "The Church of God." The fact that different titles can be given to the third division shows, however, that its subject matter is complex, and needs to be subdivided—as both Dickie and Aulén do subdivide it when they come to develop it. The second division is far more unified, as befits the central nucleus of the Christian faith; but the first division is usually subdivided into doctrines of God in himself and God in relation to the world; and it is usually preceded by an introductory discussion of reason and revelation as pathways to the knowledge of God. (In Tillich, this discussion forms the first part of the system; in Aulén, it is included in the Introduction; in Dickie, it appears as a subhead in Division I.) It is evident that some subdivision of the three main parts of the Christian faith is unavoidable, in an exposition of any length. The division here proposed is sevenfold:

I. The Knowledge of God
II. The Nature of God
III. God and the World
IV. God and Man
V. Christ the Savior
VI. The Church and the Means of Grace
VII. The Christian Hope (God's Kingdom)

The relation of this sevenfold division to the main threefold division can be seen from the accompanying diagram, where six of these divisions are roughly located on the triangular figure already used to indicate the "shape of a creed." (The *first* of the seven divisions is prefatory to the other six, so cannot be placed on the diagram. The doctrine of man is hard to diagram, as we shall see in Chapter V; it is related both to God's creation, as suggested here, and also to the process of salvation through Christ.)

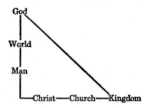

The order in which the topics of Systematic Theology are considered does not greatly matter, if it is clearly realized that *each topic presupposes what follows, as well as what precedes it.* In geometry, reasoning is linear, and the later propositions are rigidly determined by the axioms and propositions with which the whole science begins. If theology were like geometry, it would matter enormously with what topic we began; and an error in this first topic would vitiate the whole system. But as Paul Tillich points out, every religious philosophy, indeed "every understanding of spiritual things (*Geisteswissenschaft*) is circular," [29] not linear, and would betray its subject matter if it tried to escape from this circle. Methodologically, this means that neither the introduction nor any other part of the theological system is the logical basis for the other parts. Every part is dependent on every other part. The introduction presupposes the Christology and the doctrine of the church and vice versa. The arrangement is only a matter of expediency.[30]

There have been theologies which have ignored this principle, with disastrous results: God-centered theologies which have

[29] Tillich, *op. cit.*, I, p. 11.    [30] *Ibid.*, p. 11.

spoken of God quite apart from his self-revelation in Jesus Christ; man-centered theologies which have started with human experience and never got beyond it. If we were proposing to reason in linear fashion, either deductively or inductively, it might be disastrous to start with a chapter on the knowledge of God; for we might get bogged down in theory of knowledge, as so much modern philosophy has done, and never reach God at all. But if we keep in mind the inevitable circularity of theological thought, our findings on later topics will help to correct our findings on earlier topics. No theory of knowledge will be acceptable that is not congruous with the subject matter it attempts to interpret: God's redeeming love made manifest in Christ, and experienced by generation after generation of Christians as the power of a new life.

While this book follows a systematic order of topics, it does not aspire to build a theological system like Schleiermacher's or Tillich's. Its aim is the more modest one of helping students of theology to organize their own convictions in orderly style. It is hoped that this service may be rendered, whether the student holds a theological point of view similar to the author's, or one quite remote from it. By following this text, the student will be introduced to the great questions we all face, to the great answers on which Christians are generally agreed, and the live issues on which contemporary Christians must take sides. Whatever side the student takes, this ought to be a useful discipline to him.

Note. The term "neo-orthodox," much used in this chapter and elsewhere, is now under attack (*Christian Century*, May 22, 1957) and some of my critics have urged me to abandon it. I have preferred to keep it, define it, and distinguish its subtypes, as is done in Chap. II. Cf. the use of the term in Hordern's *Layman's Guide to Protestant Theology*, which is clarifying not confusing.

## II

## *THE KNOWLEDGE OF GOD*

SECTION 1. THE UNIVERSAL PROBLEM OF RELIGIOUS KNOWLEDGE

To speak of the "knowledge" of God, as most theologies do, might seem to imply a close analogy between religious knowledge and scientific knowledge, or common-sense knowledge of the things and persons that surround us. Yet it is a fundamental principle of monotheistic religion that "no man hath seen God at any time" (John 1:18), whereas the objects that surround us are perceivable by the five senses, and the scientific laws that govern their behavior are based on and tested by sense perception. Does this mean that religious knowledge is purely a matter of inner feeling or extrasensory perception?

There is an inexorable drive in higher religion which pushes us beyond the world of immediate perception, but it would be a great mistake to suppose that religion had nothing to do with this familiar visible world of "every day." Religion arises, as we have seen, out of an inescapable need to find an object of ultimate trust, a Goal of hope and endeavor, and a means of relating them, *so that this everyday life can be ordered, inspired and directed to its highest good.* The world around us is thickly populated with religious objects that can be perceived by the five senses: symbols and pictures, priests, preachers, and sacred books.

38

In polytheistic religions, the gods are represented by all sorts of "graven images," and worship is addressed to these visible, tangible objects. The trouble with such "idolatrous" worship is not that it focusses attention on a sense object, but that it directs religious trust and hope toward something too limited, too ephemeral to deserve it.

Even in primitive religion, it is important to distinguish between the visible objects used in worship and the mysterious beings symbolized by these objects: spirits good and evil, gods high and low, and the wonder-working power (*mana*) that lurks in so many unexpected places. What monotheism finally proclaims in the First Commandment, that no visible thing "in heaven above" or "in the earth beneath" (Ex. 20:4) is to be worshiped as divine, is a principle that implicitly emerges from the whole religious quest of mankind. No finite perishable thing or person can as such be made the Object of man's ultimate trust and devotion; no limited objective, realizable tomorrow, can be his ultimate Goal of hope and endeavor; no technically precise formula for solving problems of ways and means can adequately define his Way of Salvation. It is part of the evidence of man's high origin and unique destiny that none of the little, more easily knowable objects that surround him can permanently satisfy his religious aspirations. Without an act of faith, the thirst for religious knowledge cannot be satisfied.

Once man has set his aspirations free from entanglement with the things that are here today and gone tomorrow, where is he to stop in his religious quest? Can he finally stop "short of the reality upon which we and the whole structure of our lives ultimately depend"? [1] Monotheism says he cannot. But even if

[1] John Bennett, *Christianity and Our World*, Association Press, 1936. Chap. I, p. 5.

he stops somewhat short of this ultimate reality, he is already in a realm of high speculation and difficult conjecture where natural science and common-sense knowledge no longer suffice to answer the questions that inevitably arise. The dilemma is: *either* an answer that is no answer to his religious needs, because too bound to the finite realm, *or*, an answer that cannot be checked and proved like the weight of a sack of meal, or the shortest route from A to B.

It is a commonplace among sober religious thinkers that mystery (for reasons just noted) cannot be eliminated from the knowledge of God. *"Si comprehendis, non est Deus,"* said St. Augustine, which may be freely translated, "Anything you can get your mind clean around is not great enough to be your God." But does this omnipresence of mystery condemn us to *complete agnosticism* or sheer *uncontrolled conjecture* in matters of religious "knowledge"? (Double quotes would then surely have to be put around the word.) Both these alternatives eliminate themselves, upon closer examination.

1. The agnostic, defining God as "the Unknowable" (Herbert Spencer), may carefully abstain from making any *direct* affirmations about the Ultimate Being; but he cannot finally abstain (being human) from taking up some sort of religious attitude toward his world, involving all sorts of *indirect* affirmations about the "Unknowable" Ground of the world, implicit in what is said about the "knowable" phenomena that emerge from this Ground. The moment any such affirmation is indirectly and implicitly made, it becomes subject to intellectual criticism and questioning. When Spencer affirmed that the knowable world was everywhere evolving toward a more differentiated and more integrated condition, he implied that he knew a good deal about the character of the world ground.

2. Religious questions are proverbially urgent questions; they *cannot* be left in a status of "sheer uncontrolled conjecture." If religion made no difference in human life, it might be calmly left to pure conjecture—as we leave the purely fanciful question, "How many animal shapes can be found in that bank of cloud?" But since even religious skeptics are sure that *some* religious affirmations, at least, are bad and dangerous, they thus imply the possibility and necessity of some kind of controlled discrimination in the religious field, discerning good religion from bad, true from false, and so deserving the name of "knowledge."

How is controlled discrimination possible in a realm so high and mysterious as that of religion? How can one answer to the question of ultimate Reality or ultimate Destiny be known as truer or falser than another? The most general religious response to this question is, "By revelation." It is important to understand that this does not necessarily deliver us over into a realm of subjective feeling, or ineffable visions and voices, comprehensible only to mystics who have been "caught up into the third heaven." Revelation is a concept that both *relates* religious knowledge *to* the more ordinary forms of knowledge, and *distinguishes* it *from* them. Literally, it implies an uncovering (Gr. *apokalypsis*) or unveiling (Lat. *revelatio*) of hidden meaning in something perhaps many times observed in a more superficial way. In a crowded room full of veiled faces—and most faces wear a sort of veil, of impersonal unconcern—suddenly a veil is lifted, and another human face becomes full of meaning for me, perhaps in a way that will affect my whole destiny from then on.[2]

Aulén varies the classic figure only slightly when he speaks of

---

[2] The disbelievers in revelation might ask themselves whether they totally disbelieve in what is described in the famous song from *South Pacific* which tells what sometimes happens, on an "Enchanted Evening," between two human beings.

revelation as a *"transparency"* capable of being lighted up from behind. "When it is properly illuminated and the light falls where it should, then we see not only what we previously beheld, but moreover, just that which the transparency was intended to display." [3] This admirably conveys the mixture of ordinary perception and extraordinary intuition in every religious revelation. The vehicle of revelation may be a thing, an event, a person already well known in a drab, secular way ("Is not this the carpenter's son?" Mt. 13:55), but suddenly a *light from behind* brings out hidden patterns of meaning in it, and the face of God looks out at us from its depths.

Not that God is even now seen, as it were, with the naked eye. The paradox is (as Aulén goes on to say) that revelation never fully drives away mystery: "The more God reveals himself and the deeper faith looks into the mystery of his divine heart, the more he appears as the Unfathomable." [4] But now, to the one who has received the revelation and *responded in faith*, the mystery is a luminous mystery, disclosing enough intelligible meaning to call out his wholehearted commitment, and kindle his hope to know more of it as he lives longer with it. Faith and revelation thus are "corresponding concepts." [5] The unbelieving observer may stand on the very premises where the revelation takes place—let us say, at the very foot of the Cross—and see nothing.[6] Only for faith does the transparency light up. Faith *is* the lighting up. Faith is not blind; it is a form of illumination, a form of knowledge, never wholly divorced from common-sense knowledge, but piercing deeper into the heart of things.

---

[3] Aulén, *op. cit.*, p. 29.    [4] *Ibid.*, p. 47.    [5] *Ibid.*, p. 29.
[6] Cf. Pieter Bruegel's famous painting, "The Carrying of the Cross," where practically the whole throng, from playing children to dicing soldiers, are obviously unaware that the supreme revelation of God is going on in their very midst.

*Revelation and faith* are not the only concepts that have been used to interpret the process of religious knowledge. Many others have been used, in the long history of religion, such as *theophany, incarnation, prophecy, oracle.* Yet upon close examination, all these concepts will be found to say substantially the same thing, under various figures of speech. In theophany and incarnation, the invisible deity is said to *become manifest* to the senses, and even to take bodily form—but not as though his mysterious and sacred essence could be fully expressed in the visible form that manifests his presence. In prophecy and oracle, God is said to *speak forth* his Word and Will—yet not as though any divine sound could be heard, distinguishable from the human voice of the prophet, or the sound of earth's thousand voices in which he thinks to hear the echo of God's voice. The "sound of gentle stillness" (I Kings 19:12, Smith and Goodspeed) wherein the prophet Elijah heard God's voice was no sound at all, but the stillness of a believing heart, discerning God as only faith can discern him, in and through and beneath all sense impressions.

In all these different concepts, the same idea is conveyed that is conveyed by the twin concepts of revelation and faith: that man can commune with the divine Object of his trust and hope, the divine Source of his salvation, through the opening of a meaning that is conveyed in and through the sensible world, while at the same time there remains a mystery that is not dispelled. For men of faith God *shines* through, *comes* through, *speaks* through, while yet God holds something in reserve that cannot be disclosed even to men of faith, in their present mortal existence. "For *now* we see through a glass, darkly; but *then* face to face" (I Cor. 13:12). These words were written by a man who had received revelation, and whose inspired letters were destined to be included in the Sacred Scriptures.

43

We may conclude that the difficulty of getting true religious knowledge, and the difficulty of distinguishing it from quack imitations and fanatical delusions, are not manufactured difficulties, but inherent in the religious situation. If man could get along without religion altogether, he might circumvent these difficulties, and handle life as a cold, precise engineering proposition. If he could be content to worship a mortal, finite creature like himself, or still better, some limited natural object like a mountain, or the moon, he might hope to have scientifically precise knowledge of his gods. But since man wearies quickly of his gods unless he can look up to them, and since he cannot stop with mere mountains and moons, once he starts looking up, the mystery of infinity is necessarily involved in his religious thinking. To escape the difficulties of this stupendous mystery, one may retreat into the idolatry of the finite (erotic love or nationalistic frenzy) or one may refuse to commit oneself to anything, and live a simply dissipated existence; but these alternatives involve such insuperable difficulties that disillusionment drives one out of them in the end.

Is man then condemned by his own unquenchable religious thirst to close his eyes and swallow the mystery of infinity in whatever form it happens to present itself? Must he give up the attempt to discriminate between rival revelations, and simply believe the first thing he hears? In our faith-starved era, many men are doing exactly that, out of violent internal pressure to believe in *something*. It is part of the responsibility of every positive religion in such an age to make its special form of revelation persuasive to the mind as well as appealing to the heart; and this requires the working out of some sort of criterion of religious knowledge, whereby the true can be discriminated from the false in the claims and counterclaims of rival revelations. The possibility of doing this without deforming and betraying your own revelation in the process is one of the most bitterly controverted points in contemporary theology, so we shall have to postpone our discussion of it to the third (or controversial) section of this chapter. Yet on the basis of what has already been said about the general nature of religious revelation, we may venture to suggest that revelation and reason, religious knowledge and other forms of knowledge, are not hopelessly opposed to one another.

Revelation confronts us with an infinite mystery which can be penetrated only by an act of faith. Yes, but revelation conveys its vision of the meaning of the mystery in and through finite objects that can be known in other ways; and it interprets the meaning that shines through these objects in language derived from everyday experience—very much the same language used by literature and philosophy. There is thus *contact* as well as *difference* between religious knowledge and other forms of knowledge—which is all that is necessary to make some rational correlation between them conceivable.

### Section 2. The Christian Consensus Concerning the Knowledge of God

Christianity shares with other monotheistic religions the conviction that a *purely* rational approach to the knowledge of God is insufficient. Without a divine revelation received in faith, the mystery of life does not disclose its meaning. Even that highly subtle and sensitive form of reason called philosophy becomes tinged with faith and hungry for revelation, when it tries to deal with religious questions. (So, for example, at the end of some of Plato's dialogues, where rational argumentation gives way to religious "myths.") Like Judaism, the parent faith, Christianity sees the vehicle of divine revelation primarily in *historical events and personages*; indeed, the key events of Jewish history are as sacred to Christians as they are to Jews: the call of Abraham, the covenant with Jacob (Israel), the deliverance from Egypt and the giving of the Ten Commandments through Moses, the conquest of the Promised Land, its division and loss, the restoration after Cyrus' conquest of Babylon, and the persistent prophecy of a Messianic Age of justice and peace. In these events both Jews and Christians see more than the history of one nation; the hand of the One Universal God, creator and governor of all the world, is seen at work, guiding all the nations back toward their true destiny, through the leadership of one people specially called and consecrated to be God's People.

The distinctly Christian reading of this historic revelation is determined by the fact that one historical character, Jesus of Nazareth, born in the days of Caesar Augustus and crucified under Pontius Pilate, now occupies the central place in the divine-human drama of deliverance. He is the One in whom the Hebrew Law and Prophets are fulfilled, and through whom the persistent hope of Israel for the coming of a Messianic Age begins to be accomplished. His death, which at first glance appears to be proof of the failure of his mission, is seen as an act of divine sacrificial love, for the redemption of the world. His victory over death, the reinvigoration of his disheartened followers by the power of his living Spirit, and their swift missionary march from Jerusalem to Rome by the power of the same Spirit, are seen as evidence that he is now King of Kings and Lord of Lords, gov-

erning the universe at God's right hand, pending the great Day
when he shall return to judge all nations and establish God's
universal righteous rule.

Jewish categories do not suffice to express the central importance of Jesus the Christ in the Christian revelation. He is not
merely the Christ, the Messiah, the anointed agent and messen-
ger of God; he is God's "Son, whom he hath appointed heir of
all things, by whom he made the worlds . . . the brightness of
his glory, and the express image of his person" (Heb. 1:2,3);
he is God's eternal Word "made flesh" (John 1:14); he is the
very Power and Wisdom of God, become seemingly weak and
foolish for our sake (I Cor. 1:22–25). If the New Testament
Christian were asked where to look for the knowledge of God,
he would unhesitatingly answer that "the light of the knowledge of the glory of God" shines forth "in the face of Jesus
Christ" (II Cor. 4:6).

The revelation in Christ is so central in Christianity that it may
easily seem to make all other forms of revelation superfluous.
Yet there has been general agreement among Christians, in every
age, that Christ does not render the preparatory revelation in
Israel null and void; he brings it to a new focus, and opens it to
all mankind. There is also general agreement that the revelation
of God in Christ needs to be freshly interpreted and inwardly
appropriated by faith in each new generation, with the guidance
and help of the Holy Spirit, if it is to become *saving* knowledge
of God to modern men. There is more dispute (especially since
Karl Barth came on the scene) concerning the relation between
God's revelation in Christ and that natural universal revelation of
God of which the Apostle Paul speaks in several places (Romans
1:20, 2:14, 15). Usually it is regarded as an important though
subsidiary form of the knowledge of God, offering a point of

47

contact for understanding the Christian message and relating it to truth in other faiths and other fields of learning. But *the* revelation of God, all agree, was made in Christ; the Scriptures of the Old and New Testament enjoy a unique authority among all Christians because they lead up to and present his unique figure. In this sense, revelation closes with Christ and his first apostolic witnesses; no later events (till the last Great Day) will add anything essential to it; the work of the Christian Church is to *interpret* and *apply* it, not to add to it or change it.

The general Christian consensus concerning the centrality of the revelation in Christ, and its fulfillment of the Old Testament revelation, was well formulated at Edinburgh in 1937:

> We concur in affirming that the Word of God is ever living and dynamic and inseparable from God's activity. . . . God reveals Himself to us by what He does. . . . He calls and fashions His chosen people and speaks His word to His prophets and apostles, interpreting to them the meaning of His action. In the fulness of time the Word, the Eternal Son of God, is manifested in Christ our Lord, the Incarnate Word, and His redeeming work. . . .
>
> This divine revelation is addressed to man in the wholeness of his personality, and is apprehended by faith.
>
> We are at one in asserting the uniqueness and supremacy of the revelation given in Christ. . . . None of us holds that there is a revelation *outside* Christ which can be put on the same level as the revelation in Christ. But while some are prepared to recognize a *Praeparatio evangelica* not only in Hebrew but also in other religions, and believe that God makes Himself known in nature and in history, others hold that the only revelation which the Church can know and to which it should witness is the revelation in Jesus Christ, as contained in the Old and New Testaments.[7]

---

[7] *Report of the Second World Conference on Faith and Order* (Faith and Order Pamphlet No. 90), p. 8. This report is reprinted completely in Bell, *op. cit.*

It will be noted that the controversy described in the last sentence above does not affect the validity of the *Old Testament* revelation, but only that of *general* revelation (in nature, history and other religions) which Barthians commonly reject. There have, to be sure, been anti-Semitic movements in ancient times (Marcion) and in modern times (German Nazi Christianity) which have rejected the Old Testament as part of the Christian revelation, but these movements have always been decisively repudiated by the Church at large. Pius XI represented all Christendom when he said, in defiance of one such movement, "Spiritually, we are Semites."

While the Old and New Testaments are revered by all Christians as God's inspired Word, and as the principal authoritative sources on which Christian teaching should be based, there is only a partial and incipient agreement concerning the relation between Scripture and church tradition. At the time of the Reformation, there was flat contradiction between Protestant teaching, based on "Scripture alone," and Catholic teaching, based partly on Scripture and partly on tradition. Today, there has been some modification of this harsh contrast, on both sides. Protestants now commonly admit that tradition has an important and positive part to play in Christian teaching. The New Testament Gospels already had existed as an oral *paradosis* before they were written down; and on every new mission field (as was remarked by an experienced missionary at Madras in 1938) the Scriptures lend themselves to misinterpretation by cranks and sects unless a "sound tradition of Biblical interpretation" is soon established. On the Catholic and Orthodox side, it is now commonly agreed that traditions *contrary to Scripture* cannot be sound traditions. One of the two "permitted opinions" among Roman Catholics is that tradition is not (as other Catholics say) a parallel source of divine truth, separate from the Scriptures, but simply the authorized churchly interpretation *of* the Scriptures in their wholeness.[8]

Tentative expressions of this new partial consensus will be found in the Edinburgh Faith and Order Report, in Aulén's *Faith of the Christian Church*, and in the Lund Report on Ways of Worship. Edinburgh (p. 9) was very clear in its recognition that while the *living* Word precedes and creates the Church, the Church's life and tradition precede and create the *written* Word:

A testimony by *words* is by divine ordering provided for the revelation uttered by the *Word*. This testimony is given in Holy Scripture, which thus affords the primary norm for the Church's teaching, worship and life. . . . By tradition is meant the living stream of the Church's life. . . . We are at one in recognizing that the Church, enlightened by the Holy Spirit, has been instrumental in the formation of the Bible.

Aulén, similarly, declares that a sound Christian theology must recognize both the "principle of Scripture" and the "principle of tradition." It sets forth

the Christian Faith as it has been expressed through the centuries . . . positively but not legalistically dependent upon the continuous testimony of faith given through the ages, or, in other words, in the tradition. But within this tradition the writings of the New Testament occupy a special place . . . first and decisive testimony to that

[8] St. Jerome is invoked in support of this opinion. He once described the Bible as like a castle, with a key to each room, and a key to the main gate. The key to each room (each book) is sound exegesis; the key to the gate (whole Bible) is Church tradition. An excellent contemporary expression of this view will be found in Father George Tavard's essay on "Scripture, Tradition and History," in the *Downside Review* (Summer, 1954), pp. 232–44, especially the last two pages, where the danger of trusting "post-apostolic oral tradition conveying apostolic doctrines which are not included in Scripture" is expressly warned against, since Papias "in its name, repeated gossip which is clearly false" (p. 243).

deed of Christ which is the fundamental fact of Christianity. Nothing can take the place of this testimony.[9]

Many Orthodox and Catholic thinkers would agree to this conception of the New Testament as *that part of Christian tradition which gives the norm to all the rest.* There are still unresolved problems outstanding in this area, but it is fair to say that real progress toward agreement has been made in our time. The Lund preliminary report on "Ways of Worship" registers the present agreement very well:

The recognition that tradition was present and active in the formation of Holy Scripture is met by the acknowledgement that no development of later tradition will be true if inconsistent with Scripture. . . . Moreover, there is a growing recognition that tradition is not simply a thing of the past, but a living reality . . . the tenets of the Reformation are a tradition as well as those of Scholasticism. No Christian age can accept all tradition at the same time, or reject tradition as such.[10]

Among the outstanding landmarks of the Christian tradition, valuable for ecumenical theology, may be mentioned the creeds and confessions of the various churches, the findings of ecclesiastical councils, the sequence of the Christian Year, Christian art and music, liturgical and devotional literature, the lives of the saints, and the great theological systems.[11] All these are potential

[9] Aulén, *op. cit.*, p. 90.
[10] Faith and Order Commission Papers No. 6, p. 8. (A new series of Faith and Order Pamphlets begins after the Amsterdam Assembly, when the Faith and Order Movement becomes a Commission of the World Council of Churches. The old series runs up to No. 103, which is No. 1 of the new.)
[11] Some of these are seldom mentioned as sources of theology. It is part of the greatness of the new *Initiation Théologique*, now being issued by the French Dominicans (Paris: Editions du Cerf, 1952 ff.), that it uses art and liturgy as sources of theology. It also uses Canon Law, in which few non-Roman Christians would care to follow it; but William Adams Brown, in his posthumous book, *How to Think of Christ* (Scribner, 1945), has some appreciative comments on "The Lawyer's Christ" (Chap. VIII).

sources for Christian theology, since they are expressions of the Christian tradition; all are to be tested by their degree of conformity to the supreme personal norm of the Christian faith, Jesus Christ, and its supreme literary norm, the Bible (especially the New Testament).

The necessity of *creeds* and *confessions* arises from the complexity of the Scriptures, and the need of stating their message briefly, in relation to the problems of each new time. All are more or less conditioned by their time, and by the sectarian conflicts which occasioned many of them; but at least two of them (the Apostles' and Nicene Creeds) have been used for many centuries as part of Christian public worship, and as outlines for catechetical instruction in the elements of the Christian faith. Thus they have become central bearers of the Christian tradition to an extraordinary degree. No decision of an *ecclesiastical council* equals them in this respect; but on crucial disputed issues, some councils have set negative bounds to Christian thought (eliminating extreme positions to right and left) which have been generally respected ever since. This is particularly true of the Council of Jerusalem, the Council of Nicaea, and the Council of Chalcedon. These councils were "ecumenical" (representative of the world-wide Christian movement) in a very high degree; modern "ecumenical" meetings like Lausanne, Edinburgh, Amsterdam, represent the whole Church only in a prophetic, embryonic manner. On the other hand, as already observed in Chapter I, the consensus arrived at in these modern councils is a relatively *free* consensus, undisturbed by the kind of political pressure exerted by the Roman Emperors at Nicaea and Chalcedon.[12]

[12] Lest we be too complacent about this, it is well to remember that the Moscow Synod of 1948 denounced the Amsterdam Assembly (despite the free debate between Dulles and Hromadka) as dominated by political motives of an "anti-democratic" character.

Christian *art* and *music*, the *lives of the saints*, and the *literature of devotion* express the Christian tradition with something of the richness and unpruned luxuriance to be found in the Bible itself. To ignore them is to be in danger of getting a devitalized, uninspiring conception of the Christian message, to rely on them exclusively is to run the risk of leaving the message vague and formless. The value of the *Christian Year* and the *liturgy* is that they select high points in Scripture and tradition for special celebration and recurrent emphasis, thus organizing Christian worship as systematic theology organizes Christian teaching. The *substance* of the great *theological systems* is much the same as that of the Christian Year and the liturgy; while their *form* is largely borrowed from contemporary philosophies. In ancient and medieval theology, the Neo-Platonic and Aristotelian philosophies furnished the rational framework for the organization of Christian thought; in modern theology, the Kantian philosophy, while never so generally accepted, has exerted a similar formative influence on Christian thought. No one of these philosophies has ever been regarded as *the* Christian philosophy—not even the Thomistic-Aristotelian, which Roman Catholic priests are expected to study, but not follow in all its details [13]—yet in the course of the centuries, the combined influence of these philosophies has become an important element in the Christian tradition. Like all other traditional elements, it must be tested by Christ and by Scripture, while at the same time it helps to make Christ and Scripture intelligible to later generations. If Christian art and liturgy show traces of the Holy Spirit's prompting and guidance, why not Christian theology,

[13] The *Initiation Théologique*, written by Thomists and deliberately following the order of St. Thomas' *Summa Theologica*, makes it magnanimously clear that other ways of organizing a theological system are open to good Catholics. (Vol. I, pp. 278-91.)

too, even in its most severely rational passages? Cannot thought as well as emotion be inspired?

The help of the Holy Spirit is necessary not only to interpret the Christian revelation freshly to each new generation and each special social group, but to open the eyes of each new individual to its meaning *for him.* George Fox's mystical "openings" and the strange warming of John Wesley's heart were extraordinary and dramatic instances of a universally necessary Christian experience. Each genuine Christian believer has some day had it inwardly revealed to him (quietly and undramatically, perhaps) that Christ really speaks to "his condition," and calls him personally to discipleship. A professor of philosophy, looking at a picture of Christ washing the disciples' feet, suddenly realizes that "the Absolute is my valet," and becomes a Christian from that moment. More commonly, it is something in family tradition, in the teaching of church or school, in the contemporary social situation, which touches an individual and becomes the occasion of his inner illumination. Whatever the immediate stimulus may be, there is general agreement that the Spirit must light a man up from within, or he will not be capable of seeing what the Spirit is trying to reveal to him from without, in Christ and Scripture and Tradition.

Sometimes the "inner light" is so exclusively stressed by mystical Christians that other Christians are forced to stress the objective, external side of revelation, lest the historical character of the Christian revelation should be dissolved in pure "illuminism." But even those forms of Christian thought which most heavily stress the historical, once-for-all-given character of the Christian revelation find it quite consistent to stress the inward work of the Spirit in "applying" the revelation to each individual. So, for example, the Protestant Reformers balanced their emphasis on the external Word of God in the infallible Scriptures by an equal emphasis on the "inward witness (*testimonium internum*) of the Holy Spirit"—God in the soul saying, "Amen!" (so to speak) to God in history. In one form or another, this doctrine of the inner witness of the Holy Spirit appears in all Christian traditions, from Quakerism to Catholicism, and thus belongs to the ecumenical consensus concerning the knowledge of God: *God in Israel and in Jesus Christ, to whom the inspired Scriptures (and holy traditions) bear outward witness, and the Holy Spirit bears inward witness.* From this point of view, the restless gropings and questionings of the modern man can be interpreted as *God at work within him.* The God of the Bible has made man for himself, and everlastingly solicits him from without and from within, leading him back toward his True Source and Goal without ever violating his freedom.

SECTION 3. UNRESOLVED ISSUES CONCERNING THE KNOWLEDGE OF GOD

The consensus that we have been interpreting is very hard to define, as at some points (Scripture and tradition) it is barely beginning to emerge, while at other points (Scripture as "God's Word") it is being recovered after a period of confusion due to conflict between different schools of Biblical criticism. Underneath and alongside this emergent, re-emergent consensus, there is a great deal of serious and honest divergence among Christians concerning the knowledge of God. Here is the topic where the schools of Christian thought first divide in principle. Divergencies on other topics can largely, though not exclusively, be seen as logical consequences of the position taken on this one. It will be necessary, then, to examine carefully the chief alternative positions between which Christians are divided on this crucially important theme. As to what are the *chief* positions, the perspective will naturally vary from place to place. From an American perspective, the varieties of Protestantism are sharply exposed in the foreground, and the varieties of Catholicism obscured in the background; but it will be important to note differences between both Catholics and Protestants.

### A. *Catholic Positions: Roman and non-Roman*

The Roman Catholic position has such numerical strength and such logical consistency that it may be taken as the principal form of Catholicism, while non-Roman Catholicism (Eastern Orthodoxy, Anglo-Catholicism, Old Catholicism) may be distinguished from it by comparison. The Roman Catholic theory of the knowledge of God may be divided into five parts: (1) the rational "preambles of the faith," (2) the general and preliminary forms of revelation, (3) the definitive revelation in Jesus Christ, (4) Scripture and Tradition as inspired, authoritative "sources of the faith," (5) the Catholic Church, its apostolic hierarchy and its Supreme Pontiff as infallible interpreters of the faith.

1. *Praembula fidei.* That the natural light of reason rightly used can lead man to a clear knowledge of "the existence of God and the infinity of His perfections," is a position consistently maintained by the Roman Catholic Church throughout its history. Down to the time of St. Anselm in the early Middle Ages, the prevailing line of argument was Platonic and intuitive, as typically in St. Augustine. St. Anselm's *ontological* argument, that the Most Perfect Being must exist, or a still more perfect could be conceived, depends for its force on Platonic realism. St.

Thomas Aquinas perfected an Aristotelian line of argument, proceeding from the observable phenomena of nature to their unseen divine First Cause and Final Goal. His classic "five proofs" of the existence of God deliberately omit St. Anselm's ontological argument, and confine themselves to *cosmological* and *teleological* arguments: from motion to a Prime Mover, from all sorts of effects to a First Cause, from contingent realities to a Necessary Reality, from degrees of perfection to an absolute Perfect Being, from moral order to a Moral Governor.[14]

The Roman Catholic Church has never accepted the validity of Kant's criticism of these rational arguments,[15] and has condemned all purely "fideistic" or pragmatic or anti-intellectualistic justifications of faith in God; but the more Platonic, intuitive line of thought, continued in the Middle Ages by the Franciscans, has never died out and never been outlawed. It is part of the greatness of Jacques Maritain's *Degrees of Knowledge* that it starts with common-sense perception, like Aristotle and St. Thomas, but builds a logical hierarchy in which intuitive "Augustinian wisdom" and the testimony of the great mystical saints find a place of high honor, subordinate only to divine revelation. There is enough Augustinian mysticism in St. Thomas himself, and in the whole history of the Roman Church to justify this Neo-Thomistic reconciliation of Augustine with Thomas, mysticism with rationalism.

The Roman Catholics have never claimed that "reason alone, by reasoning alone," could lead man to a *saving* knowledge of God. God's holy Will for man and saving Grace can be known

---

[14] *Summa Theologica*, Part I, Q. II.
[15] *Critique of Pure Reason* (Norman Kemp Smith Edition, Macmillan, 1950), pp. 495-531. For the condemnation of Kantianism and "fideism" in nineteenth-century Catholic thought, see my doctoral dissertation on *The Philosophy of the Abbé Bautain* (New York Univ. Press, 1926), pp. 74-97.

only by revelation. But a rational knowledge of God is sufficient, as St. Paul says, to leave man "without excuse" (Romans 1:20) if he does not press on from this preliminary rational knowledge to the fuller revealed knowledge that is implied and foreshadowed in it.

2. *General and preliminary forms of revelation.* It is part of Catholic teaching that a "primitive revelation" was made to the "first men."[16] (The Church is not, however, committed to the "traditionalist" theory which finds this revelation in the early legends of all peoples.) Primitive revelation is not to be sharply distinguished from natural or rational theology. Some of the same truths are taught by reason and by general revelation—because man's moral weakness makes him fail to follow his reason without added light from above—but as early as the first chapters of Genesis, God begins to reveal the inner mysteries of his nature to men, step by step. The first announcement of the Gospel, later to be fulfilled in Jesus Christ and his Blessed Mother, is found in Gen. 3:15, where enmity is decreed between the Serpent and the Woman, and the coming of One is predicted who shall bruise the Serpent's head.[17] The whole Old Testament is not only full of clear revelations of God, but of mysterious anticipations of the full Redemption that is to come. (See for example the Old Testament tableaux in the Oberammergau Passion Play, for this persistent Catholic use of Old Testament typology.)

3. *The definitive revelation in Jesus Christ.* What the Old Testament prefigures and partially discloses is fully and definitively revealed in Jesus Christ. He is "the Truth Incarnate" (John 14:6). "He is *God*, the Truth made flesh! he is the

---

[16] Rudloff and Muller, *Petite Théologie Dogmatique à la Portée de Tous,* p. 13, Note 3. Cf. English version, *Everyman's Theology,* cited on p. 275.
[17] *Ibid.,* p. 220.

*Revelation of God.*"[18] What is here revealed has only to be faithfully preserved and rightly proclaimed, to the end of the world; it cannot be added to or changed.

4. *Scripture and tradition as "sources of the faith."* Although the Catholic faith does not rest so heavily upon the sole authority of Scripture as most forms of Protestantism, Roman Catholics claim to hold the sacred writings in equally high honor. The list of canonical books varies slightly from the Protestant, including certain books which appear only in the Greek Septuagint version of the Old Testament—Tobit, Judith, I and II Maccabees, Baruch, Ecclesiasticus, Wisdom of Solomon, and the Greek supplements of Daniel and Esther. These canonical books were all declared by the Vatican Council to have been "written under the inspiration of the Holy Spirit" and thus to "have God for their Author."[19] Divine inspiration does not imply that the human faculties and individual diversities of the human authors were destroyed by the Divine Author; the Bible remains a truly and richly human book in and through which the Word of God speaks to us. Divine Authorship does, however, imply that the Bible is unique in all literature as a source of religious guidance and inspiration, and *contains no error whatsoever, since God cannot lie.* This means that the Bible is infallible not only in matters of faith and morals, but also in *matters of fact*, provided that the facts are really basic to the revelation conveyed through them, and are not merely irrelevant circumstances.

There are problems, of course, in the detailed application of this doctrine of Scriptural infallibility. Many facts of natural and historical science appear to contradict Scriptural assertions. God

[18] Ibid., p. 13.
[19] Denzinger, Enchiridion, 1787. Freiburg: Herder, 1937 (23rd ed., ed. Bannwart).

cannot contradict himself, and all truth comes from him. It may be that the alleged scientific fact is only "science falsely so-called" and needs re-examination; or it may be that the Biblical author did not really mean to say what he seems to say. Many theories have been proposed by Catholics to reconcile these apparent contradictions. Some of them have been declared unacceptable by recent papal encyclicals,[20] though no official dogma on the subject has yet been formulated. It is unacceptable, for example, to say that *parts* of the Bible are not inspired; or that while all parts are *religiously inspired* not all are *factually inerrant*; or that the Bible has no concern for *historical facts*, but only for *eternal truths* of which inaccurate facts may be good metaphors.

The theory favored in recent Roman Catholic thought is that of "literary *genres*." Every literary *genre* has its own sort of truth; poetical truth is not the same as scientific or historical truth; ancient sacred history belongs to a different literary *genre* from modern secular history. If it would be unfair to declare the parables of Jesus "untrue" because what they relate did not happen just so, it would be equally unfair to declare Old Testament history "untrue" or the Creation story of Genesis "false," because they do not conform to the standards of modern secular historiography. Sacred history's purpose, when one properly classifies its literary *genre*, is sometimes to "point a moral" rather than to tell a precisely accurate tale; if it fulfills this purpose adequately, it is infallibly true in its own proper literary *genre*.[21]

Though Scripture is infallibly true, it is not by itself sufficient to guide us into all truth necessary to salvation. *Tradition* is

[20] Leo XIII, *Providentissimus;* Pius X, *Pascendi;* Benedict XV, *Spiritus Paraclitus;* Pius XII, *Divino afflante.*

[21] For a clear interpretation of this theory, see *Initiation Théologique*, Vol. I, Chap. II, pp. 63–73.

needed to supplement it, and is therefore, according to the Council of Trent, to be held in "equal respect."[22] Some Catholics maintain that tradition teaches important points of faith and morals not contained in Scripture—that Sunday is to be observed instead of Saturday, that certain "laws of the Church" are to be added to the Ten Commandments, and which parts of Hebrew-Christian literature are apocryphal, rather than canonical. Other Catholics maintain that Christian faith and morals are entirely contained in Scripture, but implicitly rather than explicitly, so that tradition is needed to interpret, develop and freshly apply the "deposit of faith" once for all given in Scripture. "Tradition is in a certain sense the way in which the text itself or the message of Scripture has been understood in the Church, and then applied to life."[23] In either case, tradition is indispensable.

5. *The Catholic Church as infallible interpreter of the faith.* Scripture and tradition do not stand by themselves, outside the Church. The Church as the Mystical Body of Christ, entrusted by its divine Lord with the task of teaching and preaching the Gospel until the end of the age, is in a sense the most comprehensive source of religious truth to all its members. As Scripture

---

[22] Denzinger, *op. cit.*, 783.

[23] *Initiation Théologique*, Vol. I, p. 84. The importance of tradition, even on the more moderate view, and the possibility that it may lead to conclusions very remote from the Bible's explicit teachings, may be gathered from the later distinction between *formal, explicit* revelation (given in the text of Scripture), *formal, implicit* revelation (implied in the text) and *virtual* revelation (dogmatic conclusions deduced from Scriptural revelation by means of natural truths that serve as minor premises). St. Thomas Aquinas doubted that a merely "virtual" revelation could be made a formal dogma of the Catholic faith; but the Dogma of the Assumption has now, it would seem, been officially promulgated on just such a basis. Dom Bernard Capelle, o.s.b., in his "Théologie de l'Assomption," in *Nouvelle Revue Théologique* (Louvain, 1950, pp. 1009–27) admits that there is no basis for this dogma in Scripture or in tradition down to the seventh century; it is based on an elaborate logical development of dogma, on *rationes* rather than on *auctoritates*. Cf. Chap. VI, sec. 3, *infra*.

# Christian Theology

contains and interprets revelation, as tradition contains and interprets Scripture, so the living Church contains and interprets tradition. If the Church were not infallible as an interpreter of Scripture, the infallibility of Scripture would not infallibly guide us into all truth.

The infallibility of the Church is not found equally in all its parts. The teaching function (*magisterium*) of the Church resides primarily in the clergy (*ecclesia docens*) rather than in the laity (*ecclesia docta*), though in a certain sense every Christian is called to be an apostle, and much is now being made of the concept of the "lay apostolate." [24] In the teaching function of the clergy, we must further distinguish between the *ordinary* and *extraordinary magisterium*. The *ordinary* teaching of the Church may sometimes be *universal*, when the bishops, successors of the apostles, teach the same doctrine unanimously. Whatever is thus unanimously taught is infallibly true, by virtue of Christ's promise to his apostles, even if no special official dogma is declared; whatever is not so unanimously taught is not infallible. The *extraordinary* teaching of the Church expresses itself in dogmas formulated officially, when special problems arise, either by an Ecumenical Council (the whole Episcopal College in communion with the Sovereign Pontiff) or by the Sovereign Pontiff himself. The dogmas defined by an Ecumenical Council, or by the Pope speaking *ex cathedra* (that is, "in the exercise of his function as Pastor and Teacher of all Christians, and in view of his supreme apostolic authority . . . . on faith or morals" [25]), are infallible.

It should be understood that neither the *ordinary* nor the

[24] See especially the letter, "Priests among Men," issued by the late Cardinal Suhard of Paris.
[25] Denzinger, *op. cit.*, 1839.

*extraordinary magisterium*, neither the consensus of bishops nor an Ecumenical Council nor the Supreme Pontiff, has authority to teach any new doctrine which is not explicitly or implicitly contained in the unique divine Revelation made in Christ. The function of all these interpreters is to confirm and make more explicit what God said to us in Christ. The Pope is not *impeccable* (he has his private confessor) and his ordinary utterances (such as the encyclicals) are not regarded as infallible; but all that he teaches is viewed with great respect by the bishops, as the teaching of the bishops is respected by the lower clergy, and the teaching of the clergy (ideally, at least!) by the laity. In the teaching of the living Church and its Supreme Pontiff the whole Roman Catholic system comes to a definite conclusion. "*Roma locuta est, causa finita est*"—no other church can settle doctrinal questions so finally and definitely as that. [26]

Non-Roman Catholicism agrees with Roman Catholicism concerning the provisional and partial validity of the knowledge of God that comes through the light of reason and nature, through general revelation, and through the sacred history of the Chosen People. It also agrees concerning the definitive revelation in Christ, the correlative function of Scripture and tradition as witnesses to this revelation, and the living Church as its proper interpreter. The main differences lie in the rejection of papal infallibility, and the refusal to accept the authority of so-called

[26] "Rome has spoken, the case is closed." If nothing has been said in this exposition about the inward testimony of the Holy Spirit in the believer's heart, this is because the dominant emphasis in Roman Catholic doctrine, as in Roman Catholic liturgy, is *objective* rather than *subjective*. But many passages can be cited to prove that the principle of "inner light" is neither denied nor forgotten. Cf. Guardini, *Vom Geist der Liturgie* (Freiburg, 1918), Chap. I, where the objective character of the liturgy appears as its great glory, but the rights of private feeling and initiative in worship are likewise defended. See also *Initiation Théologique*, Vol. I, pp. 264 ff., 284 ff., where the relative liberty of theology to interpret the faith subjectively, in order to "grasp" it, is defended.

"ecumenical" councils (such as the Councils of Trent and the Vatican) since the Eastern and Western Churches became divided.

Eastern Orthodox, Anglo-Catholics and Old Catholics all accept the authority of the Seven Ecumenical Councils of the ancient Church, and all are dubious of the later developments of dogma in the Roman Church, culminating in the dogma of papal infallibility (1870). Authority is not pyramided in a hierarchy coming to a point in the Pope; it resides in the acceptance of a doctrine by the *Church as a whole*. This is what is meant by the principle of *sobornost* (Catholicity) in the Russian Orthodox Church. Its nearest Roman analogy would be the "ordinary" *magisterium* of the Church in its "universal" form—except that the Roman Church means by "universal" the unanimity of the *bishops*, whereas the Russian Church appeals to the *Church at large*.[27] If this makes Orthodox dogma hard to define, and hard to distinguish precisely from heresy, it is the conviction of Eastern Orthodoxy that the deepest things in the faith are not precisely definable, but mysteries to be reverently felt out by mystical insight. Anglo-Catholicism and Old Catholicism have somewhat different attitudes toward doctrine, but both try to protect freedom of interpretation from too much interference on the part of the hierarchy. When an Anglo-Catholic disagrees with his bishop, he sometimes behaves in a very Protestant fashion.

The concern for intellectual freedom in the non-Roman churches proves that liberal theology can exist in them. An Anglo-Catholic, for example, can be both a High Churchman and

---

[27] For the meaning of *sobornost*, see Sergius Bulgakov, *The Orthodox Church*, London: Bles, 1935; cf. his contribution to the Baillie and Martin symposium on *Revelation*, Faber and Faber, 1937.

a Broad Churchman. As a matter of fact, liberalism can and does exist in the Roman Catholic Church, too. The Encyclical *Pascendi* (1907) revealed the existence of a Catholic Modernist Movement of considerable proportions. While this movement was severely denounced and largely suppressed by the Roman authorities, other forms of liberalism, usually known as "progressivism," are very strong in countries like France, Belgium and Germany, whereas conservative or "integralist" tendencies prevail in countries like Spain. The Vatican sometimes encourages progressivism (in the interest of a missionary appeal to alienated intellectuals or workmen, for example, and sometimes "applies the brakes" when it thinks the integrity of the faith is endangered—even by highly successful missions like that of the French workmen-priests. However, since liberal tendencies have larger scope in Protestantism than in Catholicism, we shall consider them mainly under that head.

B. *Protestant Positions: Conservative, Liberal, Radical and Neo-Orthodox*

1. *Conservative Protestantism* continues the original revolt of the Protestant Reformers against Catholic scholasticism, Catholic traditions, and the authority of the Catholic hierarchy. The slogan of this revolt was *"sola Scriptura, sola fide, solus Christus"*: Scripture the only formal test of truth, faith the only human requirement for receiving this saving truth, and Christ the whole content of the saving message. As worked out in the post-Reformation period, this position was not so exclusively Biblical as it sounds. Reason and nature were not wholly excluded as sources of the knowledge of God, and the Protestant confessions became the basis of a new Protestant tradition. Today conservative Protestantism takes two main forms: *confessionalism* and

*fundamentalism.* Confessional conservatism adheres strictly to the historic Protestant creeds, confessions and catechisms, and the theology that was built upon them in the post-Reformation period of Protestant scholasticism; thus it tends to be strongly Lutheran or Calvinistic, as the case may be. Fundamentalism on the other hand cuts across denominational lines, like the pietist-evangelical movement of which it is one historical outcome. Instead of insisting upon adherence to a complete system of doctrine, fundamentalism insists only upon a short list of minimum essentials, of which the first and most important is *the plenary, verbal inspiration of Scripture.* All other "fundamentals," such as the Virgin Birth, Bodily Resurrection, Blood Atonement and Physical Second Coming of Christ, represent parts of Scripture close to the center of the Gospel, where the literal veracity of the Scriptural narrative has been questioned by modern liberalism.

"The Bible alone is the religion of Protestants." This perhaps applies with approximate accuracy both to the confessionalists and to the fundamentalists. Both emphasize the Scriptural Word of God as the "infallible rule of faith and practice," sufficient by itself, without traditional supplements, to give the saving knowledge of God. This does not deny the existence of a natural and general revelation of God outside the Scriptures,[28] nor does it deny the necessity of an inward work of the Spirit, to make the human heart receptive to the Scriptural Word of God. Yet the hope of salvation does not finally rest on anything in nature or in the human heart; it rests on God's promises declared in the Scriptures. The confessionalists use the Scriptures more freely

---

[28] See, e.g., L. Berkhof, *Manual of Christian Doctrine*, Eerdmans, 1950, pp. 23 ff., for a representative conservative position on this point. Cf. Carnell, *Introduction to Christian Apologetics*, Eerdmans, 1948, Chaps. V–X.

and flexibly than the fundamentalists, resting on the infallible truth of the Bible's central message—"an unbreakable whole of which Christ is the centre"—rather than upon the infallibility of each text and word. Finally, however, both groups appeal to the written Word as the test of their faith. With Luther, Calvin and the other Reformers, they take *sola Scriptura* as the "formal principle" of all their teaching.

2. *Liberal Protestantism.* The characteristic liberal approach to the knowledge of God is through *experience*. Liberal Protestant theology inherits the pietist-evangelical reaction against a dry, scholastic emphasis on correct doctrine. What shall it profit a man if he learn the whole catechism and stifle his own soul? Schleiermacher, the father of modern liberal theology, was raised a Moravian; and his whole theology was a learned elaboration of the Moravian stress upon heartfelt religious experience. The Bible and the historic creeds do not disappear from his theology, but they are treated as crystallizations of religious experience. Only that in them which springs from firsthand mystical experience of God and can be reproduced again as firsthand experience, is genuine knowledge of God; the rest is mere speculation or accidental historic accretion.

Schleiermacher's appeal to mystical experience was not typical of the whole liberal movement. Another type of liberalism arose in the latter half of the nineteenth century, emphasizing *moral and social* rather than *mystical* experience. Under the leadership of Ritschl, Harnack and Troeltsch, Christianity was interpreted as an ethical movement aiming at a great social goal, the rule of divine love and justice on earth—a goal whose eventual attainment would be the legitimate test of the soundness of the movement. In German liberalism, the mysticism of Schleiermacher and the moralism of Ritschl were rather sharply opposed to each other; in French and Anglo-Saxon liberalism, the mystical and moral emphasis were combined and reconciled, through a general appeal to experience-of-all-sorts, in which experimental science served as a pattern and analogy for experimental religion.

The analogy between experimental science and experimental religion is developed with great clarity in Auguste Sabatier's *Religions of Authority and the Religion of the Spirit*,[29] perhaps the classic expression of the liberal Protestant position on the knowledge of God. The conservative Protestant doctrine of the infallible Book is rejected as decisively as the Catholic doctrine of the infallible Church. *Both* types of authority have a provisional, educational validity, very much as the findings of previous scientists are valid starting points for new scientific investigations; but all merely *extrinsic* secondhand truth is inferior to the *intrinsic* firsthand truth of direct observation and experiment. Both in science and in religion, authority should aim to render itself less and less necessary, by leading over into firsthand, self-evidencing experiences. The New Testament is "The Charter of the Religion of the Spirit," because it is full of the assurance that what has hitherto been believed by hearsay or by promise may now be experienced as present actuality, and what is partial in this present experience may be more fully tested in future experience.[30] The uniqueness of the Christian revelation is not denied in this doctrine; but it is found in a unique quality, reproducing itself in Christian experience from age to age, rather than in unique, unrepeatable historic events.[31]

[29] English translation, New York, McClure, Phillips, 1904.
[30] *Ibid.*, Bk. III, Chap. III.
[31] Harry Emerson Fosdick elaborates this theory of "reproducible experience" in his book on *The Modern Use of the Bible* (Macmillan, 1925), Lecture IV, "Abiding Experiences in Changing Categories."

3. *Radical Protestantism* has reacted against this liberal Protestant position in one distinctive way, while neo-orthodoxy has reacted in an exactly opposite direction, as we shall see. Liberal theology often claimed a kind of scientific validity for its conclusions, by following Sabatier's analogy between experimental science and experimental religion. One American theologian, the late D. C. Macintosh of Yale, wrote a book entitled *Theology As an Empirical Science* (1919) working out this thesis in great detail. But some who accepted the ideal of a scientific theology doubted whether the analogy strictly held; whether a moral or religious "experiment" could ever have the cogency of an experiment in a laboratory—laboratory conditions being conspicuously lacking in those spheres. Holding to the scientific ideal, these radicals became more agnostic than the liberals about the possibility of proving the main doctrines of the Christian faith, including the doctrine of God the Creator. Some of them became religious *humanists,* doubting the existence of any superhuman deity; others became religious *naturalists,* asserting the scientifically provable existence of a superhuman cosmic Process to which man can give himself in humble devotion, but doubting whether this cosmic Process can be strictly identified with any supernatural, extraempirical deity, such as the personal, transcendent Creator-God of the Bible. Both the humanists and the naturalists felt that the liberals were not logically consequent in their appeal to experience; real, consequent empiricism would have to give up its claim to establish truth in any sphere beyond the human and natural spheres, of which alone we have direct experience.

It may be fairly questioned whether religious humanism and naturalism are forms of Christian theology at all, though they may be advocated by members of Christian churches and professors in theological schools. Certainly it is hard to interpret them as expressions of the "Christian Consensus" described in Section 2; and if the description were revised to include them, it would exclude all conservative Christians. They stand on the boundary line of the historic Christian movement, partly inside and partly outside, like the ancient Gnostics and Manichees. Perhaps we might say that their position lies *inside* Christianity, so far as it is defined in tentative terms, as a partial view of religious truth; and they set themselves *outside* when they dogmatically define the human or natural sphere as the absolute limit of all possible knowledge of God. Auer's *Humanism States Its Case* contains many unchristian dogmatic assertions, but it begins with a modest plea for an anthropocentric approach to theology, which it rightly declares to be one persistently recurrent point of view in the history of Christian thought. Wieman's conception of God differs sharply from historic Christian theism, but when he remarks (as he often does) that God is always "more than we can think," he leaves room for the possibility that Christian faith and devotion reach out farther than the limited area where scientific method is valid. The intentions and loyalties of many religious humanists and naturalists are Christian, whatever may be their conclusions. To rule this radical movement out of consideration, because of its dubiously Christian character, would unduly simplify the contemporary theological situation, and dull the edge of one of its sharpest issues.

4. *Neo-orthodox Protestantism* criticizes the liberal appeal to experience at the very same point singled out by the humanists and naturalists; but it moves away from liberalism in what may be called an antihumanistic and antinaturalistic direction. Paul Tillich, who was at first associated with Karl Barth in the "dialectical theology" movement, is now hardly to be described as

"neo-orthodox," and certainly not as a Barthian; but he has articulated more clearly than anyone else the fundamental point of divergence between liberalism and neo-orthodoxy: the impossibility of dealing with God, the Unconditioned One, in terms of a logic analogous to empirical science. When you pass from man to God or from nature to God, using the scientific or philosophic logic appropriate to finite persons and things, you "thingify" God and commit idolatry.[32] The difference between religious revelation and scientific investigation is not to be bridged by the liberal analogy between experimental religion and experimental science; revelation is as inevitably paradoxical as science is inevitably logical. Kierkegaard, the paradoxical critic of all rational theology, was a better interpreter of Christianity than all the liberal reconcilers of the nineteenth century. In this negative criticism, all neo-orthodox concur.

The centrality of the Biblical revelation in Christian theology, and the incomprehensible majesty of the God revealed in Scripture, are positive emphases common to the neo-orthodox school, as they are common to the Calvin-Luther-Augustine tradition which neo-orthodoxy has revived. Beyond this point, there are great divergencies between—and within—the German Swiss school of neo-orthodoxy (Barth, Brunner), the Scandinavian school (Aulén, Nygren), and the American school (Niebuhr, Tillich). Barth himself goes beyond all other neo-orthodox thinkers (except perhaps some of his young followers) in his uncompromising reaction against the appeal to reason and experience in theology, and his uncompromising reassertion of the Reformation principle of *sola Scriptura*. To put *any* other source of truth "alongside" Scripture, *any* other revelation of God

---

[32] There is a pun here in Tillich's original German: you make a *Ding* (thing) out of *Das Unbedingte* (the Unconditioned).

"alongside" Christ, is to commit the fatal fallacy of *Nebenord-nung*, and blaspheme against the unique majesty of God. ("To whom then will ye liken me . . . ! saith the Holy One" Isa. 40:25). All "natural theology," all rational philosophizing in theology, must therefore be mercilessly cut out, like gangrene, whenever found in a theological system.

*By reducing theology to a purely "kerygmatic" form—the clarification of the Biblical message, quite apart from any attempt at "apologetic" explanation or rational justification—Barth has raised the most acute issue in contemporary theology, concerning the knowledge of God: whether reason has any significant role to play in theology at all.* American radical empiricism, as we have seen, tends to eliminate all divine revelation (whether superhuman or supernatural) in the name of scientific method. If this impairs the Christian faith by confusing God with man and nature, does not Barth's opposite reaction impair the Christian faith by raising impassable barriers between reason and revelation, man and God, nature and God? To put this question to theologians is the quickest way to classify them.

First reflections on this important issue may take their departure from the fact that Barth's own colleagues in the neo-orthodox movement are critical of his position. Emil Brunner's criticisms of his fellow Swiss are mainly three: (1) Barth is guilty of *Biblical monism.* He sees in the Scripture only the supreme revelation in Christ, and does not give scope for the relative independence of preparatory revelations, of which the first is the revelation in Creation. (2) Barth does not clearly distinguish between an illegitimate *Natural Theology* and a legitimate *Nature Theology*, based on God's self-revelation in Creation. (3) Barth's attempt to get rid of the philosophical element in his theology is unsuccessful; his writings are full of an *unconscious*

*philosophy*, highly questionable in its unexamined assumptions.[33]
Aulén, representing the Scandinavian (Lundensian) school of
neo-orthodoxy, is just as suspicious of theological rationalism as
Barth or Brunner, but it seems to him that the Swiss dialectic
theology has fallen into an *irrationalism* and a *metaphysical dualism* as remote from Christian faith as the rationalistic monism
against which it reacted. Religious paradox, he suggests, is a fruitful *tension* between seemingly opposed ideas, which ought not
lead to the irrational *contradiction* in which Barth seems to
revel.[34] Niebuhr and Tillich, leaders of the parallel movement
in America, object to Barth's position on somewhat similar
grounds,[35] but would not be satisfied with the limited scope allowed to reason in Aulén's theology. To say, with Aulén, that
the Christian faith is founded "in the divine revelation and nothing else," and that "no combination of the theses of faith and
metaphysics can be allowed," [36] is to go against the theological
method which Niebuhr has generally followed and the method
which Tillich is now scientifically elaborating in his *Systematic
Theology:* the "method of correlation." This method is based
on the principle that "man cannot receive answers to questions he
never has asked," and "has asked . . . in his very existence . . .
questions which Christianity answers." [37] The principle of this
method is in itself a rational principle, even though the questions
man asks are unanswerable in purely scientific or philosophic
terms, and though the answers Christianity gives are symbolic
and paradoxical. Since Tillich sees the divine image in man's "ra-

[33] Brunner, *Revelation and Reason*, and *Dogmatics*, I, references to Barth in
the index. Cf. my summary of "Neo-Orthodox Conceptions of Biblical Authority," in the *Journal of Religious Thought*, V (Autumn-Winter, 1948), pp.
42-56.
[34] Aulén, *op. cit.*, pp. 103, 166.
[35] See Tillich's article in the *Journal of Religion*, Vol. XV (1935), pp. 127-45.
[36] Aulén, *op. cit.*, p. 95.        [37] Tillich, *op. cit.*, I, p. 65.

tional structure," and asserts a real analogy between the divine *logos* and the human *logos*,[38] he cannot possibly exclude reason from his theological method. As for Niebuhr, his constant habit of balancing the truth in the Reformation tradition over against the truth in the Renaissance tradition [39] implies a similar safeguarding of the rights of reason, broadly conceived, against narrow irrationalism.

Niebuhr and Tillich separate themselves so decisively from Barth and Aulén on this issue, that the term "neo-orthodox" hardly seems to cover them. (If their works are listed under "neo-orthodox" in the references appended to each chapter in this book, it is for lack of a better term.) They stand "on the boundary" (as Tillich likes to put it) between left-wing neo-orthodoxy and right-wing liberalism. Just the other side of this boundary, there is a large group of liberals who have reconsidered their position in the light of neo-orthodox criticism, but remained adamant on the place of reason in theology. L. Harold DeWolf speaks for many of these "neo-liberals" when he lays down the following as the necessary functions of reason (defined as "comprehensive coherence") in a theology that fully accepts the necessity of divine revelation: "Reason required to receive revelation . . . . to decide when revelation has occurred . . . . to interpret and apply revealed truth . . . for transmission of revealed truth to others." [40] If we further note the fact that conservative Protestants have been as little convinced as liberal Protestants of the total illegitimacy of the rational approach to theology,[41] it

---

[38] *Ibid.*, p. 259.

[39] Niebuhr, *Nature and Destiny of Man*, Vol. II, Chaps. VI, VII.

[40] DeWolf, *A Theology of the Living Church*, Chap. 3. Cf. his thorough discussion of the issues raised by Kierkegaard and Barth, and his criticism of the theology of paradox, in *The Religious Revolt Against Reason*, Harper, 1949.

[41] See, e.g., Carnell, *Introduction to Christian Apologetics*, where the rational approach is strongly defended against neo-orthodox criticism.

becomes evident that Barth and (to a lesser extent) Aulén occupy a very isolated and unrepresentative position in contemporary Protestant thought, on this issue. They may yet prove to be right—"one man with God constitutes a majority"—but after occupying the focus of theological attention for a whole generation, they still have the ecumenical consensus, Protestant as well as Catholic, conservative as well as liberal, overwhelmingly against them.

## C. *Anglican Positions: High, Low, Broad and Central*

After our review of Catholic and Protestant positions, Anglicanism can be briefly dealt with, since it embraces all or most of the positions hitherto considered—held in balance within one communion, and exerting a moderating influence each on the other. The Anglo-Catholic or High Church party approximates the Catholic position in its Eastern Orthodox rather than its Roman form. The Evangelical or "Low Church" party approximates the classic Protestant position in its Puritan-Wesleyan form; but Protestant reverence for the authority of Scripture is here considerably modified by Catholic reverence for the authority of "ancient authors" and venerable traditions. The "Modernist" or "Broad Church" party approximates the liberal Protestant position as known elsewhere; but the boldest of all the Anglican liberals in the past generation, W. R. Inge, was paradoxically the very man who did most to explode the liberal cult of progress when the average Anglican believed in it.

By the "average Anglican" we mean to indicate no mythical figure, but a very substantial and important phenomenon: the presence of a large "central party" in this communion, which shares the three positions just described, without carrying any of them through to its logical limit. Catholic in its respect for tradition, Protestant in its respect for the Bible, liberal in its respect for reason and experience, this central party is perhaps more typically Anglican than any of the factional parties which contend for its support. It corresponds to the consensus of opinion among average Englishmen, which gives such continuity and stability to British government, whether the Socialists or the Conservatives are in office. The three elements in this central party's doctrine of the knowledge of God—Tradition, Scripture, and Reason—may seem hard to reconcile logically; but Anglicans are firmly convinced that they belong together and must never be separated. Rawlinson, an Anglo-Catholic, represents this Anglican consensus when he contends that the Christian faith is given to us in history and must therefore be accepted on *authority*, not improvised according to our modern likes and dislikes; but he also represents it when he argues that a *free* consensus of Christian minds, open to rational questioning, is more authoritative than one resulting from artificial repressive measures.[42]

The most representative Anglican theologian of the past generation was the late Archbishop William Temple. No figure of nearly comparable magnitude has yet appeared to succeed him. Starting as a liberal, much influenced by the Hegelian idealism of the Cairds, he became more realistic in his philosophy and more "central" in his theology as time went on, personifying the main contemporary trend of British thought, from idealistic liberalism to "classical Catholicism"—the Catholicism of the "undivided Church," to which the Ecumenical Movement under his leadership in so large a measure sought to return.[43] His Gifford

[42] See his essay in *Essays Catholic and Critical*, pp. 83 ff, and his book on *Authority and Freedom*.
[43] On the trend of British theology in the twentieth century, see my study of *Contemporary English Theology*, Harper, 1936, last chapter.

Lectures on *Nature, Man and God* are a landmark in contemporary Christian thought, standing for a theological method in sharp contrast to Karl Barth's: one that gives large scope to natural theology and general revelation (horrible example of the *Nebenordnung* Barth decries) while at the same time insisting that they end in a "hunger" which only the special revelation given in Christ and testified in the Scriptures will satisfy. His definition of revelation as "the coincidence of event and appreciation"— "divinely guided events" as the primary medium of revelation and divinely inspired appreciation of their meaning as secondary thereto—has liberated Anglican thought from Biblical literalism while keeping it anchored to the great revealing acts of God about which the Bible and the Christian Year revolve.[44]

Of all the positions reviewed in this chapter, two stand out as clearly irreconcilable with each other and with the general consensus of Christian thought: the radical empiricism of the American humanists and naturalists, and the radical revelationism of Karl Barth. The other positions are capable of being incorporated in one many-sided method, as "central" Anglicanism so clearly illustrates; but these two positions flatly contradict each other. May we not conclude that they represent corrective protests (or as Barth once said of himself, a "pinch of spice" to be taken with any theology you may happen to hold) rather than tenable theological positions?

Without *some* reference to general experience, without *some* resort to the rational criterion of "comprehensive coherence," a revelational theology becomes mere authoritative table-thumping

[44] Temple's firm conviction that such a revelational theology is consistent with a rational natural theology appears both in his Gifford Lectures (chapter on "Revelation") and in his contribution to the Baillie and Martin symposium on *Revelation*, where it clashes with Barth's sharply different view.

—and some pretty dangerous characters have thumped loudly and commanded vociferously in our time. On the other hand, general experience without specific revelation is too ambiguous to furnish decisive guidance to life, and answer the universal human question with which we started. Tillich is right; experience *receives and correlates* religious knowledge; by itself, it is not a sufficient *source* of such knowledge.[45] The practical recommendation would seem to be, then, to accept the ultimate necessity of an existential venture of faith in some specific, concrete revelation—which for Christians means faith in Jesus Christ—but to precede and follow such a venture of faith by exploring its logical implications, and that of its principal rivals, to see which casts most light upon the whole human enterprise, and offers the best promise of an answer to the three inescapable religious questions.[46]

[45] *Op. cit.*, I, p. 46.

[46] Our comparative method has not left us room to elaborate a constructive doctrine of reason and revelation, such as will be found in a full-fledged system of theology. A view that harmonizes well with the critical upshot of this chapter will be found in John Baillie's book, *Our Knowledge of God*, where the truth in the neo-orthodox and liberal theories of religious knowledge is carefully sifted. Our own view, in brief, is that the primary data for Christian theology are to be found in the uniquely revealing figure of Jesus Christ together with the history of Israel that leads up to him and the Church Tradition that interprets his significance; but the philosophy of religion, general philosophy and even the specific natural sciences, together with the commonsense experience of which all these disciplines are specializations, are all relevant to theology, and help to check its truth as the following diagram suggests:

| Sense Data | Values | Supreme Value: the Holy | Special Revelation |
|---|---|---|---|
| Science | Philosophy | Philosophy of Religion | Theology |

In this diagram, each discipline listed *below* the line has as its primary data what appears directly *above*, and as its secondary data what appears *above and to the left*. The diagram is a résumé of my chapter in the Baillie and Martin symposium on *Revelation*, to which the reader is referred for a fuller exposition.

# III

## *THE NATURE OF GOD*

### SECTION 1. UNIVERSAL OUTREACH TOWARD SOME SORT OF DEITY

IF SOME SORT of religious faith is universally necessary to man, then some sort of deity is necessary; for a deity, in the broad sense of the term, is one of the three cardinal points in every religious faith, and the most fundamental of the three: an Object of ultimate trust and devotion. Functionally speaking, there are so few real atheists that one has to seek for them long and patiently, with the lantern of Diogenes. A real atheist is a man who has found literally nothing in which to put his trust, nothing to live for or live by, nothing that gives meaning and purpose to his life as he gives himself to its service. Such a man is in a truly desperate plight, and cannot stay in it permanently. Either he will find some credible object of trust and devotion, or he will escape into the compensatory delusions that comfort the insane, or he will quite deliberately (and in this case quite rationally) decide that life is not worth living, and commit suicide. Most *professed* atheists are in no such terrible position. They have reacted, probably not without cause, against some particular conception of God; but they have found some substitute deity to which they trustfully cling: the evolutionary process, or democracy, or psychiatry, or the dictatorship of the proletariat, or something else. If all the unconscious assumptions on which pro-

79

fessed atheists act were to be systematically organized, they would amount to quite a considerable theology, different from orthodoxy, but just as full of religious trust—very often in something pathetically unworthy of trust!

The real, universal problem of God, then, is not whether any deity at all exists, but which of the infinite variety of candidates for deity that manifest themselves in the wide realm of existence is most genuinely worthy of trust and worship. All sorts of obviously existing objects such as mountains and trees, nations and kings, have been worshiped and deified; the real question is not whether they exist, but whether they deserve such trust and devotion as has been given them. The problem is not to find one possible object of worship,[1] but to find some principle of order in the chaotic throng of deities once worshiped, now worshiped, or yet to be worshiped by men, that will enable us to compare them and judge between them. It may be helpful to compare the various possible ideas of God by locating them on two infinitely divisible lines: a *horizontal* line passing from complete atheism to complete pantheism by way of intermediate positions such as humanism, and monotheism; and a *vertical* line passing from complete polytheistic idolatry (identification of God with some observable thing, person or event) to complete deism (complete dissociation between God and anything observable whatsoever).

---

[1] The recurrent use of the word "object" in the introductory section of this chapter does not prejudge the important question whether God is properly speaking an "object" at all. It may well be, as neo-orthodoxy typically insists, that only the Absolute *Subject* is finally worthy of worship, and every mere *object* is an idol. Here, as everywhere else, the Christian revelation *upsets* the universal expectation of mankind, yet at the same time *fulfills* the real needs expressed in the universal quest. Whenever we move from the human quest to the divine revelation, we reverse our perspective, and give God the final initiative. God answers the human quest for a divine object by revealing himself as Subject.

## The Nature of God

|  | | | | | Deism |
|---|---|---|---|---|---|
| | | | | | \| |
| *Nothing* to Worship | *Something* Worshipful | | *Everything* Worshipful | | Monotheism |
| Atheism | Humanism | Monotheism | "Theopantism" | Pantheism | \| |
| | | | | | Polytheism or Pantheism |

At the left end of our horizontal line is the practically impossible view already described, which says in effect, "*Nothing* is worshipful," and means, "There is nothing to which I can give myself in trust and devotion, nothing to live for or live by." At the right end is an equally impossible view which says, "*Everything* is worshipful," and implies that the world in its totality is so grand, so adorable, so altogether divine that it would be an impiety to change the slightest detail in it. These views are impossible to maintain except for moments of nauseated rejection of life on the one hand, or moments of supreme appreciation of life on the other—when everything seems temporarily to be at zero point ("completely futile") or at infinity point ("absolutely perfect," "simply gorgeous"). Whoever goes on living beyond such moments, finds that his pessimism is eventually overcome by the attraction of intrinsic goods that reawaken his desire to live; and on the other hand, no state of affairs remains permanently perfect, but develops flaws and problems demanding corrective action. Complete atheism and complete pantheism thus tend to eliminate themselves.

The elimination of these two extremes leaves open still a great variety of intermediate choices, all of which imply that "*something* is worshipful." If that "something" is solely in the realm of human relations it is a *humanistic* deity; if in the realm of natural process, a *naturalistic* deity. Monotheistic religions have generally recognized that there is something sacred, holy and worshipful in the realm of human relations ("Honor thy father and thy

mother") and in the realm of natural process ("The heavens declare the glory of God"), but they have refused to offer *ultimate*
trust and adoration to anything in these spheres. To worship the
human as such or the natural as such is to commit idolatry, monotheism declares; it is to deify something that is born and dies,
something that grows old like a garment. A god who grows old
and dies cannot hold man's ultimate trust. It is not sufficient then
to locate monotheism to the right of humanism and to the left of
pantheism on our horizontal line; it is also necessary to locate it
*above* them on the vertical line. The God of monotheism is not
a visible object in our world, alongside man and the cosmos, but
rather an invisible depth in our world, more enduring than the
human and natural events that half-veil and half-reveal this
depth.

How deep into invisible mystery must one pierce in order to
find the One True God of monotheism? To ask this question is
to discover that monotheism is a mean between irrational extremes in this dimension also. If the lower end of our vertical
line identifies the deity too closely with perishable things, so that
worship spurns such idols and soars above them, the upper end
represents such an absolute cleavage between God and world
that worship recoils before a measureless void. Technically, this
extreme is called deism. It found its classic expression in the
Creator-God of eighteenth-century natural philosophy, whose
contact with the visible world was confined to that long-past
aeon when he set up the world machine, endowing it with sufficient force to run itself forever without further divine intervention. Worship withers away before this inaccessible deity as
surely as it hungers for something deeper when offered the too
accessible deities of humanism, naturalism and pantheism. What
monotheism offers is a deity revealed *in* man and nature as their

creative Source, Depth and Ground, *above* and *beyond* the world, yet not *apart* from it.

Monotheism cannot fairly be described as a self-evident position, devoid of all rational difficulties. *No* position on either of our infinitely divisible lines is wholly free from difficulties. What can fairly be claimed is that the religious quest finds overwhelming difficulties in the atheistic, pantheistic and deistic positions, and tends to be driven by these difficulties (when they are clearly understood) in the general direction of monotheism. It may be added that there are certain general attributes which a deity must have, in order to pass the elementary test imposed by the religious quest itself: *holiness, goodness, and greatness.*

Rudolf Otto has convincingly analyzed *The Idea of the Holy* as the root idea from which all highly developed ideas of God have sprung. In its primitive form, holiness does not yet imply moral perfection in the object of worship, but only an awesome mystery, which draws the worshiper with irresistible fascination —like Moses at the burning bush—and at the same time makes him feel unworthy of drawing near without radical purification. Without this elementary attribute of holiness, which at once sets God apart and makes one yearn to be united with him, God is not God at all. A deity so clearly comprehended that all mystery is dispelled, so cozily companionable that all "fear of the Lord" is dissipated, may be a very comfortable deity but he will not long be worshiped. Man is so made that he must be able to *look up* to his deity in reverent adoration, or presently he will *look down* upon him.

A second fundamental attribute increasingly united with holiness in the higher religions is *goodness.* Ideas of goodness differ immensely, so that primitive deities sometimes look like demons to civilized men; but a completely indifferent or purely malevo-lent deity has no appeal to anyone. Typically, the images of the gods have benevolence written on their countenances. Deities are beings from whom *blessings* flow; they may be immensely great and august, but if they promise no blessings, they are not worshiped. In many primitive religions, a Creator-God is rec-ognized; but since this deity satisfies the need for *explanation* rather than the need for *blessing*, devotion passes him by, and fastens upon the little gods of sun and rain, hearth and home, who promise concrete benefits to man. The same defect dis-qualifies some philosophical conceptions of God, which answer many rational questions about the underlying structure of Real-ity, but fail to evoke religious gratitude and dependence. If I am to trust God, I must believe he is trustworthy; and this implies that he is *good* to all who put their trust in him.

A third fundamental attribute, imposed on all ideas of deity by the religious quest itself, is *greatness* or *power*. We have already noted that a god who grows old and dies is unacceptable to the worshiper. The ancient Greeks and Romans always spoke of the "immortal gods," and saw in their immortality a princi-pal mark of their deity. Other things being equal—that is to say, holiness and goodness remaining unimpaired—the greater and mightier a deity is, the more divine he is. Of course, if great-ness means remoteness and moral indifference, or power means sheer brutal violence, devotion dies and may even be replaced by horror or moral revolt. But what mankind is seeking, when it seeks God, is a Being infinitely holy, infinitely good, and infi-nitely great. The Christian revelation gives a concrete answer to this universal demand by manifesting, first in the history of Israel and then in Christ, a holiness, goodness and greatness that tran-scend and fulfill all other ideas of these divine attributes.

84

## SECTION 2. THE CHRISTIAN CONSENSUS CONCERNING THE NATURE OF GOD

The Christian conception of God has remained pretty constant through all the storms of controversy that have raged around other doctrines. It is based upon the Old Testament revelation of God as the Holy One of Israel, infinitely exalted above all the creatures he has made, yet caring for his creatures, ruling and overruling the events of history in justice and mercy, and promising eventual peace to mankind through Israel his specially chosen servant. In the New Testament, the God of Israel is further revealed as the God and Father of our Lord Jesus Christ, "God with us" (Immanuel) in a new and more intimate sense, God walking with us in the person of our Lord, God abiding in our midst through the activity of his Holy Spirit in the new community, the Church, which he has begun to gather from all nations to inherit his Kingdom.

In the Trinitarian and Christological controversies, the centrality of the new revelation in Christ was clearly established, without abandoning the old revelation in Israel or compromising its monotheism; and at the same time a point of contact was established between the Biblical idea of God as Creator and the Greek philosophic idea of God as the Absolute Being that endures beneath the multiplicity and transiency of the visible world. The consistency of this alliance between Hebrew and Greek monotheism has been seriously challenged in recent times, as we shall see; but for the classical schools of Christian theology, both Catholic and Protestant, it has held as firm as the alliance between the Old and New Testament revelations. Through all the schools of Christian thought runs the common conception of God as the creative Source and Ground of nature, the exalted Ruler of history, made man for our redemption in Jesus Christ, working on since Christ by his Spirit in the Church, toward the gathering of a City of God, a Kingdom of justice and love.

Lists of the attributes of God, and above all *classifications* of these attributes, have been very variable in Christian theology; but the actual *content* of the Christian conception of God remains relatively constant amid these variations. Sometimes the attributes of God are grouped as *metaphysical* (omnipotence, omniscience, omnipresence, eternity, etc.) and *moral* (justice, love, wisdom, truth, etc.), sometimes as *incommunicable* (without analogy in the creature) and *communicable* (analogous to human characteristics, but free of human imperfections), sometimes again as *negative* (*in*finity, *in*comprehensibility, *im*mensity, etc.) and *positive* (*all*-wise, *all*-sovereign, *all*-loving, etc). Behind all of these classifications lies the important distinction between God as the mysterious creative Source of the world, incomparable with any of the creatures he has made, and God as the Judge and Redeemer of his creatures, calling them to conform to his image and imparting to them the grace to fulfill this divine calling.[2]

That God the Creator and God the Redeemer are really one God, not two, was stoutly maintained by Irenaeus, the first great ecumenical theologian, against the dualistic denials of Marcion and the Gnostics; and it has been the cornerstone of

[2] The various *names* given to God in the Old and the New Testaments point in these same two directions. Some, like El-Elyon and Adonai (Lord) point to the exalted majesty and mystery of the Creator; others, like Living God, Savior and Father, point to his care and concern for his creatures. Sometimes a section on the divine names precedes the section on the divine attributes in theological treatises. Names express the characteristics of God in the literary style appropriate to worship; *attributes* express the same characteristics in the more abstract style appropriate to exact thought. Names and attributes should be *consistent*, they need not be *identical*.

Christian thinking about God ever since. If this fundamental distinction (and identity) are clearly kept in mind, as for example in the doctrine of the Trinity,[3] it will be evident that God must on the one hand be sharply distinguished from every finite creature, and the idea of God the Father must be protected against anthropomorphism by thinking away every finite limitation from the divine attributes; while on the other hand God must be conceived as One who could call man into the fellowship of the covenant by his eternal Word, actually "join the human race" in the Man of Nazareth, and stay with humanity by the power of the Holy Spirit. This requires that God should have both metaphysical and moral, both communicable and incommunicable attributes; and it requires that there should be both a negative and a positive relation between the two sets of attributes. The doctrine that man is made in the divine image suggests the kind of balance that should be kept between these different attributes. It justifies the attribution of creaturely qualities to the Creator, provided that (a) all merely creaturely limitations are removed, and (b) the analogy between the creature and the Creator takes the form of a "how much more" proportion, as in one of Jesus' best-known sayings: "If ye then, being evil, know how to give good gifts unto your children, *how much more* shall your Father who is in heaven give good things to them that ask him?" (Matt. 7:11).

If these precautions are observed, it does not greatly matter how long or short a list of divine attributes is used, nor precisely how they are grouped. Aulén's grouping in *The Faith of the Christian Church* [4] is particularly impressive and helpful: holi-

---

[3] The doctrine of the Trinity will be more explicitly discussed in Chap. VI, on "Christ the Savior."

[4] Pp. 120–60.

*ness*, not as a particular attribute, but as the background of all the attributes; *power*, *judgment* and *love* as attributes standing in a certain tension with one another, a tension which must neither be too easily eliminated, nor pushed to the point of flat contradiction; *love*, in the special sense of the kind of self-giving *agapé* revealed in God's saving act in Christ, as the central unifying attribute with which the others finally must harmonize. (God's judgment is "the wrath of love," and his sovereign power is the "sovereignty of love").

It is noteworthy that Paul Tillich, whose theology is as deliberately philosophical as Aulén's is deliberately antiphilosophical, comes at the climax of his discussion on "The Reality of God"[5] to a threefold emphasis on the Divine Holiness, the Divine Power and the Divine Love, quite similar to Aulén's: "God's holiness is not a quality in and of itself; it is that quality which qualifies all other qualities as divine. His power is holy power; his love is holy love."[6] William Newton Clarke said substantially the same thing in different terms when he gave his memorable definition of God[7] as "the Personal Spirit, perfectly good, *who in holy love creates, sustains and orders all.*" (Italics added.) Beneath all varieties of terminology and differences of method there is a deep consensus concerning the essential attributes of the Christian God.[8]

It is important to observe that the three fundamental attributes of God stressed by Aulén, Tillich and Clarke correspond exactly,

---

[5] *Op. cit.*, I, pp. 271–89.     [6] *Ibid.*, p. 272.     [7] *Outline*, p. 66.

[8] This consensus still holds, even if we admit that certain attributes derived from Greek philosophy are formally inconsistent with the Biblical conception of God. The *intention* of Christian theology has always been to describe the Biblical Creator and Redeemer by these philosophical terms—as Scriptural footnotes clearly bear witness. The *meaning intended* is always believed to be consistent with Scripture, even where the *terms employed* are inappropriate to their intention, and need to be revised.

but with a new and heightened meaning, to the three attributes of holiness, goodness, and greatness demanded by man's universal religious consciousness of any deity that is to be worthy of worship. Holiness now means the specific kind of holiness manifested by the Holy One of Israel in his dealings with his People, and by the Holy Spirit in the New Testament. Goodness now means love, of the specific sort (*agapé*) taught and lived by our Lord. Greatness now means something quite different from the greatness of the "Kings of the Gentiles"; it is the power of service and sacrifice, which looks to the world like weakness, but in the end leaves the Alexanders and Napoleons looking like petty politicians.[9] It takes faith for modern men to learn to bow before the God who manifests himself in these specific attributes; but when they do so learn, they recognize that they have found what all the world is seeking, and are bound to communicate the good news to all.

While there is a real and enduring consensus among Christians concerning the attributes of God, every one of them is capable of being interpreted in an unbalanced way that threatens to destroy faith in God, and provokes theological opposition. The omnipotence of God can be perverted into tyranny, provoking the Arminian protest against Calvinism. The holiness of God can become deistic remoteness, provoking a reaction that may move toward the opposite extreme of pantheism, as happened in the idealistic philosophy and theology of the early nineteenth

---

[9] In Pascal's fragment on the three "orders" of greatness—the physical order, the mental order, and the "order of charity," he has these impressive words about the divine greatness revealed in Christ: "Jesus Christ, without property and without scientific productivity either, is unique in his order of holiness. He gave us no invention; he did not reign as king; but he was humble, patient, holy, holy to God, terrible to the demons, without any blot of sin. O, with what great pomp and what prodigious magnificence he came, to the eyes of the heart, the eyes that see Wisdom." (E. Havet, *Pensées de Pascal*, p. 347.)

century. The love of God can be divorced from justice, provoking a new emphasis upon divine wrath and judgment in the neo-orthodox school. The personality of God can be so anthropomorphically conceived that Henry Nelson Wieman's conception of God as Process appears as a protest against this excessive personalism. In times past, schools and parties have divided over these issues. Many fruitless controversies have begun to engender a more becoming modesty and caution in modern theologians. So, for example, John Dickie is quite typical of modern Calvinists when he refuses to push divine omnipotence and omniscience to the point where they endanger the freedom and responsibility of God's creatures. "The religious interest at stake in the idea of the Divine Omnipotence," he explains, "is simply this, that if we are to have adequate assurance that God's purpose cannot fail, God must be Lord over all things and all men, and able to make all things and all men serve the coming of His Kingdom." Concerning the Divine Omniscience, he says, "The two fixed points within which our thought must move are *first* that God's knowledge like His power is all-sufficient for the accomplishment of His World-purpose, and *second* that man is truly responsible for his actions." [10] With such a statement, modern Arminians would not find much fault. It is in fact very similar to the Edinburgh statement (above p. 25) to which theologians of many different churches and parties were able to agree.

Not only is it difficult to maintain a perfectly balanced interpretation of each attribute, but still more to maintain a perfectly balanced harmony among *all* the attributes of God. What Aulén calls "tension" always to some extent prevails among them. When theologians become aware of such tension, they may handle it

---

[10] Dickie, *op. cit.*, pp. 104–6. Cf. John Oman's fuller discussion of the same issues in *Grace and Personality*.

in different ways. A highly rational type of theology may be so deeply convinced of the ultimate unity of God's character that it will attempt to deduce all or most of the attributes from one fundamental attribute—thus eliminating the scandal of disharmony but probably impoverishing the richness of the Biblical revelation. Neo-orthodox theology, reacting against such rationalism and stressing the paradoxical character of the Biblical revelation has sometimes followed an exactly opposite course, heightening the tension among the attributes instead of trying to eliminate it—as though the truth about God were best expressed in a series of crashing discords, where every Yes was immediately contradicted by an equal and opposite No. The simplicity of the Gospel is as much obscured by this procedure as its depth is obscured by the other. (After all, the parables of Jesus are part of the Bible!) If a genuine ecumenical consensus concerning the divine attributes has been preserved through all the history of Christian thought, it has been because theology has generally avoided both of these extremes, and followed a procedure nearer to Aulén's own: not prematurely eliminating all paradoxes from the Christian idea of God, when both sides of the paradox are deeply rooted in Christian revelation, but trusting that in God all apparent contradictions are finally resolved, and trying to see and show the consistency between power and justice, justice and love, love and holiness, as a partial confirmation of this ultimate trust.

SECTION 3. UNRESOLVED ISSUES CONCERNING THE
NATURE OF GOD

A. *The God of Greek Metaphysics and the God of
the Bible*

It would be unprofitable to make a comparison of all the
schools of Christian thought, on a topic where so little fundamental disagreement exists.[11] The main issue now seriously under
debate in this field is not an issue on which Catholics are divided
from Protestants, or Calvinists from Arminians, or liberals from
conservatives, but one which cuts across churches and parties in
a most extraordinary way: the question whether the Greek metaphysical conception of God as Absolute Being can really be reconciled with the Biblical conception of God as the Almighty
Father and Creator.

The scholastic theologians of Christendom, both Catholic and
Protestant, have generally assumed that Greek and Hebrew
monotheism were natural allies, and have thought it possible to
give Biblical texts in support of conceptions of God's nature historically derived from Greek speculation. Here and there they
have made corrections in Greek ideas, to make them more compatible with Biblical ideas: the possibility that God's Logos could
become flesh, for example, as Plato did not allow; and the possibility that God should know and care for the world as Aristotle's God did not. It did not occur to them, however, that the
Absolute Being of Greek philosophy and the Creator-God of

[11] L. A. Zander, writing from the Eastern Orthodox point of view, remarks
in his *Vision and Action* (London, Gollancz, 1952, p. 141) that "at the present
time dogmatic disagreements about God are not the source of confessional differences and do not, in fact, divide Christians." This judgment would be accepted by most students of contemporary theology, whatever their denomination or school of thought.

Biblical revelation were really incompatible ideas; so, while maintaining the general Christian consensus concerning the attributes of God, they have loaded the list pretty heavily with attributes such as simplicity, aseity, absoluteness, perfection and the like, derived from Greek metaphysics. The most striking example of this is the opening part of St. Thomas Aquinas' *Summa Theologica*, where the five famous arguments for the existence of God are followed up by a long train of logical inferences concerning the precise nature of the Unmoved Mover or First Cause or *Actus Purus* to which these arguments point. The more specifically Christian attributes of God are not finally omitted; but they come so late that they are obscured and minimized by comparison with the Aristotelian concepts that dominate the approach. Luther protested against this whole method in the name of a more Biblical and more religious type of theology, but Protestant scholasticism (Lutheran as well as Calvinistic) brought it back.

Ever since Hegel pushed the philosophical approach to theology to extreme lengths, a critical reconsideration of the role of Greek philosophy in Christian theology has been under way. Ritschl and Harnack devoted a great part of their work to detecting and exposing Greek influence upon Christian thought, and denouncing it as an almost unmitigated evil. Karl Barth, who has reacted against Ritschlianism in most respects, has continued the Ritschlian opposition to the Greek philosophic element in Christian tradition. While the Ritschlian and Barthian "revolt against reason" is not shared by most contemporary theologians, there are many Christian thinkers who consider that particular Greek ideas were taken over too uncritically into the Christian doctrine of God, in such a way as to threaten the harmony and balance of the divine attributes.

93

William Adams Brown maintained against Ritschl that the Greek idea of the Absolute was consistent with the Biblical idea of God as Creator and Father; but he contended in his inaugural address [12] and throughout his career that the unique revelation of God in Christ had been pushed to the periphery of Christian thought by Greek metaphysical concepts, and needed to be restored to the center. Father Laberthonnière was not sweepingly antiphilosophical; but he contended that the typical Greek conception of God was a last abstraction, an idea of ideas, derived from the search for Something Changeless beneath all change, whereas the Living God of authentic Christianity is really active in the struggles of history.[13] Professor Charles Hartshorne of Chicago, an empirical theist of the Whitehead school, maintains that the Greek idea of "perfection," when taken over into the Christian idea of God, logically destroys all relationship between God and his creatures, and can only be kept as an ingredient in the Christian idea on the condition that *absolute* perfection be replaced by *relative* perfection.[14] Emil Brunner considers that the most perilous of all Greek concepts is that of the absolute "simplicity" of God, derived from Neo-Platonism by way of Pseudo-Dionysius. Strictly speaking, this concept not only forbids all anthropomorphism in the idea of God (such as is common in the Old Testament) but all distinguishable attributes whatsoever.[15] It tends, we may say, to replace the God Paul preached to the Athenians with the Unknown God they had "ignorantly worshipped" before hearing the Gospel at all. It is very remarkable that these criticisms of Greek metaphysics come

[12] "Christ the Vitalizing Principle of Modern Theology"; cf. *Christian Theology in Outline*, pp. 74–78, 89–100.
[13] Laberthonnière, *Réalisme chrétien et idéalisme grec.*
[14] Hartshorne, *Man's Vision of God*, Chap. I, "The Formally Possible Doctrines."
[15] Brunner, *Dogmatics*, I, *The Christian Doctrine of God*, Chap. XVII.

not from one school of Christian thought only, but from a liberal Protestant, a Catholic modernist, an American empiricist and a Swiss neo-orthodox. When the smoke comes from so many different quarters, it is time to turn in a general alarm.

The issues in this controversy will become clearer if we summon four witnesses, two for the prosecution and two for the defense. For the prosecution: Aulén and Brunner. For the defense: Tillich and Ferré. The division in this group of theologians is a fact as significant as the unity of the group just named above; for they are all to some degree influenced by Swiss and Swedish neo-orthodoxy. Evidently, this is not only a controversy which unites members of different parties, but one which divides members of the same party. That is to say, it is an academic controversy, not likely to split the Church, but likely to clarify Christian thought in all churches and parties.

Aulén's purely fideistic, revelational approach to theology requires him to reject all alliances between theology and metaphysics, whether in ancient or medieval or modern Christian thought. Platonism, Aristotelianism, modern idealism, *and the existential philosophy which rejects all these systems*, are equally incompatible with Christian faith. "The paradoxical character of the affirmations of faith is purely *religious*," he insists. "It is misinterpreted and perverted when it becomes logical or metaphysical. The paradoxes then become an end in themselves, and the result is an irrationalism that is foreign to faith . . . . A metaphysically oriented rationalism is opposed by a metaphysically oriented irrationalism." [16] The attempt of scholastic theology to make a rational adjustment of all paradoxical tensions in the idea of God ends in a blurring *compromise*; the attempt of liberal theology to remove all tension by humanizing the idea of

[16] Aulén, *op. cit.*, p. 103.

God and making love all-controlling results in obscuring the sovereign majesty of divine love, and weakening its opposition to evil;[17] the existential and dialectic theology which opposes both these types of rationalism falls, as just stated, into an exaggeration of paradox equally foreign to Christian faith and revelation.

All metaphysics, of whatever school, inevitably perverts the Christian idea of God. "The metaphysical conceptions of God which have appeared in history may be divided into two representative groups: the deistic, which emphasizes the transcendental, and the pantheistic, which emphasizes the immanent conception of God . . . . In either case, man is simply confronted with the idea of causality, and faith's living conception of God is lost." [18] Any combination of, or middle term between, these two types of metaphysics fails to correct their errors, since it still operates in a sphere of bloodless categories quite alien to vital faith. In a word, "faith has really nothing to do with metaphysics," and any theology which admits *articuli mixti*, even partly based on metaphysics, issues in utter confusion.[19]

Brunner's position differs from Aulén's in that he admits the possibility of metaphysical terms being rightly used to define the Christian conception of God, and objects only to the uncritical use of such terms in a sense really inconsistent with Biblical revelation. For example, the term "absolute," in the sense inherited from Greek philosophy, represents the abstract impersonal "It" at which the mind arrives when it strips away all change and variety from the world. Even the idealistic concept of absolute *Spirit* represents "our final *object* of thought," not the Creator and Lord described in the Bible. Yet to describe this Creator and Lord, the term "absolute" is not only useful but in-

[17] *Ibid.*, pp. 126–29.    [18] *Ibid.*, p. 155.    [19] *Ibid.*, pp. 13, 14.

dispensable. He is in fact "absolute" in a far higher sense than the God of speculative philosophy, who is always *relative* to the world or the self from which the concept is ultimately abstracted. He is the Absolute Subject. Even the highly metaphysical concepts of *aseitas* and *actus purus* are similarly capable of being used in a sense which describes and safeguards the freedom and spirituality of the God of the Bible.[20]

The charge brought by Brunner against traditional theology is not, then, that it has used metaphysical terms, but that it has used them *unconverted*. Every philosophical attempt to think one's way to Ultimate Being leads necessarily to conceptions which strive inconclusively with one another, and are inconsistent with the Christian God; but many of these concepts are capable of being converted to Christian use and baptized, so to speak, into the name of Christ. This is the nature of the purge that Brunner labors so earnestly to accomplish, whereby the metaphysical elements in the idea of God *are not eliminated but redefined and severely subordinated to the Biblical elements.* So to speak, philosophy is now to become for the first time what the medieval scholastics falsely supposed it had become in their systems, the *handmaid* of revealed theology. She is to have no mind of her own but look only to her mistress for guidance, since every attempt at a philosophy independent of revelation leads necessarily to error and idolatry.

Tillich and Ferré differ from Brunner as well as from Aulén in their defense of *philosophical theology* as a proper branch of Christian theology, *connected* with Biblical theology but not completely *dominated* by it. They deny Aulén's contention that religious faith has "nothing to do with metaphysics," and his assertion that the only possible forms of metaphysics are the

[20] Brunner, *Dogmatics*, I, Chap. XIII.

deistic or the pantheistic outworking of the category of causality. As they see it, the problem of being and existence, being and becoming, being and nonbeing (the metaphysical or better the "ontological" problem) is inextricably bound up with the religious problem, and cannot be evaded by theology.

God, says Tillich, is man's "ultimate concern"; and only a God who is "Being itself," the ultimate Reality who is at once our creative Ground and transcendent Abyss, can finally satisfy this ultimate concern, remove the anxiety of finitude, and give us the "courage to be." The structure of being discovered by philosophy determines the "meaning of being" discovered by religion's existential grapple with life, and vice versa; philosophical absolutes are finally derived from the same religious experience which gives birth to the idea of God. There is no need of defining ultimate Being in terms of causality, or substance, or any other limited category; no need of freezing it into immobility as Parmenides did. God can and must be defined as beyond the contrast of cause and effect, essence and existence. He is the unconditioned "ground" (*not* the finite "cause") of every existent; the creative "power of being" in all that comes to be; yet not to be identified, except symbolically, with anything whatsoever in the finite world. That God is "being-itself or the absolute" is the only "nonsymbolic" statement, the only "direct and proper" statement that can be made about God. "Other assertions about God can be made theologically only on this basis." Hence the immense and fundamental importance of this ontological element in the concept of God; it alone is properly a "concept"; all the other elements are symbols that point beyond themselves.[21]

The difference between Tillich's type of philosophical theol-

[21] Tillich, *op. cit.*, I, pp. 11–14, 18–28, 230–41. Cf. II, pp. 9–12 (changed view).

ogy and Ferré's is mainly one of approach. Tillich begins with the ontological element in the concept of God, and then adds the Biblical attributes of holiness, love and power, as Thomas Aquinas does. Ferré begins with the central concept of Christian revelation, *agapé*, whose unique meaning Nygren and Aulén have so ably pointed out; then he develops its implications until they make contact with the metaphysical realm, and suggest a definition of being, becoming and nonbeing. Christian faith thus makes use of a Christian philosophy to work out its own meaning. "If the Christian faith is not always to suffer from alien systems," says Ferré, "it must produce its own"; [22] and this evidently means a systematic application of the central Christian concept of *agapé* to the problems of ontology and cosmology. Love is defined as "the form of being which acts out of complete concern not only for all, in all dimensions of life, and the conditions which sustain, promote and enhance life, but also for ever new life and new conditions of life." [23]

Applying this definition to the categories of being, Ferré finds that a God of love both *is* and *is not*; he is "self-existing and self-directing energy," but "requires an object of concern" that is finite, and so participates in nonbeing. "The need to create and to forgive is not the weakness but the strength of love. Nonbeing, then, is the condition for, and the occasion of, love as being. It is like the vacant lot next to an institution in need of enlargement!" [24] The interpersonal relations of the Trinity are not a sufficient field for divine *agapé*; God needs a needy world as a field for his creative and redemptive activity. Starting from this angle, Ferré quickly comes in contact with the Whiteheadian conception of God as process, and accepts with reservations

[22] Nels Ferré, *The Christian Understanding of God*, p. 6.
[23] *Ibid.*, pp. 15, 16.     [24] *Ibid.*, p. 17.

the idea of a growing God. "Potentiality is intrinsic to love." [25] Moreover, God cannot be absolute in a sense that denies *relations*; and if God has relations with the finite world, it means that *God has a body*, that he *begets children*, that he *gives his Spirit* to his finite creation. Here is real philosophical boldness in a Christian thinker.

Ferré consciously prefers his own approach to Tillich's. "Start with being as ultimate, and arrive at no adequate doctrine of becoming; start with becoming as ultimate, and find no real interpretation of being. Start with love as ultimate, and being and becoming are both inherent within His nature; being and becoming are then abstractions from the fullness of reality." [26] Looking at both approaches objectively, one may say that the danger of Tillich's is that of Hegel's, to make philosophy swallow up Christian theology, and reduce the distinctive Christian ideas to figures of speech illustrative of an abstract system; the danger of Ferré's is the opposite danger of drawing the Infinite down into the realm of the finite, and absolutizing the relative.

After listening to these four witnesses, what have we to say about the case under judgment? Is the philosophical conception of God compatible with the Biblical, or not? Let each reader judge for himself, perhaps after studying more of each witness's testimony than we have cited here. Our own judgment is, in brief, that metaphysical concepts are not *irrelevant* to the Christian doctrine of God as Aulén charges, but are *dangerous* to it, as Brunner charges, unless criticized and "converted" by being brought into vital interaction with the Christian revelation.

If anyone still thinks that faith has "nothing to do with metaphysics," let him read Tillich's impressive discussion of "the divine power and the creature," [27] or his Terry Lectures on *The*

---

[25] *Ibid.*, p. 18.    [26] *Ibid.*, p. 29.    [27] *Op. cit.*, I, pp. 272-79.

*Courage to Be*, where the power of absolute being to overcome anxiety and strengthen the heart of the believer is described in terms that every man of faith will recognize as truly religious. As for the dangerousness of bad metaphysics, and the ease with which one can get sucked down and lost in that boggy domain, both Tillich and Ferré will gladly admit that Brunner is right; that even the greatest Christian thinkers have gone astray in that region, and even the most time-honored lists of God's metaphysical attributes need to be carefully scrutinized in the light of Biblical revelation. This admission does not amount, however, to a renunciation of the special task of philosophical theology, as a relatively independent discipline, the colleague and not the mere handmaid of Biblical theology. After all, the relative independence claimed by Tillich and Ferré for philosophical theology can hardly be refused by Brunner, seeing that he has claimed a similar independence for God's various forms of self-revelation, as against Barth's insistence that the revelation in Christ is the one and only revelation.[28]

A balanced concept of God is so hard to maintain that each approach to it needs to be checked and controlled by other approaches: the central revelation in Christ by other stages of revelation within the Bible; the Biblical revelation as a whole, rich in concrete imagery, by the abstract researches of philosophic theology into the structure of being. Throughout the history of Christian thought, as we have seen, a balance of this sort has been fairly well maintained between the metaphysical and moral, communicable and incommunicable attributes of God. If Ritschl, Barth and Aulén had made good their sweeping charges against metaphysics, it would appear that this whole balance was a falsi-

---

[28] Brunner, *Dogmatics*, I, Chap. III, which is a résumé of the similar argument in *Revelation and Reason*.

fication of the Christian idea of God. With the collapse of their indictment, the Fathers, the scholastics and contemporary theology appear once more to be in substantial agreement concerning the nature of God, while all schools of thought are still required to re-examine and revise such dangerous metaphysical concepts as characterless simplicity, tyrannical omnipotence, and static perfection. If a purely metaphysical God is a cold abstraction, a wholly unmetaphysical God is a finite idol, whose worship violates the First Commandment.

If the opponents of the Greek philosophical element in the Christian concept of God should finally withdraw their objections, would all serious conflict be removed from this fundamental sphere of Christian doctrine? Would the general Christian consensus then stand forth, free from all tensions and controversies? It would be too much to expect any such results to follow automatically. As we have already seen, the balance between the various attributes of God, metaphysical and moral, incommunicable and communicable, is notoriously difficult to maintain; and there is no present agreement between the advocates of deliberate paradox and the advocates of rational adjustment, as to the best method of maintaining this balance.

Among the advocates of rational adjustment, there is unusual readiness in our time to accept drastic limitations upon the divine omnipotence, omniscience, etc., and frankly accept the idea of a "finite-infinite God" as the best way of reconciling God's metaphysical supremacy with his moral attributes. Besides those already mentioned in this chapter, Berdyaev of Paris, Brightman of Boston and Montague of Columbia may be cited as resolutely philosophical thinkers who were led to this bold theory in their endeavor to balance the attributes of God, and above all to preserve God's goodness in the face of evil. We shall encounter this view as a serious contemporary alternative when we discuss the problem of evil in Chapter IV. Meanwhile we must note that this so-called "finitistic" solution is opposed by an "absolutistic" school, which believes that an infinite, omnipotent God can also be just and loving, if we properly understand our terms and properly recognize the limits of human thought on these high themes.

## B. *In What Sense Is God Personal?*

In addition to the very general issue we have discussed, concerning the metaphysical element in the Christian idea of God, there is a more specific issue on which many Christian theologians are significantly divided: the sense in which God may be called "personal." That God is in *some* sense personal—that he is no mere subpersonal thing or force, but what the Bible calls a "living" God, confronting man with an inescapable call to worshipful devotion and loyal service—is generally granted by all schools of thought. This being the case, there is no likelihood that the more or less academic issue we are about to discuss will ever split the Church; but there is nevertheless strong tension between those theologians who declare that God's personality, analogous though not commensurable with human personality, is his most fundamental attribute, and those who regard such an analogy between divine and human personality as perilous if not idolatrous.

As an illustration of the first of these two attitudes, we may cite Professor Peter Bertocci's treatment of "The Conception of God in Western Thought," in his *Introduction to the Philosophy of Religion*.[29] In his summary of the divine attributes as commonly understood in Christendom, he for the most part agrees

[29] Prentice-Hall, 1951.

with Aulén, and with others we have quoted above, in Section 2; but at one significant point he differs: where Aulén puts *holiness* as the background of all other divine attributes, Bertocci puts *personality*. "The essence of God's nature, according to the western conception, is that he is an infinite, perfect Mind or Person[30] . . . . that his being had inner conscious unity, that he knew what he was doing, . . . enjoying complete unity of aim and activity[31] . . . . To summarize, the central affirmation of God in Judeo-Christian thought is that he is a Person, an everlasting self-dependent unity of thinking, feeling, and willing"—though of course free from the "imperfections to be found in human nature."[32] Any such clear-cut affirmation that God "is a Person" is deliberately and not accidentally absent from Aulén's treatment of the same topic. "The use of the word person as applied to God did not come into theology," he remarks, "until relatively late."[33] It is open to Schleiermacher's objection that it makes God "too thoroughly human," and is clearly a figure of speech rather than an assertion that God is literally a person. This figure of speech guards against the tendency to make of God "an abstract idea" or "some force of nature," and it protects man's fellowship with God against "dissolution of personality into the infinite" and against "all tendencies to understand God's 'grace' in a more or less material sense."[34] Still it is plain that Aulén uses this figure with great caution, and prefers to say that holiness rather than personality constitutes the fundamental background of God's nature.

Bertocci's view must not be regarded as peculiar to himself, or to the Personalist school of thought which he represents. Though not universal in liberal Protestant theology, as the ob-

---

[30] *Ibid.*, p. 306.    [31] *Ibid.*, p. 308.    [32] *Ibid.*, p. 309.
[33] Aulén, *op. cit.*, p. 159.    [34] *Ibid.*, p. 160.

jections of Schleiermacher and the Hegelians would prove, it is very widespread, especially in America. William Newton Clarke in his *Outline* defines God as "the personal Spirit, perfectly good, who in holy love creates, sustains and orders all." [35] William Adams Brown in his *Outline* groups the attributes of God under three principal heads, one of which is "Attributes of Personality." [36] Henry Churchill King in all of his theological works [37] takes the personality of God so seriously and so literally that he describes the ideal relationship between God and man in terms of a strict analogy with human friendship: first, "deep community of interest"; next, "mutual self-revelation and answering trust"; finally, "mutual self-giving." The thoroughly personal character of the God-man relationship is likewise emphasized by Brunner and other neo-orthodox theologians, who believe that Martin Buber has rightly described the religion of the Bible as always involving an "I-Thou" and never an "I-It" relationship between man and God.[38]

As theological personalism is not confined to any one school of thought, but cuts across the differences between liberalism and neo-orthodoxy, so also the opposition to it arises not from any one quarter, but from positions as diverse as the religious naturalism of Henry Nelson Wieman, the systematic theology of Paul Tillich, and the theosophical speculations of Nicholas Berdyaev. Let us consider their objections in the order named.

Wieman has consistently avoided personalistic terms in all his writings, believing that they involve an evocative, emotionally comforting but inaccurate use of language, inimical to clear

[35] P. 66.   [36] Pp. 102-5.
[37] See especially *Reconstruction in Theology*, Macmillan, 1901, and *The Laws of Friendship, Human and Divine*, Macmillan, 1909.
[38] Brunner, *The Divine-Human Encounter*, Westminster Press, 1943; Buber, *I and Thou*, Edinburgh: Clark, 1937.

thinking about the supremely meaningful Reality whereon man's highest good actually depends. He has defined this Reality in constantly shifting terms—in his early writings as a "value-making Process" or "integrating Process" at work in the world at large; in *The Wrestle of Religion with Truth*, as Whitehead's "Principle of Concretion," or that "order of existence and possibility" by which each thing that is or can be "shares in all and all in each"; [39] finally in *The Source of Human Good*, his most definitive work, as "creative good," or "the creative event . . . . always and absolutely good . . . . in the sense of creating value . . . a creative power in history which is able to conquer and to save." [40] It will be seen that these shifting definitions point to the same superhuman cosmic Reality from slightly variant angles; but all carefully avoid speaking of this Reality as a Person.

Wieman has expressed his objections to personalism most clearly in *The Growth of Religion*.[41] Speaking for his own school of thought, he remarks, "The new naturalists are like the new supernaturalists in holding fast to the reality of God, but they seriously question the character of personality in God." [42] God creates and sustains personality in man, but this does not mean that God is himself a person. "God does respond to the intimate needs and attitudes of each individual personality. But a being that is ready to do that for every different individual personality cannot be a personality . . . . God does catch up the intimate and secret outreachings of the human heart. But to represent God as a personality would be to give him a character that would make such ministrations impossible by reason of the essential limitations of personality." [43]

If we ask social psychologists and anthropologists what actu-

[39] Pp. 185-89.    [40] Pp. 299-309.    [41] Harper, 1938, pp. 359-65.
[42] *Ibid.*, p. 360.    [43] *Ibid.*, p. 361.

ally *does* create and sustain human personality, we shall get an answer which has deep theological significance: "growth of community between the individual and his environment . . . a living matrix of connections which flower into meanings and which generate personality in the individual, which sustain it, which respond to its deepest outreachings, which enrich it and bring it to highest development . . . when the person maintains the right attitudes of responsiveness and is kept free of undue self-concern." [44] This personality-producing matrix is God, or at least "the work of God," at the observable level. God so conceived is "more rich and pervasive than any personality could ever be." [45] Human persons dwell in God, and God's love "encompasses and fosters and dwells in the personalities of men . . . meaning by love that whole system of connections of mutual support which keeps all the cells and organs of the body working together . . . brings innumerable sources of life into the organism . . . brings the riches of thought and feeling to the individual from his social environment and from the accumulated meanings of the past . . . innumerably complicated connections of mutual support, ranging from atoms to great historic cultures . . . made of living, dynamic, delicately responsive bonds which move and change and transform one another in deep and delicate response to the changing needs of each individual." [46]

"God, then," concludes Wieman, "is not a personality, but God is more worthful than any personality could ever be. God is not nature and he is not the universe, but he is the growth of living connections of value in the universe." [47] It is proper to call God "he" not "it" since he is superior not inferior to personality. It is proper to call him "Father" since he "creates human per-

[44] *Idem.*
[46] *Idem.*
[45] *Ibid.*, p. 362.
[47] *Ibid.*, pp. 362–63.

sonality . . . makes us all brothers . . . bestows a great love upon each of us." [48] But his love involves no "visceral contractions and glandular modifications," like human love, and is only remotely analagous to it. "What God may have in the way of consciousness or super-consciousness or beyond consciousness, we do not know. We do know the mighty gentleness, we know the tender care which characterize his being. . . . Why do we think . . . God must have the sort of viscerally controlled consciousness that we have or else be less than we. . . . God in the mystery of his being is probably much greater than any wish we could have for him. Surely we do not think greatly of God when we insist that he be like us." [49]

Wieman's "behavioristic theology" (as it has been called) stands in some respects at the opposite pole from Tillich's theology of "being-itself." One stresses the immanence, the other the transcendence of God; one sticks close to the empirical evidence, the other plunges boldly into ultimate metaphysics—or to use the preferred term, "ontology." It is all the more impressive, in view of these contrasts, to find Tillich objecting as strenuously as Wieman to theological personalism. The passage in question occurs at the end of *The Courage to Be,* where Tillich claims that "absolute faith," the only kind that can courageously face radical doubt and ultimate meaninglessness, implies a conception of God that transcends the personalistic categories of ordinary Christian theism.

"Theism" is of course an ambiguous term. As Tillich uses it, it has three possible meanings: (1) "unspecified affirmation of God"; (2) "the divine-human encounter . . . person-to-person relationship with God"; (3) "a doctrine of God which transforms the person-to-person encounter with God into a doctrine

---

[48] *Ibid.,* p. 364.          [49] *Ibid.,* pp. 364–65.

about two persons who may or may not meet but who have a reality independent of each other." [50] The first form of theism Tillich calls "irrelevant"—except to politicians, who find it cheap and easy thus to invoke "God" in public speeches. The second he calls "one-sided," because it ignores the mystical element in Biblical religion and historical Christianity, to concentrate exclusively on its nonmystical side: "personalistic passages in the Bible and the Protestant creeds, the personalistic image of God, the Word as the tool of creation and revelation, the ethical and social character of the Kingdom of God, the personal nature of human faith and divine forgiveness, the historical vision of the universe, the idea of a divine purpose, the infinite distance between creator and creature . . . the person-to-person character of prayer and practical devotion." [51] As for the third form of theism, it makes of God a mere idol, "a being beside others . . . *a* being, not being-itself"; and God so conceived turns me into an object of tyranny as I have turned him into an object of idolatry.

At this point we are strangely reminded of the indignation with which Nicholas Berdyaev, again and again in his works, upbraids "positive" or "rational" theology for presenting a portrait of God which justifies atheistic rebellion.[52] The cure for this danger is the same for Tillich as for Berdyaev: balance "positive" with "negative," "rational" with "mystical" theology. A theology that is to face down ultimate despair and overcome the threat of meaninglessness by the "power of being" must be at once personal and mystical, says Tillich. It will not deny the reality of that personal encounter with God on which Brunner

[50] *The Courage to Be* (Yale Univ. Press, 1952), pp. 182–84.
[51] *Ibid.*, p. 183.
[52] See *Truth and Revelation* (Bles, 1953), Chap. III, where (as often) the technical terms *kataphatic* and *anaphatic* are used to describe these opposing types of theology. See also Chap. I, "An Undevout Meditation," in *The Divine and the Human* (Bles, 1949).

and Buber lay such stress; but it will say, "The God above the God of theism is present although hidden in every divine-human encounter . . . neither object nor subject and . . . therefore above the scheme into which theism has forced him. . . . Personalism with respect to God is balanced by a trans-personal power of the divine." [53]

One thing is common to the perspective of Wieman, Tillich and Berdyaev, despite their many differences: a deep appreciation of the mystical element in religion, and its implications for theology. It would appear, then, that the unresolved issue between the theological personalists and their opponents is ultimately the issue between an ethical-rational and a mystical-metaphysical interpretation of the Christian faith. This issue emerged at the very beginning of the history of Christian thought, as Harnack and many other historians have pointed out, and it has never been fully resolved. All that one can say with assurance is that in authentic Christian mysticism, the personal encounter between God and man is never eliminated, and the ethical-social element in religion is not by-passed but strongly affirmed; while in authentic Christian personalism the organic, vine-and-branches relationship between God and man, and the indirect, more impersonal relationships between God and man are likewise recognized.

[53] *Ibid.*, p. 187.

# IV

## *GOD AND THE WORLD*

Section 1. Does Cosmology Present a Religious Problem?

From the first cardinal point in every religious faith, the idea of God, a perpendicular line drops toward the horizontal line of natural, historical events on which we live. This perpendicular, vertical line is the line of relationship between God and the world. What it represents, varies from faith to faith. In monotheistic faiths, it represents the divine creative activity, which brings the world into being, and the divine providential activity, which sustains and orders the world and guides it toward its destiny. In some other faiths, the world is regarded as eternal, and the work of God (or the gods) is confined to ordering an already given environment. Sometimes the relationship between God and the world is purely external, as in deism. Sometimes it is purely internal—from the world's hidden depths to its visible surface appearances—as in pantheism. Whatever the conception of God or of the world, there must always be some line of relation between them. Having already explored the Christian conception of God, we have now to consider the meaning of the term "world," and how the two terms are related.

The "world" is the environment that all men have in common, whatever their faith or lack of faith. Cosmology, or the ordered knowledge of this world, is therefore to a large extent a neutral, nonreligious field, from which religious controversy can be and ought to be excluded. The natural sciences have cultivated special parts of this common field, special aspects of this universal environment, by methods so impersonal and abstract that whoever faithfully adheres to them is bound to come to the same results under the same conditions, whether he be Moslem or Hindu, capitalist or socialist. For theologians to assert that the thrice-checked outcome of a chain of scientific observations and experiments cannot be so, if it chances to differ from the assertions of a sacred book or an ecclesiastical council, is as foolish and futile as it would be for them to charge the multiplication table with heresy. Within its own limited field, the secular cosmology of natural science is as impregnable to theological criticism as it is irrelevant to religious problems.

The fact that religious controversy has actually arisen after great revolutionary discoveries in natural science—the globular shape of the earth, its revolution around the sun, the law of gravitation, the mutability of species—suggests that there are areas of cosmology where religious interests are really involved. The tragic "conflict between science and theology" springs from inaccurate definition of boundaries between such areas of vital involvement and the neutral areas described above. All the natural sciences were originally parts of philosophy, which always was and always will be a controversial field. The boundaries between the neutral field of exact science and the controversial field of philosophy are so hard to fix with finality, that violations of scientific territory, such as have occurred in the Copernican and Darwinian controversies, are best understood as defense reactions against threatened invasions from the other side. Scientific theories can never be completely disentangled from conscious or unconscious philosophic assumptions. (The rejection of biological theories in Soviet Russia on ideological grounds, makes this particularly clear.) When a really revolutionary scientific theory arises, its popular interpretation usually includes some highly questionable philosophic "over-beliefs,"[1] which appear to be logically involved in it but are not really essential to it. Giordano Bruno thus blew up the apparent implications of Copernican astronomy into a complete cosmic philosophy, and Herbert Spencer did the same with Darwinian biology. While theology is bound to respect the neutrality of natural science, it cannot escape its duty to challenge and expose destructive cosmic philosophies masquerading as "scientific."

By speaking of "destructive" cosmic philosophies, we do not mean to imply that there is only one truly "religious" cosmic philosophy (say, the idealistic) and all philosophies inconsistent with this are to be regarded as "destructive." The mere fact that religion has survived the destruction of many "religious" philosophies is sufficient to discount this monopolistic theory. If we make the German distinction between *Weltbild* ("world picture") and *Weltanschauung* ("world view") we may go so far as to say that no particular world *picture* is essential to religion; but there are certain world *views* so incompatible with the religious attitude that they must be described as "destructive." The clearest example of a religiously destructive world view is materialistic mechanism, which logically results in a devaluated universe where religion stifles because there is literally nothing worthful to worship, nothing to live by, nothing to live for. It is important for theology to point out that this destructive world

[1] This term is borrowed from John Langdon-Davies, who has written the whole history of the science-theology conflict from this angle, in *Man and the Universe*, Harper, 1930.

113

view is philosophic, not scientific; Lucretius made a stronger case for it in terms of ancient prescientific atomism than can be made in the modern scientific setting. Its final disproof is that it not only destroys religion but destroys all meaning in life—all goodness, all beauty, all objectively valid truth—and so incidentally destroys its own claim to be true.

The destructive effect of materialistic mechanism is due to its rigid exclusiveness. It will admit no other substance than matter, no other process than mechanical cause and effect. In order to escape its destructive consequences, theology does not need to deny matter and mechanism (redefined, of course, in terms of the New Physics) as real cosmic factors; it needs only to assert the operation of other real factors—which leaves the door open to a variety of possible cosmic philosophies, all compatible with religion. The universal religious concern in the field of cosmology is simply that nature should permit man to find God, or be found of God; that it should not be so conceived as to exclude the reality of *any* divine Object of devotion (materialistic mechanism) or so as to cut off the devotee from his God (deism) or so as to locate God "everywhere in general, nowhere in particular" (pantheism). We have already noted in Chapter III that the difficulties of deism and pantheism tend to drive religious thought in the general direction of monotheism, whose conception of God's relation to the world avoids both the pure transcendence of deism and the pure immanence of pantheism. Between these destructive extremes, religious thought is free to consort with many different cosmological systems. *Cosmology, in other words, is not an independent topic in theology; it is simply a part of the doctrine of God. What concerns religious thought is the world as related to God, not the world in itself.* Other aspects of cosmology—the details of the *Weltbild*, and even the broad outlines

of the *Weltanschauung*—may be liberally borrowed from contemporary science and philosophy, and replaced from time to
time when they "wax old like a garment," without risking the
destruction of any essential element of religious faith.

### SECTION 2. THE CHRISTIAN CONSENSUS CONCERNING GOD AND THE WORLD

If a particular *Weltbild* were an essential part of the Christian
Faith, it would be difficult if not impossible to define any consensus concerning it. The vicissitudes of the Christian *Weltbild*,
from Biblical times to the present era, have been simply stupendous.

The Biblical writers show no such interest in natural phenomena as the Greek philosophers; they *perceive God in time*, as
Victor Monod has put it, *and not in space;* [2] yet they assume a
picture of the natural world similar to that held by neighboring
peoples in the Near and Middle East: a flat earth, overarched by
the solid inverted bowl of the sky, in which the stars are fixed
like driven nails, while the sun, moon and planets "wander" over
the surface in complicated paths; a reservoir of waters above the
"windows of heaven," and another "great deep" beneath the
earth, by whose downpouring and upgushing streams, the earth
may be completely flooded (Genesis 7:11).

In Ethiopia and in Zion City (Illinois) there are still Christian
theologians who declare that the Christian faith is destroyed if
this flat-earth cosmology is given up; but long ago, it was given

[2] Victor Monod, *Dieu dans l'Univers*, Paris: Fischbacher, 1933, Chap. I.

up by the overwhelming majority of Christian theologians, when Christian thought came in contact with the Aristotelian-Ptolemaic *Weltbild*, elaborated by a long series of scientific observers and discoverers in ancient Alexandria. How stubbornly the Biblical cosmology persisted after contact with Alexandrian cosmology began, may be inferred from the *Christian Topography* of Cosmas Indicopleustes, a widely traveled and well-informed Christian geographer of the sixth century A.D. Cosmas adheres firmly to his own special version of the flat-earth cosmology, according to which the shape of the whole world resembles the boxlike structure of the Tabernacle in the Wilderness, and the variations of day and night in different seasons are explained by the hypothesis of a mighty mountain peak in the north, behind which the sun passes at different heights in summer and winter. By the thirteenth century, however, Dante and Aquinas have accepted the Aristotelian-Ptolemaic cosmology, and have found it notably congenial to the hierarchical patterns prevailing in feudal society, in the Church, and in theology: hell (nadir-point of imperfection) at center of earth, earth at center of universe, all imperfection bounded by the sphere of the moon, rising degrees of perfection in successive, concentric spheres beyond the moon (planets, sun and stars) each controlled by its own appropriate rank of guardian angels, till at last the empyrean sphere, seat of God's throne (summit of all possible perfections) bounds and consummates the whole.

The "Copernican" and "Cartesian" revolutions have rudely shaken this medieval *Weltbild*, displacing the earth and man from their astronomical-theological centrality, and transforming the universe from a hierarchy of values into a uniform system of mechanical pushes and pulls, in which the status of spiritual values becomes highly problematical. However, by the early eighteenth century, such leading Christian thinkers as Newton and Leibniz have completed the model of the "world machine" down to the last cog (setting it in a framework of absolute space and time) and have found various ways of reconciling their Christian faith with an acceptance of this seemingly soulless system. The modern idealistic movement in philosophy, from Kant and Fichte through Hegel and Lotze, has generally continued to accept the Newtonian "world machine" as its portrait of the external, phenomenal world, while subordinating this whole world to a spiritual, inner world that is half-hidden, half-revealed by its forbidding outward appearance.

Since Darwin's *Origin of Species* (1859) we have been passing through another major revolution in *Weltbild*, whose destructive effect on the "world-machine" cosmology is already visible, while its ultimate constructive implications are still hard to estimate. With the passing of fixed species in biology, the world has assumed a fluid character that would have dizzied Sir Isaac Newton. When to this Darwinian fluidity we add Einsteinian relativity and the Heisenberg principle of indeterminacy, all resemblance between the world of Newton and the world of today seems to become "purely coincidental"—though we are assured that for average-size operations, as distinct from subatomic and supergalactic, the laws of Newtonian mechanics are still approximately correct.[3]

It is hard to find any consensus at all between the world pictures of Cosmas Indicopleustes, St. Thomas Aquinas, Sir Isaac Newton and Alfred North Whitehead; but there is far more consistency between their world views. Despite many sharp shifts

---

[3] For a more detailed review of the phases through which cosmology has passed since Copernicus, and some typical reactions to each phase, see my *Theism and the Scientific Spirit*.

of emphasis, due to variations in the prevailing cosmological climate, Christian thinkers have remained relatively stable in their world views, since they have preserved a common view of God's *relationship* to the world. William Adams Brown has offered a brief and striking formula for this Christian consensus in cosmology, which constitutes one of his best contributions to ecumenical theology: *"real existence, dependence, and adaptation to the Christian end."* [4]

Brown was a "critical idealist" in philosophy; but he recognized that idealistic pantheism's reduction of the world to a mere appearance or expression of the divine activity, having no "real existence" in the sight of God, stood outside the Christian consensus. To this extent, the Christian view of God's relationship to the world is "dualistic": God and nature are not one and the same (*Deus sive natura*) but two. Yet there are forms of dualism as alien to the Christian consensus as pantheistic monism: those that deny the "dependence" of the world on its Creator and Sustainer, or its "adaptation" to serve God's eternal Purpose revealed in Christ. Historically, Christian thought (especially *liberal* Christian thought) has veered back and forth between pantheistic monism and deistic or finitistic dualism; but it has persistently refused to settle down in these extreme positions. Brown's formula for the Christian consensus, properly understood, would satisfy Catholics and conservative Protestants as well as liberal Protestants.[5] To test it out, let us consider its implications for the doctrines of Creation and Providence.

"In the beginning God created the heavens and the earth" (Gen. 1:1). The exact meaning of the Biblical idea of creation

[4] *Outline*, Chap. XIII, pp. 198 ff.
[5] For a conservative Protestant view in essential harmony with the formula, cf. Berkhof, *op. cit.*, pp. 96, 111.

cannot be determined by a definition of the Hebrew verb here used. On the face of it, the Creation narrative describes how God's Spirit brooded over a dark, formless, watery Abyss and began to bring light and order into it. The question of the origin of the Abyss is not raised, for this is not a piece of philosophical speculation, but an expression of religious faith in God as the Lord and Source of the ordered universe. It is clear, however, that the Creator is never confused with his creatures, in Biblical faith, and transcends them in such a manner that they "really exist" over against their Source, while at the same time they remain "dependent" on his ever-present creative power. As for the "adaptation" of the world to God's purpose, this is unmistakably indicated by the phrase, "and God saw that it was good," repeated at the end of each day's creative work.

When the Biblical faith later confronted philosophical speculation about God and the world, it became further clarified. Neither Stoic monism nor Platonic dualism was satisfactory to it—the former, because it identified the divine World-Soul so closely with the world as to endanger the separate existence of the creatures; the latter, because it treated matter (*hyle*) as an intractable second principle of creation, so independent of the Creator that he could never fully subdue it to his good purposes. Rejecting these alternative world views, the Christian Fathers declared that God created the world "out of nothing"; i.e., neither out of his own divine substance nor out of any sort of pre-existent stuff. This view does not commit Christian thought to any crudely anthropomorphic or magical conception of God's creative power—as though the Creator snapped his fingers and cried Abracadabra!—nor does it profess to offer any intelligible explanation of the creative process; it simply declares that the stuff as well as the structure of the world has God for its Author.

While many modern Christians hesitate to use the phrase "out of nothing" because of its irrational sound, there is a large Christian consensus in favor of the general position to which it points: that God neither spins the world out of himself, nor carves it out of alien, recalcitrant matter, but brings its elementary units into being, and combines them in orderly structures.

How and by what stages the elementary units of our existing world emerge from the divine creative matrix, and are combined to form the objects that we see and the persons that we are, is more a scientific and philosophic than a religious problem. There is no Christian consensus about such matters, comparable to that which affirms simply that God is the Creator of "heaven and earth and all that is therein." Pre-Darwinian "special creation," Darwinian "natural selection," Bergsonian "creative evolution," Lloyd Morgan's "emergent evolution" and Whitehead's "principle of concretion," contend with one another as more or less adequate interpretations of the creative process. One important point of consensus appears in the midst of these contending theories, however: *creation is not simply once-for-all, but in some real sense continuous.*

Even on the "special creation" hypothesis, with its doctrine of unchanging species, every new-born individual is more than the product of his immediate parents; he is a new work of God in and through his parents. And since the creative process will not reach its goal until this present world is reshaped into that "new heaven and new earth" in which God's "Kingdom, power and glory" are at last to be fully expressed, authentic Christian piety cannot possibly be content to reverence the world as it now is, as though it were God's finished work of creation. Neither in six days nor in six aeons could the whole mighty scope of God's creative work be revealed. As St. Augustine long ago declared,[6] the act of creation cannot possibly be conceived to have occurred and been finished "in time"; but only on the border line of eternity, where time itself comes into being. While St. Augustine's lead has not been universally followed, there seems to be a growing consensus in our generation that God is now and everlastingly the Creator. This consensus is bounded on the one hand by the deistic view that God is no more active in the world, once he has made it, and on the other hand by the pantheistic view that the world is eternally re-created out of its own divine depths.

Concerning God's providential sustenance and government of the world he has made and is making, there is deep agreement. Here again, William Adams Brown's three principles help to define the consensus. He himself correlates the doctrine of providence with the principle of *dependence,* as he correlates the doctrine of creation with *real existence;* but on closer examination it will be seen that all three of his principles come into play in both fields.

Too exclusive correlation of providence with dependence has been the bane of Christian thought on this subject. If the world process is simply and absolutely dependent on what Calvinism calls the divine "decrees," then both the freedom and the real existence of the finite creatures are imperiled. All action becomes predetermined by divine action, till at last God becomes the sole Actor in the cosmic drama, and the Author of evil as well as good. When Zwingli accepted divine evil-doing as the unavoidable conclusion of his doctrine of divine Providence, he set himself outside of the Christian consensus. Even the most convinced predestinarians, from St. Augustine to Calvin and beyond, have

[6] *Confessions,* Bk. XI, Chaps. XII, XIII.

struggled manfully to avoid this fatal conclusion. The *West-minster Confession* speaks for them all when it declares, "God from all eternity did . . . unchangeably ordain whatsoever comes to pass; yet so as thereby neither is God the author of sin, nor is violence offered to the will of the creatures. . . ." [7]

If man "really exists" in relative independence, and if the world process is "adapted to the Christian end," then Christians are substantially at one in a conception of "dependence" upon divine Providence that is not mechanical nor slavish. Man has a real but limited sphere in which he is allowed and even called by his Creator to exercise rational foresight and control—a finite providence, which is capable of serving the ends of the infinite Providence. Man is also capable of turning these same high powers against God's Providence and treating God as his Adversary; but he is not able to defeat God's purpose in the end. In ways consistent with man's relative independence and moral responsibility, God is bringing human history under his control and making even the wrath of men to praise him. In this divine strategy, the chosen People of God are believed by all Christians to play a centrally important role. Through their witness in word and in deed, God extends a persistent call to his rebellious children to come out from their proud Cities of Destruction into the present humiliation and final blessedness of the City of God. It makes a great difference, of course, whether God's final purpose is to gather all mankind into his Kingdom and to redeem the whole universe, or only to save a few "chosen vessels" *out* of mankind, and *out* of the world. On this question of ultimate eschatology, Christians are not agreed, as we shall note in Chapter VIII. But on either view, the world process is "dependent" on God's providential control and "adapted to the Christian end,"

[7] Chap. III, opening sentence.

God and the World

while respecting the "real existence" and limited freedom of God's creatures.

In the Credo of the United Church of Canada, written by Calvinist Presbyterians and liberal Congregationalists in ecumenical conversation with Arminian Methodists, the present Christian consensus concerning God and the world is well expressed:

We believe in God, the eternal personal Spirit, Creator and Upholder of all things.

We believe that God, as Sovereign Lord exalted above the world, orders and overrules all things in it to the accomplishment of His holy, wise, and good purpose. . . .

So we acknowledge God as Creator, Upholder, and Sovereign Lord of all things, and the righteous and loving Father of men.[8]

It will be noted that in this statement the creating, sustaining and governing activity of God are brought into close relation with one another. In consistent deism, creation is a finished operation, after which the world runs by its own resident forces and the Creator retires into inactivity, from which retirement he emerges only at the end of history to award prizes and inflict punishments. In pantheism, God's work is only to sustain the world (his permanent body) by his indwelling presence; neither creation nor government is possible in any thoroughgoing way for a deity who does not transcend the world. In the ecumenical statement just cited, God is "exalted above the world," but at

[8] Cited in John Dow, *This Is Our Faith*, opposite p. 1. Dow comments as follows: "God is a transcendent God neither external to and aloof from His world nor chained and limited within it. He is the great Sovereign overlord, who has called the world out of the void and can always call it back again, an Almighty One constricted by no sinister arbitrary chain of fate, but who holds in His sure hands all events, One moreover who is a hearer and answerer of prayer, able and always willing to respond to the call of man" (p. 16). This ecumenical creed and its commentary by John Dow are published by the Board of Evangelism and Social Service, United Church of Canada, Toronto, 1943. See also the excellent brief Catechism published by the same board in 1944.

the same time inwardly sustains all his creatures. Thus he re-affirms and maintains their real existence, while never surrender-ing the power to order and overrule the creatures he has made, by means that do not violate their relative independence. We may say that both his sustaining activity and his governing activ-ity are creative and infinitely resourceful, not mechanically coercive and repetitive but full of newness, while remaining self-consistent through the dominance of one unwavering Purpose. Paul Tillich suggests this same great idea by the captions he uses to summarize his doctrine of God and the World: "God's Origi-nating Creativity, God's Sustaining Creativity, God's Directing Creativity." [9] While there are many features of his powerful presentation which are peculiar to himself or to his school of thought, he surely represents the general Christian consensus when he maintains the consistency between providence and *prayer:*

God's directing creativity is the answer to the question of the meaning of prayer, especially prayers of supplication and prayers of intercession. Neither type of prayer can mean that God is expected to acquiesce in interfering with existential conditions. Both mean that God is asked to direct the given situation toward fulfilment. The prayers are an element in this situation, a most powerful factor if they are true prayers. As an element in the situation a prayer is a condition of God's directing creativity, but the form of this creativity may be the complete rejection of the manifest content of the prayer. Nevertheless, the prayer may have been heard according to its hidden content, which is the surrender of a fragment of existence to God.[10]

[9] *Op. cit.,* I, pp. 252–70.
[10] *Ibid.,* p. 267.

## Section 3. Unresolved Issues Concerning God and the World

Creation, providence and prayer are doctrines where there is a large "common core" of agreement among the Christian churches. It cannot be said, however, that there is agreement concerning the proper adjustment between these doctrines and the contemporary state of scientific knowledge and human history. The violent controversies aroused by the Darwinian theory in the latter part of the nineteenth century have somewhat subsided, but many of the issues then raised have continued to divide theologians in our century, while the focus of attention has moved from natural history to human history, and from biology to physics and psychology.

The tension between the Biblical world picture and the modern world picture has perceptibly relaxed since the rise of the new physics, but no clear consensus has emerged as to how the two are to be reconciled. The *miraculous* elements in the Biblical world picture, and the prominence it gives to *angelic and demonic beings,* continue to present problems for Christian thought, perhaps not so insoluble as they seemed at the turn of the century, but at any rate still unresolved. On another issue over which the Darwinian era was greatly perplexed—*the problem of evil*—it must be confessed that the tension has mounted rather than diminished. Natural evil is still hard to interpret, while moral evil has taken on new power to horrify and dismay, since atomic fission and psychologically refined methods of torture have so dreadfully multiplied man's capacity to destroy and degrade.

Monistic idealism, on which so much liberal theology was

based at the turn of the century, has proved unable to handle these issues, and pluralism of various sorts, including dualistic diabolism, has become a powerful trend. The repopularizing of Satanism and demonry as partial explanations of evil has reopened many minds to belief in the existence of superhuman spiritual beings, both angelic and demonic—a belief which had practically died out in liberal Protestant circles. While most of the debate on these issues has been between liberal and conservative Protestants, the emergence of new faith in miracles, angels and demons among some leading Protestant thinkers creates new possibilities of ecumenical conversation between Protestants and Catholics— who have never ceased to believe that miracles occur *now*, and angelic or demonic influences play upon human life *now*, as truly as in Bible times.

## A. *Reconciliation of the Biblical and Contemporary World Pictures*

The problem of reconciliation in its present form has been well posed by Otto Dilschneider.[11] Modern man, he believes, is too fundamentally alienated from his cosmos to feel at home in the world again without a fundamental rethinking of the relationship between the Christian movement and its cosmic environment. On the side of the Church, this alienation is due to a narrowing of the Christian message from the cosmic outreach it had in the New Testament to an exclusive concern with the individual soul and its relations with God. In terms of the Pauline epistles, it may be said that the Western Church, since Augustine and Luther, has come to live too exclusively in the sin-and-justification framework of *Romans* and *Galatians*, ignoring the cosmic Christ of *Colossians* and *Ephesians*—whom the East-

[11] *Das Christliche Weltbilt* (Gütersloh: Bertelsmann, 1951).

ern Orthodox Church has never forgotten and the "younger churches" of India are freshly commending to our attention. Meanwhile, on the side of secular culture, a world picture has been built up where man feels himself lost, and the fields of knowledge no longer hang together. Neither conservative theology with its stubborn reassertion of the ancient-medieval *Weltbild*, nor liberal theology with its tendency to "de-mythologize" the old *Weltbild* in favor of the new, can adequately solve the problems or heal the alienations from which we all suffer. What is needed is a new Christian world picture, in which Biblical insight into the meaning of the creation and modern data from the natural and social sciences really *interpenetrate*.

The theological foundation for this reconciliation is to be found in the cosmic Christ of Paul and John, who is God's Word or Wisdom, whereby the world was originally made, and its coherent unity, purpose and meaning still consist—"the central meaning wherein all the problems of meaning that man raises in respect to the cosmos are comprehended . . . . the Pantocrator who comprehends the whence and the whither . . . . the Alpha and the Omega, the beginning and the end." [12] For lack of such a center of meaning, the Western cosmos has lost its integrity, and the fields of knowledge have drifted beyond the legitimate autonomy of specialized study (*Eigengesetzlichkeit*) into the illegitimate autonomy of proud self-sufficiency (*Eigenmächtigkeit*). The cosmic Christ will not force the facts of any science, but will reintegrate those facts about a center of cosmic meaning and a goal of cosmic destiny that are beyond the reach of any empirical science. Just what such a reintegration will imply, Dilschneider can only faintly foreshadow, from the fruitful collaboration now just beginning between "anthropological

[12] *Ibid.*, pp. 123–26.

medicine" (as practiced by Weizsäcker of Heidelberg) and "pastoral medicine" (as practiced by Tournier and other Swiss physicians).[13] Beyond that one concrete suggestion, and an appreciative reference at the end to Karl Heim's constructive thought in this field, this book does not move toward the realization of the program it lays down.

We may illustrate the diversity of cosmological views now current among Christians with particular reference to the problem of *miracle*, on which so much else hangs. Fundamentalists give great prominence to the miraculous elements in the New Testament narrative, as those which must above all be accepted, if authentic Christianity is to be preserved. Conservative evangelicals would generally agree with the late Dr. E. Y. Mullins of Louisville that the greatest peril in facing the scientific world picture is to allow the supernatural "irreducibles" of the Gospel to be so reduced as to fit into a naturalistic scheme.[14] Many conservatives would accept Louis Berkhof's doctrine (common to Protestant and Catholic Scholastics for centuries) that God the first cause can at any time by-pass all secondary causes (those that science describes) and "produce extraordinary effects by a simple act of His will, and that without violating the order of nature." If man can counteract the law of gravitation without disturbing it, by throwing a ball into the air, how much more can the omnipotent God do as he wills with the laws he has made.[15] Most liberals, on the other hand, would agree with the late Professor Macintosh of Yale that "if miracles to prevent natural disasters ever happen or have happened, they ought to occur much oftener than they do"; but if frequent miraculous suspensions *did* occur, "the whole orderly system of nature

[13] *Ibid.*, pp. 288–309.   [15] Berkhof, *op. cit.*, p. 116.
[14] Mullins, *Christianity at the Crossroads*, Doran, 1924.

would be upset and the development of intelligence and moral character made impossible." Prayer itself would degenerate into magic under these conditions.

Prayer is the right religious adjustment, and there are objective effects following the right religious adjustment which would not be experienced without it. This is the dependable human experience of the answer to prayer. But it is also a dependable human experience that the heavens are as brass toward any petition that asks for what is against the laws of nature. There is a law of prayer and its answer. But there is no place in the best possible kind of world for the arbitrary interruption of the established natural order.[16]

The opinions just cited reflect the tension between conservative and liberal views of miracle, as they stood in the first quarter of the twentieth century. Much has happened, both in science and in theology, to diminish this tension, but without producing a clear new consensus. The deterministic conception of the laws of nature, on which the impression of their absolute dependability and inviolability so largely rested, has been thrown in question by the Heisenberg Principle of Indeterminacy and other new developments in the field of science. Theologians, meanwhile, have begun to throw off the domination of that monistic "everythingism" (whether pantheistic or naturalistic in character) in which C. S. Lewis sees the principal modern obstacle to faith in miracles.[17] So far have some neo-orthodox theologians gone in reaffirming the transcendent majesty and sovereignty of God, that *all* his operations become unfathomable miracles for faith, instead of "dependable" in Macintosh's sense. For Aulén, "the unfathomable is not something which lies by the side of the comprehensible, but that which faith perceives is by its nature

[16] Macintosh, *The Reasonableness of Christianity* (Scribner, 1925), p. 98.
[17] C. S. Lewis, *Miracles: an Introductory Essay*, concluding section.

incomprehensible even to faith." Luther was right, he says, in seeing in the act of divine forgiveness, "an inscrutable mystery, a miracle which defied all description." [18] For Barth, all God's dealings with his creatures, especially the Incarnation, are so profoundly mysterious that he finds no difficulty in accepting the Virgin Birth as a "miracle" that fittingly conveys the central meaning of the Christmas "mystery"—the feminine passivity of the human and the masculine activity of the divine in the coming of Christianity.[19] In its general openness to the miraculous, which it sees potentially "breaking in" everywhere, neo-orthodoxy thus tends to abandon any attempt to correlate or reconcile the natural and supernatural orders, as conservative and liberal theology in their different ways have both tried to do. Charles Raven in his Gifford Lectures complains that neo-orthodoxy diverted attention from this task of reconciliation, just when conditions were becoming favorable for its accomplishment.[20]

The most thoroughgoing attempt in our time to correlate and reconcile the scientific and religious world pictures has been made by the dean of German Protestant theologians, Karl Heim. As early as 1904, when mechanistic naturalism still held the field, he addressed himself to this problem in his *Weltbild der Zukunft*: either, he declared, a new *Weltbild* would appear, in which religious certitude would be possible, or religious faith would retreat to the vanishing point.[21] Now, in his eightieth year and crippled by a paralytic stroke, he has made himself master of the new physics in all its technical details, and correlated it

---

[18] Aulén, *op. cit.*, pp. 100–101.

[19] Barth, *Dogmatics in Outline*, Chap. 14.

[20] Raven, *Natural Religion and Christian Theology*, Vol. I, *Science and Religion* (Gifford Lectures, First Series, Cambridge Univ. Press, 1953), pp. 202, 212.

[21] See my discussion of Heim's earlier works in *Contemporary Continental Theology* (Harper, 1938).

with the Biblical world picture in two very striking books: *Christian Faith and Natural Science* and *The Transformation of the Scientific World View* (1953).

The basis for Heim's scheme of correlation was already laid in *God Transcendent* (1936), where he dealt with God's relation to the world in terms of a theory of *dimensions*. Not only the various dimensions of the objective space-time world of physical science, but also "my" objective world and "thine," "I" and my objective world, and above all "I" and "Thou" as living centers of consciousness, are separated from one another by "boundaries of content" that separate parts of the same space. An extra space or dimension permits phenomena to occur which seem miraculous from a more limited perspective but involve no actual violation of the laws of that realm; for example, an inhabitant of three dimensions can mystify the inhabitants of "Flatland" by passing from A to B without traversing the line between them—simply by detouring through that third dimension which the Flatlanders cannot perceive. "I" and "Thou" continually transcend the world of the objective sciences in the same way, without violating their laws. How is it, then, with God and the world? We expect Heim to say that God lives in a dimension that includes and transcends all other dimensions; but this application to God of "intramundane Forms of Intuition" seems to him to lead inevitably to idolatry or pantheism; so that in the end he declares divine transcendence to be absolutely *sui generis*, and God unknowable except by revelation.

In *Christian Faith and Natural Science*, Heim picks up the same analysis of dimensions and spaces, but this time he dares to declare that the God of Hebrew-Christian Monotheism inhabits "suprapolar space"—a kind of space that bounds all other spaces, but is not bounded or limited by them in return. Thus the dangers of pantheism and idolatry are avoided, and Heim can stress the *analogy* as well as the *difference* between divine transcendence and human transcendence, as he did not in his earlier book. In *The Transformation of the Scientific World View*, Heim makes plain that the world of the new physics is no closed mechanistic-materialistic system, like the world of the old physics, but an open universe conceivably penetrable to human or divine free will. Matter, the "absolute object," hard and self-contained like the proverbial billiard ball, has been reduced to energy and light; and whether light is a wave or a particle cannot be discussed without some reference to the knowing subject. Absolute space and time, meanwhile, have been displaced by the theory of relativity, and absolute determinism replaced by the principle of indeterminacy. In such an open universe, miracles are not "suspensions" of natural laws, as they are in Thomistic (or Protestant) scholasticism, but *voluntary acts coming from a dimension beyond the objective dimension to which the sciences are confined.*

An act of will, performed in faith, nothing doubting, enables me to raise my hand—unless some paralysis or neurosis breaks the mysterious connection between my ego and my body in their distinct but related dimensions. There is much evidence that similar acts of will, performed in faith, may sometimes enable me to heal my body, to heal others by kindling a like faith in them, and even to affect persons and objects in distant places. "Seen from within, nature is a war of living powers of will," [22] and natural miracles are possible whenever a finite will becomes hypnotically sure of its objective. In the Christian sense, however, a real miracle means that God's "higher will" dwelling in suprapolar space, and therefore omnipresent to all spaces what-

[22] Heim, *Transformation of the Scientific World View*, p. 191.

soever, becomes a participant in the cosmic battle of wills, and prophetically asserts "the supremacy of God and His Plenipotentiary over the world of demons," [23] as it was in the beginning and shall be at the end. Only through sensitiveness to God's will, acquired through much prayer, can one discern the difference between divine and demonic miracles. Both kinds are constant possibilities in our living and open universe.

To confront Heim's frank avowal of faith in the constant possibility of miracles as the prophetic breaking in of a new divine order, or the equally clear-cut avowal of C. S. Lewis's book on *Miracles*, is to realize how far Christian thought is from general agreement on this subject, despite the "transformation of the scientific world view" and the theoretical oneness of the universe. Miracle faith is common among small Protestant sects, but the major denominations tend to treat it as superstitious. Macintosh's objection that miracles ought to be more frequent, and if they *were* frequent would destroy God's dependable providence, is still widely felt.

It will be noted that demonic wills are for Heim as much a part of the cosmic process as human wills, and the divine will. In this respect he represents a marked trend of our generation to recover an aspect of the Biblical world picture closely bound up with its miracle faith. One of the soberest and best-disciplined thinkers of our generation, Paul Tillich, has given encouragement to this trend in his essay on "The Demonic," [24] by which he means a "super-individual and yet not natural power" [25] bursting through the natural cosmic balance between vitality and form, and moving toward destruction. Like Heim, Tillich be-

[23] *Idem.*
[24] Tillich, *The Interpretation of History,* Scribner, 1936, pp. 77–122.
[25] *Ibid.*, p. 88.

lieves in demonic ecstasy and demonic miracle as well as in their divine counterparts; and he sees no conflict between such beliefs and a critical use of reason: "No conflict between different dimensions of reality is possible. Reason receives revelation in ecstasy and miracles; but reason is not destroyed by revelation, just as revelation is not emptied by reason." [26] It is a remarkable fact that Harold DeWolf, a theologian of the Boston Personalist tradition (that is to say, a liberal of liberals in his background), now seriously discusses the existence of angelic and demonic beings, and regards it as "probable." [27] A generation ago, most liberals would not even have mentioned the subject. The new trend ought not of course to mean the uncritical acceptance of stories of miracles and spirit possession, in or out of the Scriptures; but it does indicate that there is now room in the universe for a dimension of dramatically conflicting wills, human and superhuman, co-existing and interacting with the dimension of orderly sequence and dependable control in which science and technology do their characteristic work.

## B. The Problem of Evil

"The existence of evil," says Berdyaev, "is not only the obstacle to our faith in God, for it is equally a proof of the existence of God, and the proof that this world is not the only nor ultimate one. The experience of evil directs man's attention towards another world by arousing in him a discontent with this." [28] This paradoxical statement helps to explain why Christian thought is so persistently divided in its treatment of the problem of evil. Some theologians attempt to work out a theod-

[26] *Systematic Theology*, I, pp. 117-18.
[27] *A Theology of the Living Church*, pp. 127-29.
[28] *Freedom and the Spirit*, London: Bles, 1944, p. 158.

icy which proves, like Leibniz's, that this is "the best of all possible worlds"; others stress the dualistic conflict and travail in the present world order, and the hope of a radically new heaven and earth. The general Christian consensus excludes complete pantheistic identification of God with the world-as-it-is, and also excludes complete dualism between God and world, whether of the deistic or of the Gnostic-Manichaean type. Between these extremes, there is still room for wide divergence between devout loyalty to the existing world order as divinely ordained in all its details, and revolutionary insurgency against it, as under the foul tyranny of "The Prince of this World." This divergence exists in various forms and degrees, both among conservatives and among liberals.

Louis Berkhof's conservative Calvinism illustrates how close to practical pantheism Christian thought can go, while expressly denying theoretical pantheism. When he defines divine "concurrence" as *"that work of God by which He co-operates with all His creatures and causes them to act precisely as they do,"* and when he adds, "God is operative in every act of His creatures, not only in their good but also in their evil acts," he admits that he cannot "fully explain" why, then, "God's concurrent action involves no responsibility on His part for the evil of men." [29] Against such Calvinistic near-pantheism, Bishop Aulén's Lutheran neo-orthodoxy, despite his general attempt to bridge the gulf between the Lutheran and Calvinist positions, breathes forth dualistic defiance: "Islam proclaims the fatalistic doctrine that everything that occurs is the inscrutable will of Allah, but this is not the language of Christian faith . . . . Faith refuses to attribute to God that which the Gospel attributes to Satan." There is for him a divine concurrence in all the events of the world

[29] Berkhof, *op. cit.,* p. 114.

process, but not so as to make God's creatures "act precisely as they do." Aulén puts the distinction strikingly when he says, "God does not will everything that happens but he wills something in everything that happens . . . even in relation to that which opposes him." [30] Not only in *Christus Victor* but in all his writings, Aulén warmly contends for a "dramatic," provisionally dualistic view of the cosmic conflict between God's will and the God-opposing powers of "sin, death and the devil" —a dualism limited only by the faith that these powers are not co-eternal with God, but have already been overcome in principle by Christ, and shall ultimately be subjected to complete divine control in the coming Kingdom for which we pray.

Among liberal theologians, a similar divergence can be seen in a friendly dispute which still divides the Personalistic school of thought at Boston University. The late Edgar Brightman, maintaining the immanence of the personal God in the world process, was led by his concern to understand how "surd evil" could exist in God's world to formulate his doctrine of "The Given." By this he meant a recalcitrant element in God's own nature—a "non-rational" and "non-voluntary" [31] factor in his being which God must struggle to control, bit by bit, somewhat as a man struggles to subject his "unformed sensory qualia" to the control of his reason and will. Brightman's successor in the chair of philosophy at Boston, Peter Bertocci, continues to defend this "finistic" conception of God as offering a better explanation than any "absolutistic" view of such phenomena as *"actual limitation of human ability," "superfluous consequences of maladjustment"* and *"natural evil which produces more harm than*

---

[30] Aulén, *Faith of the Christian Church*, pp. 196, 197.
[31] Brightman, *Philosophy of Religion*, pp. 336, 337.

*good.*" [32] DeWolf, his theological colleague, disagrees with Bertocci, and prefers a more "absolutistic," less dualistic solution of the problem of evil. It may help to expose the real issues in this field if we notice just how and why DeWolf differs from Bertocci concerning Brightman's doctrine.

Both Bertocci and DeWolf agree that Brightman's doctrine of "The Given" is superior to Plato's doctrine of the cosmic "Receptacle" (with whose recalcitrant "matter" the creative Demiurge had to struggle) in that "The Given" involves no final and insuperable dualism between God and the world stuff.[33] Moreover, the doctrine that God simply *cannot* now overcome all evil (because of an impediment in his own nature) but is steadily set toward the eventual mastery of evil, has some indubitable advantages, admitted by both parties. It places God *"unconditionally with the sufferer and against the pain,"* and it offers a *"clear defence of God's goodness,"* [34] while not denying his power to triumph in the end. Yet DeWolf is troubled by the fact that this doctrine pushes dualism back from human nature and cosmic process into the very nature of God, thus gratuitously introducing "a new self-contradictory relationship at the very source of being." [35] He argues that only an omnipotent God can kindle "the absolute dependence or unconditional trust . . . characteristic of religious experience, at its more profound and creative levels." [36] If Hosea, or the Second Isaiah, or Jesus, or Paul, had not believed that suffering was in some sense divinely purposed, they would never have reached those profound interpretations of its redemptive meaning which still sustain us in our darkest hours. It is better, then, to *define* omnipotence so as

---

[32] Bertocci, *op. cit.*, pp. 415–18.
[33] *Ibid.*, pp. 425, 426 and DeWolf, *Theology of the Living Church*, p. 134.
[34] DeWolf, *ibid.*, p. 132.      [35] *Ibid.*, p. 134.      [36] *Ibid.*, p. 135.

to eliminate nonsensical implications, inconsistent with divine wisdom or goodness, and in the last resort to take refuge in the mystery of God's ways, rather than to turn to the desperate expedient of a finite God. To this Bertocci replies, in substance, that the only God for whom we can care is One who cares for us, and is thus involved in finitude.

> If we suffer, God cannot be conceived as not suffering. If we are incomplete, he still has work to do. When we ask for a God complete in every respect, do we know what we ask? [37]

It is evident that the considerations which thus polarize Christian thought, both conservative and liberal, into two contrasting standpoints, are not easily united into one synoptic view. The practical problem of overcoming evil drives Christian thought to trust in an absolute, infinite, omnipotent Helper and Protector; but when the logical consequences of this conception are drawn out, they appear to lead to a view of Providence that makes God responsible for evil, and so raises grave theoretical problems for faith in such a God. Dualism relieves God of responsibility for evil, but appears to threaten his ability to overcome it.

The situation is complex and paradoxical. Either the paradox must be left unresolved, or two aspects of God's dealing with the world must be sharply distinguished, and so related that they can be simultaneously true. Many contemporary Christian thinkers have attempted such a reconciling distinction; e.g., Leslie Weatherhead's distinction between the primary and secondary will of God,[38] and Tillich's distinction between God as the Ground of Being and as the Abyss of Being.[39] Such distinction

---

[37] Bertocci, *op. cit.*, p. 439.
[38] Weatherhead, *Thinking Aloud in War-time*, Abingdon Press, 1940, VIII.
[39] Tillich, *Systematic Theology*, I, p. 156.

is implied in many interpretations of the doctrine of the Trinity: as Father, God is absolute Source and absolute Ruler of the whole world process; as Son and Spirit, he is involved redemptively in the world process, bears a cosmic Cross in his heart, and struggles painfully up from darkness to light, "with groanings that cannot be uttered," in every soul that seeks his help. We must postpone full consideration of this great and difficult doctrine until we deal with Christ the Savior in Chapter VI.

Meanwhile in Chapter V we shall encounter a polarity in Christian thought related to the one just discussed in the conflict between divine sovereignty and human responsibility. Here, as already noted, ecumenical discussion since Edinburgh 1937 has agreed that neither side of the paradox can possibly be given up, and both sides must be maintained, though no formula of reconciliation is fully satisfactory to all parties. Implicitly, this agreement applies to the problem of evil, too. No universally satisfactory solution of it has ever been offered; but neither the "absolutistic" nor the "finitistic" solution can clearly defeat its rival without seriously crippling the Christian faith at some essential point.

# V

## GOD AND MAN

### SECTION 1. THE UNIVERSAL PROBLEM OF MAN

WITH the doctrine of God and Man, we approach the second cardinal point that is to be found in every religious faith: the point of intersection between the line that descends vertically from God toward the world and toward man, and the line that runs horizontally from man-as-he-is toward man-as-he-hopes-to-be. Here is the point where the doctrine of God and the doctrine of salvation meet at right angles. Strictly speaking, we do not arrive definitely at this point of right-angled intersection until we reach the doctrine of the Savior. It is the Savior through whom God and man are brought into a right-angled relationship; until he comes, they stand (if the play on words may be forgiven) in a confused, wrong-angled relationship.

To vary the mathematical figure, we may say that until the Savior arrives on the scene, the vertical line between God and man is a *double* line. The line of God's search for man comes down from above and intersects the line of history at a proper right angle; but the line of man's search for God is a crooked, wavering line, shooting up at an angle that widely diverges from the perpendicular. Only in the Savior, and those who follow him, will the two lines become one; meanwhile man's life is pulled in different directions, and torn with contradictions. What he is divinely meant and impelled to be, and what he is, are two different things. It is with this highly problematic situation that the doctrine of God and Man is concerned.

Man is always and everywhere a problem to himself. His nature is complex and his destiny hard to foresee. The ancient Orphics described him as "child of earth and of starry heaven," and all his tangled thought about his nature gives forth confused echoes of that ancient judgment. Not only does his nature appear to be curiously compounded of stardust and common clay, but his behavior is distressingly contradictory. He sets up great goals, pursues them with incredible skill and amazing energy— and then turns traitor to his own high purposes. Ovid the playboy and Paul the apostle confirm each other's description of human perversity, across the gulf that separates their outlooks on life. "I see and approve the better, I follow the worse"— "the evil that I would not, that I do."

Greek philosophy and modern scientific anthropology have contributed much to man's objective knowledge of himself, but without dispelling the mystery of his complex nature and strange behavior. Aristotle gave a classic description of man— hard to improve on, even yet—as a "rational animal" and a "political animal," like other animals in having the same five senses and the same biological appetites, but unique in his capacity to reason logically, to envisage ideal ends, and to organize socio-political systems in the service of such ends. Modern anthropology, psychology and sociology have filled in many new details concerning the family tree which links early mankind to other animal species, the conditioning process whereby human skills and character traits are developed, and the structures and functions of human society. All such details are of interest to religious thought, and in a full theological system would have to be included and interpreted, as Aquinas included and interpreted Aristotle's doctrine of man in his Christian *Summa*. By themselves, however, apart from all consideration of man's ultimate Source and Goal, the various sciences of man yield only a secular anthropology, as remote from religious anthropology as the physical and biological sciences are from religious contemplation of nature. When all its objective findings are in, secular anthropology still leaves the deepest problems concerning man untouched and unsolved. Given the rational animal of Aristotle or the tool-making, language-using, culture-producing animal of modern scientific anthropology, how are we to comprehend his humble yet lordly position in nature, his self-accusing conscience, his intimations of a destiny different from that of the beasts that perish?

No one has stated the universal human problem more poignantly than Blaise Pascal in his *Pensées*. As an apologetic for the Christian faith, Pascal's *Thoughts* are inconclusive, but as a deep-probing analysis of the human situation, they have fascinated saints and skeptics alike. In relation to the vast extent of nature, Pascal's man is simply lost between the infinite bigness of the world and the infinite littleness of its component parts— "a middle term between nothing and everything"—yet by his power of thought this fragile, easily destructible being dominates the world that dwarfs him. "Though the universe should crush him, he would still be greater than the universe, for he would know he was being crushed." Here in his relation to the physical world, man's unique combination of greatness and meanness (*misère*) appears; but even more clearly in his moral nature. He is as full of rascalities and deceitful dodges as Montaigne found him to be; yet he is capable of a moral greatness (in

the "order of charity") that lifts him as far above mere intellectual greatness as the power of his intellect lifts him above the
mere physical greatness of nature, or the military greatness of
vulgar conquerors. Greatness and meanness so contradict each
other in man that Pascal calls him a monster, a chimera, the
glory and shame of the universe. No one-sided philosophy can
interpret this contradiction; the cynical naturalism of Montaigne
falsifies the human portrait as unfairly in one direction as Epictetus the Stoic (who sees in man a little Zeus, a little piece of the
divine Reason) falsifies it in the opposite direction.

Despite the classic balance of this portrait of man, drawn at
the very beginning of the modern era, modern philosophy has
continued to alternate between two opposite views of man, reminiscent of Montaigne and Epictetus. Naturalistic philosophy,
based mainly on the findings of the natural sciences, tends to
assimilate man to the cosmic forces that condition his existence,
and ultimately reduces him to a helpless, meaningless nonentity
("nihilism"). Idealistic philosophy, insisting upon the creative
power of mind over matter, assimilates man to the divine Mind,
and elevates him to membership in the Godhead ("titanism").
Pascal might say that, discontent to be "a middle term between
nothing and everything," man alternates between thinking himself nothing and thinking himself everything.

Neither of these extreme views could finally prevail over the
other: when cosmic determinism seemed (toward the end of the
eighteenth century) to reign supreme, Kant reasserted man's
freedom; when Hegel's idealism saw the Absolute first coming
to self-consciousness in man, Darwin humbled man again. The
conflict between nihilism and titanism is not yet ended; yet the
frequent defeats sustained by both sides in the long combat tend
to cancel out the two extremes, and force upon one the convic-

tion that man is no mere mote on a minor planet, and no immortal god either, but some sort of "middle term" between these two, as Pascal himself suggested. Further than this, philosophic agreement is hard to reach, and a venture of religious faith is necessarily in order—not to replace or set aside the known scientific facts about man, but to interpret them in the light of some total vision of life's meaning.

The answer which the problem of man requires is so general and comprehensive, that it is possible to regard the doctrine of man not as one particular topic in theology, but as one side of *every* topic. This is the way Paul Tillich handles it; man appears, so to speak, on the hither side of God, of Christ and of the Spirit-in-the-Church, as the one who cries out for just what they have to give. All theological doctrines are answers to the problem of man from this perspective. Without denying this wider view, we shall here limit our consideration to *man's relationship to God as a topic by itself*, preceded by the doctrine of God and the World, and followed by the doctrine of Christ the Savior. The Christian answer to be given in this chapter is not, therefore, the answer to all religious problems at once, but just the answer to the question, "What place is man called to fill in the cosmic scheme; how has he missed his calling; and from what must he be saved if he is to be restored to his true destiny?"

## Section 2. The Christian Consensus Concerning God and Man

In our time the doctrine of man has become so important and so problematical that it has figured increasingly in ecumenical discussions. The whole field of social ethics, to whose fresh cultivation the Life and Work school of ecumenical thought has been dedicated, revolves about the doctrine of man. Whether the problems considered be those of education, or international politics, or race relations, or economic justice, the positions taken always presuppose (whether consciously or unconsciously) some particular doctrine of man. It was natural and proper, therefore, that among the preparatory volumes for the Oxford Conference of 1937 on "Church, Community and State" was a symposium on *The Christian Understanding of Man*. Let us examine this symposium as our principal indicator of the extent of agreement concerning God and man between contemporary Christians, despite all the sharp tensions and controversies that still persist among them—some of which have actually been renewed and heightened in the present generation.

Part I in the symposium, concerned with present-day thought currents outside the churches, can be briefly summarized. (1) The *scientific* account of man is incomplete, though valid within its limits. It cannot be invoked to prove either the Christian doctrine of man or its opposite. When Bertrand Russell invokes it to prove "that man is the product of causes that had no prevision . . . the outcome of accidental collocations of atoms," he forgets that "the scientist's world, or any naturalistic extension of this, cannot hold a single scientist or a single truth," [1] and therefore contradicts its own truth claim unless set in a larger context where universal truths and values have standing. No author in this volume claims that this larger context can be fully explored by science alone. (2) There is general agreement, too, about the insufficiency of "humanitarian modernism"—by which is principally meant John Dewey's view of man as self-in-soci-

[1] *The Christian Understanding of Man,* London: Allen & Unwin, 1938, pp. 4, 40.

ety, "arbiter of his own destiny" through creative intelligence and co-operative effort, needing no help from any superhuman power. Man's hunger for infinity and his capacity for demonry cannot be understood on this basis; because it denies these factors in man's nature, humanitarianism of this type "condemns its own best impulses to continual thwarting and recurrent disaster." [2] (3) As to the *Marxist* conception of man, it is again clearly insufficient, from the Christian point of view, whatever relative and partial truths it may contain. This view places man in "dialectical" relations with nature and the social order, so that one may say, "if man is the product of nature, nature is also the product of man," or alternatively, that man is both the product of and the remolder of the economic and social order in which he lives. From this perspective, not only the superhuman relationships and eternal destiny of man disappear, but the personality of man disappears in a "sum-total of social-economic relations," and the "inner life" of man is "absorbed into the community." [3] The consensus here is only negative, but to that extent helps to bound and define the Christian view of man.

What then is the positive consensus among Christians concerning those human problems that science, humanitarianism and Marxism cannot solve by themselves? In Part II, four theologians of various backgrounds speak to this question. The fundamental paper, by Emil Brunner, already rewritten several times as a result of ecumenical criticism, is supplemented by three other papers, contributed by an Anglican, an American Congregationalist, and a French Barthian. On some issues, such as the proper relationship between the Christian Revelation and the natural self-knowledge of man, there are real differences among the four contributors, rising to the point of flat contradiction

[2] *Ibid.*, pp. 63, 80–81.          [3] *Ibid.*, pp. 90, 137.

between the Anglican and the Barthian views.[4] This makes all the more impressive the fact that in their main outlines the four accounts of man's place in the scheme of things, and his present predicament, are practically identical. Let us try to state the points of agreement in orderly fashion.

Man's essential nature, in the Christian view, is defined by three cardinal relationships to God, who is his Creator, Judge and Redeemer.

1. As the *creature* of God the Creator, man is finite and mortal, like other mere creatures, and belongs to the order of nature; but he bears the image of his Creator in a special sense. Other creatures may mirror the glory of their Creator unconsciously in their structure; but man, as Brunner puts it, is a "responsible" creature, a person capable of personal confrontation with God, and conscious "response" to God. In this basic fact, man's "chief end" is already indicated: he is made for fellowship with God. But since man's love for the invisible God "cannot be exposed in a concrete way towards God himself . . . God gives him his fellow-man as the recipient of this love." [5] Thus man is made to honor his Creator by loving his neighbor; and also by asserting a finite "dominion" over nature that mirrors his Creator's infinite Lordship over the world.

2. In the sight of God his Judge, man is a *sinner*. It has somehow become second nature for him to oppose the will of God, and thereby to fall into contradiction with his fellow men, with himself and with the world. This is not a condition to which God has fatally condemned mankind, but a perversion of the nature and destiny of man as God created him, for which man

---

[4] Cf. Austin Farrer's Anglican position on this issue (*ibid.*, pp. 190 *et seq.*) with Maury's Barthian position (pp. 250, 259–65).
[5] *Ibid.*, pp. 157–60.

himself is responsible. It is a misuse of the great powers with which God has endowed man, so that he dishonors his Maker instead of glorifying him, hates and oppresses his fellows instead of loving and serving them, is inwardly at war with himself, and becomes the slave of those natural and temporal forces he was meant to dominate. So long as man remains impenitently in this condition, he remains under the condemnation of God his Judge.

3. The same God who is man's Judge is also his Redeemer from sin and his Regenerator into a *new humanity* of which Christ is the head. The Cross of Christ is at the same time God's final judgment upon sin and God's all-sufficient outpouring of his reconciling love and redemptive grace.[6] In so far as man responds to this divine love and grace, and is incorporated into Christ's new humanity, he is delivered from the contradictions that make of him such a "monster" as Pascal describes, and he is redirected toward his true destiny, which is "to glorify God and to enjoy him forever."[7]

We may speak, then, of a "four-fold state" of man: his state of "integrity," as created; his state of "corruption," as fallen into sin; his state of "grace," as a member of Christ's new and restored humanity; and the state of "glory" toward which he moves in faith and hope, with occasional foretastes of coming triumph. All of these states may be regarded as overlapping and to some extent simultaneous. Although Barth has sometimes (as in his controversy with Brunner over nature and grace) spoken as though the image of God was now entirely destroyed in man, his disciple Maury plainly says that man remains God's creature, "enveloped" in God's providential care, and "above all, God

---

[6] Cf. Maury's statement of this paradox, *ibid.*, pp. 255–57.
[7] *Westminster Shorter Catechism*, Q. 1.

does not cease to speak to man, that is to treat him as His image, as being responsible before Him." [8] Martin Luther put the simultaneity of man's second and third states into the classic phrase, "*simul justus et peccator*"; while the state of glory, as already indicated, casts occasional gleams of brighter light upon the state of grace.

This overlapping or simultaneity of man's various conditions in God's sight needs to be understood, if the high degree of consensus actually existing on this subject among Christian theologians is not to be lost in needless confusion. Sometimes the depravity and lostness of man's state of corruption have been described in terms which sound as though God's original good creation in him had been utterly destroyed; but this idea would have shocked St. Augustine himself, who was convinced that every corruption was a lapse toward nothingness, so that the mere existence of any being was a proof that there was *some* good left in it. All such descriptions are really abstractions from the complicated truth of man's condition; they need to be read with the saving clause, "but for the grace of God."

Actually, for every school of Christian thought, God's grace never ceases to operate in and upon man—(1) in the sense of an original gracious bestowal of the divine image, never withdrawn and still to be seen (if not in more positive forms) in the awful grandeur of man's revolt; (2) in the sense of an almost unbelievable patience of the divine Providence, sustaining man's powers even when they are turned against the Creator, and finally, (3) in the full sense of the "grace of the Lord Jesus Christ," which has always been part of God's disposition toward man, even under the Old Covenant, long before it was fully revealed on the Cross. To refer once more to St. Augustine, it is

[8] *Op. cit.,* p. 255.

clear that the realm of saving grace now called the Christian
Church is for him continuous with a "City of God" that began
with Righteous Abel, just after man's expulsion from Paradise,
and has never lacked some saving remnant to represent it
throughout the course of human history.

We may say, then, that as God remains unchangeably man's
Creator, Judge and Redeemer, so man (despite his finite change-
ableness and wayward affections) typically and universally bears
three characters in one, at every stage of his career: God's highest creature, destined to exercise dominion over the other creatures; God's most rebellious creature, cursing the world he was
meant to bless, and living in guilty alienation from himself, his
fellows and his divine Source; and the special object of God's
redemptive grace, evermore healed (if he will) of the bruises
God's judgment has inflicted, and evermore delivered (if he
will) from the traps and prisons into which his own stubborn
steps have led him.[9]

"If he will." Here we touch upon one of the most problematic factors in human nature, about which there may always be
some dispute, but upon which the Edinburgh consensus has
nevertheless shed some clear light: the freedom of the human
will. Negatively the Edinburgh balance between divine sovereignty and human responsibility implies that any view of human
nature, theological or scientific, which treats free will as a completely negligible factor in human affairs, and so transfers all
responsibility for sin from man's shoulders to God's, stands outside the Christian consensus. Positively, enough genuine freedom
must be attributed to man to enable him to respond affirmatively

---

[9] We here make abstraction from the "state of glory," since it is not typical
of man's persistent condition, and since it represents the final future outcome
of God's redemptive grace.

to the divine grace when it persistently and persuasively knocks at his door. On the other hand, divine sovereignty implies that man possesses only a strictly limited freedom, subject to God's final control. Whenever man tries to be absolutely "master of his fate," and "captain of his soul," and thus sets his will above God's, he begins to lose the limited freedom that God has given him and ultimately finds himself the captive of some evil habit or powerful social demand to which he has given himself in the attempt to escape from God's will. From such captivity, all schools of Christian thought warn man that he cannot deliver himself by his own unaided will power.

It is not necessary to insist that man's will power becomes literally *extinct* when he sins, or that there is literally "no health" in him anywhere. Anglican theology, in spite of the somber phraseology of the General Confession in the *Book of Common Prayer*, is more hopeful than other schools of Christian thought concerning the surviving powers of unregenerate man, and the possibility of summoning him to "stand upon his feet" rather than to wallow in his own filth and misery; but even Anglican theology (or Thomistic) is quite clear about the impossibility of man's saving himself from sin and its consequences. Austin Farrer, representing the Anglican position in the Oxford symposium on *The Christian Understanding of Man*, describes the godless man as containing many sound elements of character "which having lost their King . . . elect a president" [10] and so get on with a semblance of order and goodness; but with all such reservations against the doctrine of "total depravity," he concludes that man's natural goodness cannot deliver him. Every sinful act involves "guilt which cannot be weighed, much less atoned, by man." Although "the roots of all the virtues" are in natural man,

[10] P. 194.

151

"it is none the less only by supernatural aid that they can at last be saved alive, not to say brought to perfection." [11]

The view of man's predicament here implied—that he needs deliverance above all from *moral and religious wrongness* (sin) and cannot meet this need without turning to God for forgiveness and renewal—is at the center of every Christian definition of the word "salvation." Of course, it is not *only* from sin that man needs to be saved. As we pass from the Old Testament on through the history of Christian thought, many other meanings cluster about the word "salvation": deliverance from injustice and oppression (O.T.), from the demonic powers that beset an evil age (N.T.), from ignorance and mortality (Greek Fathers), from temporal and eternal punishment (Latin Fathers), from unbelief and fear (evangelical Protestantism), from the danger of social collapse and collective suicide through misused scientific knowledge and technological power (contemporary). None of these secondary meanings of salvation is to be rejected out of hand as unchristian, provided only that it is consistent with the conviction that sin is the chief root of the evils from which man needs to be saved. Since Anglican thought is notable for the balance it keeps between loyalty to traditional verities and openness to new insights, we may appeal to another Anglican author, the late Canon O. C. Quick of Oxford, for a contemporary summary of man's predicament that might be acceptable to most Christians.

In his book on *The Doctrines of the Creed*, Quick distinguishes four principal answers to the question, "What is the fundamental evil from which I must pray to be delivered?" They are death, pain, ignorance and sin. The religions and philosophies of ancient Greece "wavered between the first and the third" of the answers.

[11] *Ibid.*, p. 197.

Buddhism unhesitatingly "fastened on pain as the fundamental evil in the world." Now, we may agree "that all four of these are genuine evils, and that a complete salvation, if such were possible, would deliver us from them all"; yet we must insist, as Christian thought has insisted in every age, that sin is "the true fount of all evil, the one enemy to be fought without compromise or truce, in deliverance from which all salvation is to be achieved even through the willing acceptance of pain and death." [12] We may say of pain and of error what St. Paul said of death, that their *sting* is sin, and when this sting is drawn these other evils can be borne and overcome.

The Christian doctrine of forgiveness and atonement is relevant to all four of these, through its primary relevance to the problem of sin. Finding in Christ a divine "self-emptying" love that even "descended into hell" for the sake of sinful man, it sees in sin a "rejection of God's love" far worse than mere disobedience to God's moral law. Finding through God's love in Christ the healing as well as the diagnosis of this major human evil, it finds at the same time victory over pain and death, and all other ills to which human flesh is heir. "God's love, in man for man, has won the final victory over death and through death," [13] and so implicitly overcome all possible enemies of mankind.

While the Christian consensus concerning God and Man falls short of unanimity at some important points, it is sufficiently clear in its main outlines to offer a clear challenge and needed corrective to the modern view of man in both of its contradictory moods. To the presumptuous "titanism" that has prevailed through much of modern history, the Christian doctrine presents the warning that man is only a finite creature, who derives his being from a Source and his meaning from a Chief End above

[12] Quick, *op. cit.*, pp. 193–95.     [13] *Ibid.*, pp. 208–13.

and beyond himself. To the despairing "nihilism" that so largely prevails since the ominous dawn of the "atomic age," it offers the assurance that man is not merely a child of nature but also a child of God, made in the divine image and destined to rule over nature benignly, if only he will accept God's righteous kingdom (Matt. 6:33) as his Chief End, and God's grace as his constant reliance.

This is a judgment of faith, but it penetrates all the tangled facts of scientific anthropology and human history with a searching light that gives one courage to believe that it is, as John Macmurray suggests, the truth of these very facts.[14] T. Z. Koo, in a memorable address at the Oxford Conference, expressed this judgment in terms of the philosophy symbolized in Oriental flower arrangement: a blossom at the top for heaven, a blossom halfway down for man, a blossom near the bottom for earth. When man subordinates himself to the will of heaven, he is supreme upon earth; when he forgets his respect for heaven, he loses his dominion over earth. This is the same judgment classically expressed in Psalm 8. God has given man a dignity "a little lower than God" and has "set all things under his feet"; yet if he forgets to honor the supreme excellence of God's name in all the earth, things presently will get him under *their* feet! Then, only God's grace can deliver him from the bondage into which he has fallen.

SECTION 3. UNRESOLVED ISSUES CONCERNING GOD AND MAN

There is thus a considerable agreement among Christians concerning the position of man in God's world, the fact that he tends tragically to miss his high calling, and the centrality of sin among

[14] *The Christian Understanding of Man*, pp. 220-25.

the imprisoning forces from which he needs deliverance, if he is to be restored to his true destiny. At one point, however, there is a continuing controversy in Christian thought, which has appeared in various forms at different periods in Church history, and flared up again in our own time: over the doctrines of the Fall and Original Sin.

"In Adam's Fall we sinnèd all." These words from the *New England Primer* express so familiar a view of the solidarity of all mankind in the sin of "our first father," that it is hard to read Genesis 3 without reading in this view. Critically examined, the early chapters of Genesis do not contain any doctrine of Original Sin, but only a series of wondering reflections upon "the origin of death and suffering."[15] Jewish thought was very slow to interpret Adam's transgression as a fall of the whole human race; only in the Apocrypha and Pseudepigrapha do we find the author of IV Ezra attributing the *Yezer Hara*, the pull of evil desire in man, to his first father: "O thou Adam, what hast thou done! For though it was thou that sinned, the fall was not thine alone, but ours who are thy descendants!"[16] Opposed by other Apocryphal writers, this view found considerable acceptance in Rabbinical theology, but was never so consistently developed in Jewish as in Christian thought. St. Paul's theory of the "two Adams" (I Cor. 15, Rom. 5), used by Irenaeus as the framework of his theory of "recapitulation," was finally built up by St. Augustine into that full-fledged doctrine of Original Sin to which Western Christian thought has constantly referred from then on. St. Augustine is the main source of our Western doctrine of Man, Sin and Grace, both in its Catholic form and its Protes-

[15] Samuel S. Cohon, article on "Original Sin," *Hebrew Union College Annual*, XXI, p. 281.
[16] *Ibid.*, p. 289.

tant form; but it is important to note that his views have always met with serious opposition, from his own time to ours.

In his own time, it was of course Pelagius who offered the fiercest opposition to the Augustinian theory. Like all their later successors, the Pelagians made their principal objection against St. Augustine's inconsistency in imputing *guilt* for acts which (by his description )were presently beyond man's power of control, since Adam lost free will for all his descendants when he committed the first sin. "We must ask," says Pelagius' disciple Coelestius, "whether sin comes from necessity or from choice. If from necessity then it is not sin; if from choice then it can be avoided." [17] This objection can never be answered by any theory which asserts the absolute present bondage of the human will— as Luther did in his controversy with Erasmus. Yet the Pelagians, in their proper concern to maintain man's moral responsibility for sin, were led to assert his freedom in terms so unrealistic as to contradict the facts of life—as though man were as free after an act of sin as he was before, or as though the persistent power of sin in human history could be reduced to "the power of evil example"! Even modern liberal critics of Augustinianism, such as F. R. Tennant, freely admit that Pelagius was "atomistic" in his conception of particular sinful acts, each deliberately willed and quite independent of one another; and that Augustine safeguarded better than Pelagius "the existence of sin as a habit . . . the social nature of man and the solidarity of the race." [18] Thus Augustine undoubtedly won the first round in the great debate, though he did not persuade the Catholic Church to sanction all his corollary views, such as double predestination. St. Thomas, while accepting predestination, combines it with human respon-

[17] Augustine, *Anti-Pelagian Works*, Vol. I, p. 315 (Dods edition).
[18] Tennant, *The Origin and Propagation of Sin*, Chap. I.

sibility by insisting that man remains a "rational being," capable
of natural goodness though not supernatural, even after the
Fall.[19] This so-called "semi-Pelagian" view, better described as
"semi-Augustinian," is still the prevailing Catholic view.

A second round in the great debate over Augustinianism took
place under Protestant auspices, and considerably narrowed the
disputed territory between the opposing parties. No one could
claim that the gulf between Calvin and Arminius was as wide as
that between Augustine and Pelagius. While concerned like Pelagius to maintain the reality of man's freedom (and thereby to
safeguard the justice of God) Arminius insisted unlike Pelagius
upon man's deep dependence upon the divine grace: "No one,
except God, is able to bestow salvation; and nothing, except free
will, is capable of receiving it."[20] The five Arminian "remon-
strances," against unconditional predestination, limited atonement, total depravity, irresistible grace, and the inevitable perse-
verance of the saints, did not deny man's final dependence upon
the sovereign will of God, but insisted (as John Oman's modified
Calvinism later did) upon the graciousness of God's grace, which
does not mechanically override man's freedom but rather presupposes it. While Arminians thus conservatively restated the
Pelagian side of the debate, the Calvinists did not maintain all the
more problematic features of St. Augustine's position. Like other
Protestants, they regarded his view that original sin is propagated
by natural generation as tainted with unchristian asceticism and
monkish prejudice against sex. Instead of biological heredity, it
was "federal headship" that connected Adam's sin with ours, for
many Calvinists.

[19] Thomas Aquinas, *Summa Theologica*, Part I–II, No. 2, Q. 85, Art. I.
[20] Arminius, *On the Free Will of Man and Its Powers*, cited in DeWolf,
*op. cit.*, p. 166.

A third round in the great debate over the Fall and Original Sin began in the latter part of the nineteenth century, when Darwinian evolution and Biblical criticism cast doubt upon the historicity of the whole traditional framework of these doctrines. If Adam and Eve are mythical figures and the Garden of Eden a mythical locality, if human history begins with a rise from brutish ignorance and innocence instead of a fall from original righteousness and perfection, what becomes of the Augustinian theory? F. R. Tennant, as a Christian evolutionist, summarizes the vulnerable points in the Augustinian view under four heads:

a. With regard to the original righteousness of Adam before the Fall, it is now evident that this does not correspond to any historical state of affairs, but is a reading-back of later ideals into what was actually a state of premoral innocence.[21]

b. With regard to Adam's transition from created goodness to actual sin, it is inconceivable that a creature so perfect as described should have behaved as he did. "If actual sin in us presupposes a sinful state, it is hard to see why the same inference should not equally apply to the case of the first man."

c. With regard to the alleged catastrophic effects of Adam's first transgression, educators do not agree that *one* misstep destroys character so fatally or so finally.[22] A really decisive and tragic fall is generally the result of a *cumulation* of sinful acts; it is not the first act but some later one that is the most heinous and destructive.

---

[21] William Adams Brown in his *Outline*, Chap. XV, points out how each school of theology describes Adam's primitive state of righteousness in exact correspondence to its ideals for the Christian life.

[22] Charles Hodge, *Systematic Theology*, Vol. II, Chap. VII (The Fall) disagrees with this; one transgression, he says, "as effectually involves spiritual death, as one perforation of the heart causes the death of the body, or one puncture of the eyes involves us in perpetual darkness."

d. With regard to the transmission of Adam's sin to his descendants, no "acquired characteristics" are thus biologically transmissible. *Social* not biological inheritance accounts for the universal spread of sinfulness in the human race.[23] Both in the individual and the race, sin originates at that relatively late date when nonmoral brute impulses, necessarily self-regarding in their infantile form, begin to conflict with conscientiously accepted moral laws and standards. Sin is "simply the general failure to effect on all occasions the moralization of inevitable impulses," once law and conscience have made us aware of a higher nature within us—what Archdeacon Wilson has called "the evolutionary and Divine force that makes for moral development." [24] Sin is not a fall, then, but a failure to rise from animal innocence to conscious self-control when God awakens us through law and conscience to the awareness of our more-than-animal nature and destiny.

One might suppose that under such a withering fire of criticism, the Augustinian theory would simply lie down and die. Actually, it has been dramatically revived in our generation. Purged of what Reinhold Niebuhr calls "literalistic errors," transmuted from "an event in history" into "an aspect of every historical moment in the life of man," [25] the Augustinian doctrine of man's fall into original sin has won the adherence of some of the most subtle and sophisticated minds of our age. Neoorthodoxy and liberalism now fully agree with each other that Adam is the symbolical "representative" rather than the historical ancestor of the human race; but on this new basis, Augustinianism's essential truth appears to many of our leading Christian thinkers to stand forth more clearly than ever before. Since no

[23] Tennant, *op. cit.*, Chap. I.    [24] *Ibid.*, Chap. III.
[25] Niebuhr, *Nature and Destiny of Man*, Vol. I, p. 269.

one has more ably championed the cause of this neo-Augustinianism than Reinhold Niebuhr, let us see how he states it in the first half of his Gifford Lectures on *The Nature and Destiny of Man*.

Niebuhr approaches his constructive doctrine of man by making a long preliminary run (Chapters I–IV) over the history of thought upon this topic, mowing down modern conceptions of man with acute and ruthless criticism before attempting to rise above them on wings of Biblical revelation.

Medieval Catholicism made a temporary and somewhat artificial synthesis between the Biblical view of man and the classical Greek conception of man. Since the Renaissance, the modern mind has disentangled the classical idea of man from all definitely Christian associations, and carried it out to such hopelessly contradictory conclusions that its inadequacy is now clearly exposed. The idea is, in Aristotle's classical formulation, that man is a "rational animal." Modern idealism or rationalism has stressed one side of this conception, and concluded that man is a divinely creative intelligence, capable of indefinite progress in the mastery of his environment and of himself. Modern naturalism has stressed the other side of it, and concluded that man is simply an animal, determined like all other animals by his natural environment. Modern romanticism has attempted to synthesize naturalism and idealism by finding man's uniqueness and divinity not in his reason but in the impulsive and emotional life which bridges the gulf between body and spirit. The feud among these three schools of thought can never be resolved unless we recognize, with Christian thought, that man is both a child of nature and a child of God; that there is nothing bad or beastly about his body, and nothing necessarily good or divine about his mind; that his uniqueness is to be seen not in something subra-

tional but in something super-rational: a capacity for "self-transcendence" and self-judgment that springs from his sense of creaturely humility and responsibility in the sight of God.

The most serious inadequacy of the modern mind is its inability in the face of the plainest facts to recognize *the sinfulness and
weakness of mankind.* This is due to the fact that science gave man
a sense of security and power, which he falsely applied to his own
moral nature. If chaos appeared in his life, he played hide-and-
seek with it, sometimes fleeing with the idealists from the chaos
of nature to the harmony of creative mind, sometimes with the
romanticists from the chaos of civilization to the harmony of un-
spoiled nature, but never admitting to himself that the root of
chaos lay deep and ineradicable within human nature itself. From
this critique of the modern conception of man there emerges, by
contrast, the conviction that man must be a strange compound
of both nature and spirit, and his spirit must have higher reaches
and deeper abysses in it than Greek and modern rationalists ever
dreamed of in their philosophy. This conviction is transformed
from a bare pattern into a rich doctrine when we consider it in
the light of the Christian revelation, which embodies three major
insights into human nature, according to Niebuhr:

(1) It emphasizes the height of self-transcendence in man's spiritual stature in its doctrine of "image of God." (2) It insists on man's
weakness, dependence, and finiteness . . . without, however, re-
garding this finiteness as, of itself, a source of evil in man. . . . (3)
It affirms that the evil in man is a consequence of his inevitable though
not necessary unwillingness to acknowledge his dependence, to accept his finiteness and to admit his insecurity, an unwillingness which
involves him in the vicious circle of accentuating the insecurity from
which he seeks escape.[26]

[26] *Ibid.,* p. 150.

It takes but a single chapter (VI) to expound the first two of these insights, which stand in paradoxical contrast to each other. The "image of God" in man stands for the freedom and self-transcendence of man, which are dissipated and lost unless he recognizes his responsibility to a Being who infinitely transcends him. The creaturehood of man stands for his bondage to nature and implication in temporality, which forever forbid him that "deification" which Greek theology (more Platonic than Christian) falsely promises. But if man's creaturehood forever separates him from deity, it has likewise nothing so evil about it as this same Greek theology (cf. its modern apostle, Berdyaev) sometimes suggests. Sex and death are not the result of a Fall, but part of God's good creation.

Concerning the third insight, on Sin, Niebuhr discourses eloquently and at great length (Chaps. VII–X). All his well-known shrewdness in the unmasking of human self-deception and the location of hidden springs of wickedness comes into play in these memorable chapters. But so colossal is his exposure of human weakness that his usual tone of scorn is modulated, as he proceeds, to one of brooding compassion and tragic irony. With Kierkegaard, he finds the occasion of sin in *anxiety*. "Anxiety is the inevitable concomitant of the paradox of freedom and finiteness in which man is involved. Anxiety is the internal precondition of sin. It is the inevitable spiritual state of man . . . the internal description of the state of temptation." [27] If anxiety could be overcome by trust in God—which is always an "ideal possibility"—there might be no sin. *Unbelief*, then, is the prime root of sin. It expresses itself in *pride*, which tries to achieve security without God, by elevating the finite self to a position of infinite importance that does not belong to it. Pride expresses

[27] *Ibid.*, p. 182.

itself in *rebellion* and intellectual *presumption* toward God, and *injustice* toward fellow men, which between them upset the harmony of creation. It expresses itself also in an intellectual, moral and religious self-congratulation that cannot be maintained without *self-deception*. It compounds itself into *collective egotism* in state and Church. When exposed and humiliated it flees into *sensuality*, but finds no escape. Thus three dimensions in sin which have traditionally been recognized in Christian theology—sensuousness, selfishness and godlessness—all find their place in Niebuhr's theory.

In spite of all specific inequalities of guilt, sin is a universal plague that guarantees *equality in sin* to every son of man. The technical term for this inevitable equality in sin, despite the ideal possibility of escaping sin, is *original sin*. Its meaning is perverted when it is regarded as a hereditary taint transmitted from a single point in history, the Fall. Rather, the original righteousness of Adam before the Fall and the subsequent depravity are both factors in every human experience. The uneasy conscience of the race is a perpetual testimony to an original righteousness that is never wholly lost, but typically expresses itself in a sad, self-transcending judgment, in moments of contemplation after each action, that *I was wrong and cannot help my wrongness*. Original sin meanwhile is the same state of affairs viewed from below upwards, out of the midst of that mass of egotistic impulses, self-deceptions and sensuous escape mechanisms which holds man enthralled. It is inevitable; but it is morally rather than naturally necessary, and we cringe with the knowledge of that fact, even as we yield.

"Inevitable but not necessary." Niebuhr knows, of course, that he speaks paradoxically when he thus speaks of sin. Like Kierkegaard and Barth, he believes all the ultimate truths about life are dialectical—too complex to be expressed except in apparently contradictory propositions. He intends, however, to put the "inevitability" of sin in a form paradoxically consistent with human freedom and responsibility. "The ultimate proof of the freedom of the human spirit is its own recognition that its will is not free to choose between good and evil."[28] This sounds as though such freedom were only freedom of despair; but Niebuhr adds that when such sober self-knowledge leads (as it may) to godly repentance instead of ungodly remorse, the way is open to a new life in which "fruits meet for repentance" are really brought forth—which however "does not prevent the self from new dishonesties in subsequent actions."[29] This tiny ray of hope that freedom-to-know-I-am-not-free may grow at least sporadically into real freedom-under-God, is all that Niebuhr admits in his volume on *Human Nature*. But it is only fair to add that in *Human Destiny* Niebuhr presents a view of man-under-grace which significantly expands this ray of hope. Here at least it becomes clear that God's grace is not only the grace of forgiveness for man's inevitable yielding to original sin, but also the grace which empowers man to live a new life so long as he really puts his trust in God, instead of in himself or some other finite idol.

Niebuhr's diagnosis of the disease of sin has been enormously influential, outside of his own school of thought. Particularly that part of his analysis based upon Kierkegaard's *Concept of Dread*, which shows how anxiety, in itself not sinful, easily becomes sick with the dizziness of man's high elevation above nature, and inevitably leads him (but for the grace of God) either to exalt himself proudly, or to dash himself down into animality so as to escape responsibility—all this corresponds so closely to

[28] *Ibid.*, p. 258.    [29] *Ibid.*, p. 259–60.

modern man's actual consciousness of his tragic dilemma that it is unforgettable, once read. When taken in conjunction with Paul Tillich's further analysis (in *The Courage to Be*) of three sorts of anxiety which are inevitable and "existential" for all men—the anxiety of *death*, the anxiety of *guilt*, and the anxiety of *meaninglessness*—this analysis shows persuasively how man is inevitably driven to sin by his anxieties, unless or until he turns to God as the strength of his life and his portion forevermore. Psychiatry confirms this diagnosis in a hundred ways. This may not be the whole truth about man, but surely it is important and needful truth, which "pertains to salvation."

Contemporary Arminianism's attitude toward the neo-Augustinianism of Kierkegaard, Niebuhr and Tillich is in fact a *correction* and *supplementation* of it rather than a flat rejection of it. This attitude is well expressed in Harold DeWolf, whose Arminian pedigree is unmistakable, both as a Methodist and as a liberal. In his *Theology of the Living Church*, he is severe with Augustine and Calvin for imputing original sin to man while denying him sufficient freedom to make him really responsible.[30] He is suspicious of resort to paradox, where anything so basic as man's freedom is at stake, and he fears that Pascal (with an obvious allusion to Kierkegaard and Niebuhr) slipped over from paradox into sheer irrationality when he claimed that a doctrine of original sin that "shocks our reason" is the only thing that keeps us from being "incomprehensible to ourselves." [31] Yet in dealing with Niebuhr's positive teaching he is very appreciative. He acknowledges that "Reinhold Niebuhr and others have shown many of the ways in which this dreadful sense of insecurity

---

[30] On Calvin, cf. pp. 175, 176; on Augustine, p. 197.
[31] *Ibid.*, cf. his general criticism of the method of paradox in *The Religious Revolt Against Reason*.

leads to the seeking of false self-assurance in wealth, social power, military force and other earthly idols." [32] His main criticism is not that this is false, but that it is an oversimplification. Niebuhr's claim that pride is *the* "basic sin," throughout the Bible, will not bear examination. "The fact is there is no single, universal definition of the basic motive of sin in the Scripture. . . . The Greek Apologists' ideas of sin as irrationality, idolatry or sensual passion and the modern liberal ideas of it as greed or folly or denial of love are not simply imported into the Christian stream of thought; they were all there from the beginning." [33]

Having made clear his Arminian reservations and amendments, DeWolf proceeds to list seven "truths symbolized" in the Augustinian doctrine of original sin: (1) "Every human being is born in indebtedness to God. . . . By the very nature of his existence he lives solely by the grace of God." (2) "All human beings suffer temptations to sin and disabilities in resistance to it which result from the sins of past generations . . . straight back to the parents in whom the possibility and actuality of sin first occurred." (3) "In our experience, from the dawn of moral consciousness, we do not find it equally as easy to be true to our duty and to be false to it. . . . Movement toward moral perfection is upstream." (4) Experience and observation "make it reasonable to believe that all human beings who have long lived at a responsible level of development are actual sinners." (5) "We need to repent not only of our formal sins, the choices we have made in contradiction of our own ideals. . . . If I do not now repent of the materially sinful choice which I once made in ignorant sincerity"—like Paul sincerely collaborating in the stoning of Stephen —"I am now easily winking at a choice which I believe to be contrary to God's will." (6) "For similar reasons we need to

[32] *The Theology of the Living Church*, p. 196.    [33] *Ibid.*, p. 185.

repent of the sins of others with which we find ourselves identified . . . by sharing in their economic or other advantages, by
our loyal self-identification with groups that have sinned. . . ."
(7) "Our acts . . . express systems of habits, ideas and motives
. . . persistently identified with ourselves. . . . Many of the more
sensitive and thoughtful souls have dwelt more sorrowfully upon
their sinful *condition*, than upon any particular deeds. This is as
it should be, so long as the connection with sinful choice is kept
clean and strong." [34]

When Arminianism goes as far as this in appreciation of the
truth in the Augustinian tradition, the ancient antagonism is in
a fair way to be reconciled. Comparing the distance between
Niebuhr and DeWolf with that between Calvin and Arminius,
and that in turn with the chasm between Augustine and Pelagius,
we cannot help noticing a marked degree of convergence between the first and third rounds of the great debate. If Niebuhr
and DeWolf were perfectly representative of the two rival
schools of thought in their contemporary forms, the war between
them would be almost over. That, of course, is not entirely the
case. There are conservative Protestants who would insist that
if the Bible is really the Word of God, Adam must be a historical
character, and his Fall a dated fact. While Roman Catholics are
not so committed to Biblical literalism, they are cautious about
any interpretation of Genesis that sounds too "mythical"; and
particularly among the Jesuits, the assertion of man's freedom
and power to collaborate with God's grace in his own salvation
goes much beyond the Arminian position.[35]

[34] *Ibid.*, pp. 199–200.
[35] The debate between the Jesuits and the Dominicans on this issue is roughly
parallel to that between the Arminians and the Calvinists, but both Catholic
parties are several degrees farther away from the Augustinian position, which
has been repeatedly condemned in modern times. See Cath. Encyc. articles
*Jansenism, Baïus.*

Still farther away from the Niebuhr-DeWolf understanding are the Eastern Orthodox, who have scarcely felt St. Augustine's influence at all. They cling stoutly to a view of human freedom that Western thought might call "Pelagian," while at the same time holding out a hope of man's eventual "deification" which Niebuhr flatly denounces as presumptuous.[36] If the Eastern Orthodox delegates could subscribe to the Edinburgh consensus on divine sovereignty and human responsibility, it was only because the terms of agreement were very broad, and no particular formula was proposed for reconciling the two sides of the paradox. Nothing is more necessary than for Eastern and Western theology to continue to converse on this issue, so as to make the consensus between them more explicit. The passionate defense of freedom by Dostoevski and Berdyaev has made a profound impression on Western thought, which must be duly digested, and balanced with the truth in Augustinianism.

[36] *Nature and Destiny of Man*, Vol. II, pp. 131–33.
For a fresh and original discussion of all the main issues discussed in chap. V, and a searching re-examination of both St. Augustine and Pelagius in the light of Biblical theology, see *Hardness of Heart* by Cherbonnier (Doubleday, 1955).

# VI

## *CHRIST THE SAVIOR*

SECTION 1. THE UNIVERSAL PROBLEM OF MEDIATION

WITH the subject of Christology, we come to the second main article of the Christian Creed, co-ordinate in importance with theology and eschatology. In terms of the triangle of faith, Christology corresponds to the right angle where the vertical line of divine creativity, divine judgment, divine grace, rightly intersects the horizontal line of human need, human sin, and human destiny. While the doctrine of Christ is the most unique thing in Christianity, distinguishing it from all other faiths, the problem to which Christ is the answer is an inescapable problem in every faith: the problem of *mediation*.

Some concrete manifestation of God's presence and power, some mediator or process of mediation between God and man, is found in all faiths. Without this, faith's vertical upreach toward God and its horizontal outreach toward some Goal of hope and endeavor do not rightly intersect; no actual divine-human intercourse can take place; no saving "grace" or transforming power is stepped down from the divine to the human plane, and released at the point where it is needed. Between God and man there is a dead switch. Man looks at his God and his Goal from afar off ruefully, and cannot go to his Goal with the aid of his God.

There is a struggle at this crucial point of intersection, as Paul Tillich points out,[1] between the contrary pulls of two great religious demands: between the *ultimacy* of the divine object of faith, and the *concreteness* required of any divine power which is to make vital contact with human needs. Only the *ultimate* Being can finally hold man's adoration; only a *concretely mediated* Being can touch his life. If ultimacy triumphs over concreteness, then the deity becomes remote and inaccessible; if concreteness triumphs over ultimacy, idolatrous deification takes place. Only by some sort of divine-human mediator can these two demands be reconciled; only by some sort of trinitarian formula can the role of such a mediator be consistently thought through.

The character of the mediator and nature of the process of mediation will of course vary with the conception of God and the conception of man's actual condition and final destiny. A crucified Messiah is "foolishness to the Greeks"—and to all mystical religions of escape from time to eternity—because such religions do not find God in history at all, and the notion of a divinely anointed historic Leader is meaningless to them. A crucified Messiah is a "stumbling-block to the Jews" because, although they find God in history, they look for the divinely anointed Leader to triumph immediately instead of meeting with temporal defeat.[2]

Nevertheless, both "Greeks" and "Jews" have concepts of mediators that raise the trinitarian issue. The ineffable One who is the ultimate God of the Neo-Platonists is mediated to mankind through three stages of emanation, that draw nearer and

[1] *Op. cit.*, I, pp. 221 *et seq.*
[2] On the contrast between mystical religions where "a Christ is not expected" and prophetic religions where "a Christ is expected," read the classic discussion in Reinhold Niebuhr's *Nature and Destiny of Man*, Vol. II, Chap. I.

nearer to the concrete: the World-Mind, the World-Soul, and finally the junction between the World-Soul and the individual souls. The God of Hinduism, fathomless in his ultimate nature (neuter Brahman), has three mediating forms or faces: Brahma the Creator, Vishnu the Sustainer, Shiva the Destroyer. Buddhism started with a rather agnostic theology intent only on the diagnosis and cure of human suffering, but in its Mahayana form it has developed a kind of trinitarian doctrine of the Buddha-nature: first, the heavenly Buddhas, glistening with light in their supernal "Buddha-fields"; next the historic Buddhas, bringing the principle of enlightening to earth in each new era; finally the living Buddhas and Bodhisattvas helping to perpetuate it on earth like the Pope and the saints. Jews are proverbially strict in their monotheism; yet they have filled the space between the ultimate, transcendent God and the human plane with such concrete entities as the Word, Wisdom, Spirit, Will, Presence (Shekhinah) of the Lord, supplemented by angelic messengers and finally by the Messiah conceived as the Son of Man from heaven. While they wait the coming of the Messiah, Torah functions for them as Jesus the Christ functions for Christians—i.e., as concrete manifestation of God and perennial source of strength. Mystical sects of Judaism have gone further, elaborating long chains of mediators that completely bridge the gulf between heaven and earth and satisfy the hunger for concrete contact with God.

If pantheistic and monotheistic deities have a tendency to reach down toward concreteness through chains of emanations, choirs of angels, prophetic messengers, avatars and incarnations, humanistic deities have a contrary tendency to undergo apotheosis and reach up toward ultimacy. The Egyptian kings, Alexander the Great, Augustus Caesar and his successors, are familiar examples of ancient monarchs claiming divine worship from their subjects. The emperors of China and Japan illustrate the same tendency at the other end of the inhabited globe. The absence of serious belief in a superhuman divine realm fails to check this irrepressible tendency. In our own day, Italians with no religion but Fascism have attributed divine omniscience to their Duce—"Mussolini is always right"—while agnostic Germans have adored Hitler as the incarnate Superman, and (most amazing of all) the embalmed body of an atheist receives religious adoration in the Red Square at Moscow! Lest this tendency to political idolatry be thought limited to the totalitarian state, the figure of Woodrow Wilson may be cited as a democratic hero who was in process of apotheosis, on both sides of the Atlantic, between his triumphal landing in Europe and his tragic failure at Versailles. "Savior, Prince of Peace, divine-human Mediator" are terms that might seriously be applied to these human leaders by many of their adoring followers.

The danger of self-deception and ultimate disillusionment here is real and terrible, as we all know. Yet the danger is no greater now in a world littered with broken wreckage of Messianic hopes, than it actually was in the time of Jesus the Nazarene, when Caesar was Savior to the Romans, and in Israel hardly a year went by without some new political Messiah calling, "Lo here!" or "Lo there!" It takes an effort of historical imagination to put ourselves back in the days before our Jesus was first called the Christ; but such an effort is a necessary introduction to the universal Christian teaching that this was indeed "the Christ, the Son of God." We are saying that in him the universal "desire of nations," so often miserably disappointed in ancient and in modern times, the desire for a divinely anointed Mediator, Leader, Savior, who would bring mankind out of darkness into

God's perfect light, has actually been realized. This is "he that was to come," and we look for no other.

## SECTION 2. THE CHRISTIAN CONSENSUS CONCERNING JESUS CHRIST

Ever since Peter's confession at Caesarea Philippi (Mt. 16:16), the main body of Christian believers have been substantially united in their answer to the question, "Who is Jesus?" They regard him as *the divine-human Savior of the world, the Man in and through whom God turned the course of history and reconciled a rebellious world to himself.* From his coming they date their calendars, *Anno Domini* or *Anno salutis humani*.[3] This faith is the very center of the Christian religion, as we noted when attempting to define Christianity in Chapter I. Every ecumenical assembly, from Nicaea to Evanston, rediscovers it as the nucleus of common Christianity around which divided Christians can cluster, while without it there is no clear basis of Christian unity at all.

"Thou art the Christ, the Son of the living God" (Mt. 16:16). This classic confession does not state the whole Christian understanding of Jesus, even within the New Testament; but it states a basic element in the Christian view, which has persisted like a "rock" in the later history of the Church. Quite apart from the vexed question of his own "messianic consciousness" (which may never be fully solved) Jesus has always been regarded as the person who fulfills the Messianic hope which runs through the Old Testament even while disappointing that form of the hope which

---

[3] My college diploma is so dated, "in the year of human salvation 1917." The more common *Anno Domini* (A.D.) has the same implications.

was most popular in his day—the Messiah as the Son of David who was to overthrow the Roman oppressor and restore the Kingdom of Israel. Peter himself was infected with this false hope, as his horrified rejection of the idea of a suffering Messiah (Mt. 16:21-23) makes evident; nevertheless his confession stands and is everlastingly confirmed by the Church.

Jesus in the eyes of the Church *is* the Christ, the Messiah, the divinely anointed Prince who fulfills the Hope of Israel and restores his Father's Kingdom in defiance of all usurpers. He fulfills the Law, he renews the Covenant, he realizes the visions of the Prophets—though in a form that perplexes the loyal sons of the Old Covenant, and constitutes a "rock of offence" for them, from that day to this. Instead of coming in glory, to liberate the world at one stroke, he comes in humiliation, "lowly and riding upon an ass" (Zech. 9:9) to fulfill Deutero-Isaiah's vision of the Suffering Servant of God, by whose stripes the nations are healed. All four Gospels were written to express and kindle the belief that Jesus is in this sense "the Christ, the Son of God" (John 20:31), and the Epistles and Apocalypse presuppose this belief even when they go beyond it. That Jesus is "the Christ" means that God's plan of redemption, which began already with Moses and the prophets to call men back into right relations with their Creator, reaches its decisive point in him, and now needs only to be preached, extended and applied to all mankind.

If this "pre-Easter" confession of Peter were the whole Christian answer to the question "Who is Jesus?" it might almost be summarized in the words which the Master himself applied to his forerunner, John the Baptist: "a prophet, and more than a prophet" (Mt. 11:9). Like Amos and Isaiah, John and Jesus spoke the Word of God by direct insight, instead of relying on chains of precedent like their scribal contemporaries; but they went beyond all prophets in announcing the actual arrival of that Day of the Lord which the prophets saw from afar. John heralded and Jesus accomplished the actual laying of the cornerstone of God's eternal Kingdom on earth, an event which cannot be repeated and makes Jesus forever unique. But this is not yet the half of what the "post-Easter" sections of the New Testament affirm about Jesus the Christ. In the light of the Crucifixion and Resurrection, Peter himself makes the further confession (Acts 2:36) that Jesus, the one whom his people crucified as a blasphemer, had been raised from the dead and exalted to God's right hand, as "both *Lord* and Christ." All the "post-Easter" parts of the New Testament echo this faith; "Jesus is Lord" can be called the first ecumenical creed of the Church. The implication is that "all power . . . in heaven and in earth" (Mt. 28:18) has been given to him; that he now rules the world secretly from God's right hand, as he shall hereafter rule it publicly, "until he has put all enemies under his feet" and destroyed death, "the last enemy" (I Cor. 15:25, 26).

A third confession follows swiftly upon the second, within the bounds of the New Testament. If Jesus is now and hereafter clothed with divine authority, he must have proceeded from God and been uniquely close to God, from the very beginning. Not only was his birth brought about by "the power of the Most High" (Luke 1:35), but even before his birth there was something in the very being of God that was already moving out toward his advent. His Cross, according to the Apostle Paul, expresses the "power of God, and the wisdom of God" (I Cor. 1:24). The Fourth Gospel begins with the great declaration that in Jesus God's creative and redemptive "Word was made flesh and dwelt among us . . . . full of grace and truth" (John 1:14); that is, God's own outgoing nature, which creates, sustains and blesses all the creatures he has made, becomes man for our salvation in this particular historic individual. In the Epistle to the Hebrews we see the swift passage from the affirmation of the Lordship of Jesus to the affirmation of his deity, in the memorable opening words:

In many and various ways God spoke of old to our fathers by the prophets; but in these last days he has spoken to us by a Son, *whom he appointed the heir [Lord] of all things, through whom also he created the world.* He reflects the glory of God and bears the very stamp of his nature, upholding the universe by his word of power. HEB. 1:1–3.[4]

In the great Christological controversies which agitated the Church for several centuries after the Age of Constantine, the meaning of this New Testament faith in Jesus as the Christ, the Lord, and the incarnate Word of God was clarified in opposition to certain views that threatened to destroy it. Against Arius, who described the Word which became Flesh in Jesus as only the first and highest of God's creatures, the Council of Nicaea decided that the Word was "God of God, Light of Light, very God of very God, begotten, not made, being of one substance with the Father"; [5] i.e., God himself coming forth from himself to redeem mankind.

Against various views that threatened the reality, the integrity or the unity of Christ's human nature, the Council of Chalcedon decided that he was one person with two natures, distinguishable but not separable—the divine Word of God living, speaking and acting in a completely human being.

It cannot be said that all obscurities in the doctrines of the Trinity and the Incarnation were cleared up at Nicaea and Chal-

[4] R.S.V. Italics mine.
[5] Philip Schaff, *Creeds of Christendom,* II, p. 58.

cedon, nor that all serious dissent was ended. That is not the effect of any ecumenical consensus, whose function is rather to exclude destructive extremes and define a general area of agreement, within which many rival theories still co-exist. Yet it is remarkable how unbroken is the loyalty of most Christian denominations, even yet, to the Nicene and Chalcedonian doctrine of Christ's divine-human person: One God in three distinguishable expressions, "hypostases" or "persons"—Father, Son and Holy Spirit—who in the fullness of the times became united in one person with the real, historic human being, Jesus of Nazareth, called the Christ, not destroying his humanity thereby, but showing the world for the first time what real humanity, God-oriented humanity, was meant to be. The Protestant reformers never rejected this doctrine, while rejecting so much else in Catholic teaching; and when they were faced with the Unitarian doctrines of Servetus and the Socinians, they rejected the doctrines as decisively as the Catholics did. Liberal Protestantism has indeed been considerably divided on the Christological issue, and been sharply critical of the Greek metaphysical concepts employed at Nicaea and Chalcedon; but when the Ecumenical Movement brings liberal and conservative Protestants together with non-Roman Catholics in a new quest for Christian unity, the basis for that unity is again and again rediscovered in the divine-human Christ, son of Mary and our brother according to the flesh, Son of God according to the divine Word that dwells in him.

It is true that the formula of invitation used by the Faith and Order Movement since it was launched in 1910, and retained by the World Council of Churches as part of the terms of union between the two movements—Faith and Order, Life and Work—whose marriage gave it birth, is open to serious objection and misunderstanding. To invite only those churches into ecumenical conversation which "accept Jesus Christ as God and Savior," might seem to limit acceptance to those "monophysite" churches of the East which believe that the humanity of Jesus was completely dissolved in his deity—"as a drop of vinegar is dissolved in the ocean." Or again, it might seem to neglect the elementary distinction between "God" and "Son of God," which makes careful Christian educators caution their church-school classes against saying "Jesus is God" without qualification. Actually, the phrase has been accepted by Christian churches which have no leanings to monophysite views, just as the same phrase has been used by the World's Y.M.C.A. since 1855, as a blunt, rough-and-ready expression of the faith that the "one foundation" of the Church, and of every Christian movement, is not just a great human teacher of long ago, but *Christ the Lord, the incarnate Word of God, the divine-human Savior of the world.* The Faith and Order Movement, from its first meeting in Lausanne, has made very clear what is meant by the blunt phrase. At its first meeting in 1927, this movement, called together by this phrase of invitation, issued a memorable statement of "The Church's Message—the Gospel," in which it referred to the Gospel as "the gift of God to sinful man in Jesus Christ," and saw this gift bestowed when "the eternal Word of God became incarnate, and was made man, Jesus Christ the Son of God and the Son of Man, full of grace and truth." [6] The following year, consciously summarizing the Lausanne message, the Jerusalem meeting of the International Missionary Council—another important expression of the Ecumenical Movement—issued the still more striking statement, "Our message is Jesus Christ. He is the rev-

[6] Conveniently cited in W. A. Brown, *Toward a United Church* (Scribner, 1946), p. 211.

elation of what God is and of what man through him may be-
come." [7] Again at Edinburgh, in 1937, just before uniting with
Life and Work on the basis of that same crabbed phrase, the
Faith and Order Movement interpreted it as follows:

> We acknowledge that all who accept Jesus Christ as Son of God
> and their Lord and Savior, and who realize their dependence on
> God's mercy revealed in Him, have in that fact a supernatural bond
> of oneness which subsists in spite of divergences in defining the
> mystery of the Lord. . . .
> We are one in faith in our Lord Jesus Christ, the incarnate Word
> of God. We are one in allegiance to Him as Head of the Church
> and as King of Kings and Lord of Lords. We are one in acknowledg-
> ing that this allegiance takes precedence of any other allegiance that
> may make claims upon us.[8]

In view of these clear interpretations, the basis of the World
Council of Churches should not repel any but Unitarian Christians, and may be said to summarize the present consensus of
Christian faith in Christ's divine-human person, very well indeed.
Its form may be objectionable, but its intent is generally accepted, and it is doubtful if at this date any proposed amendment
will greatly improve it as a minimum basis of agreement, on
which each church can build its further affirmations. Such at
least has been the experience of the Y.M.C.A. with its identical
formula of admittance, which has been reconsidered for nearly
a century without being improved upon.

For the Ecumenical Movement to accept Jesus Christ ("Son
of God . . . Lord and Savior . . . Incarnate Word of God")
as its very foundation, does not automatically assure theological

---

[7] *Ibid.*, p. 213.
[8] Edinburgh Report, Chap. III, sec. viii, and concluding "Affirmation of
Unity" (cf. *ibid.*, p. 220). Cf. also the Edinburgh decision to unite Faith and
Order with Life and Work "on the basis of the doctrine of the Incarnation."
Bell, *op. cit.*, p. 286.

agreement among its members upon such doctrines as the Incarnation, the Trinity and the Atonement. The Edinburgh Report just cited couples its solemn affirmation of oneness in Christ and supreme allegiance to Christ with a candid (and accurate) admission of the existence of "divergences in defining the mystery of the Lord" among those who sign the affirmation. The remarkable fact about this central Christian faith, today as always, is that it never stays peacefully settled, but has to be reasserted and restated in the midst of heated theological debate, in every generation. Perhaps this is one indication that Jesus the Christ is no dead fact, to be peacefully laid to rest and permanently memorialized, but a living Fact, posing profound and disturbing questions to each new age.

The best indicator of the amount of theological consensus now existing on the doctrines of the Incarnation and the Trinity is the extraordinarily cordial reception that has been given to D. M. Baillie's *God Was in Christ*. Not only among Scots and Presbyterians, but among American and Continental Protestants of many different denominations and among Anglican and other "Catholic-minded" Christians as well, the book has evoked almost universal acclaim and general assent. This is all the more remarkable because, though irenic in spirit, Baillie does not evade controversial questions, and takes sharp issue with some of the leading theologians of our time, including Barth, Brunner, Bultmann, Heim and Tillich. This happily illustrates the fact that in order to contribute to ecumenical theology, a Christian thinker need not abdicate his personal judgment, nor minimize his honest disagreements. What has evoked such world-wide acclaim and assent cannot possibly be the *whole* of Baillie's book, but only its *main theses*, which even those thinkers whom he attacks would generally agree to be sound and salutary. Let us try to analyze these main theses, since they appear to have become part of the current ecumenical consensus.

1. The "return to the historical Jesus" in late nineteenth-century and early twentieth-century theology has made a permanent, not a temporary contribution to Christian thought, which must not be carelessly thrown aside in the current neo-orthodox reaction against the liberal theology of that period. It has in principle made an "end of docetism," [9] and re-established more firmly than ever before the principle for which the Early Fathers contended against the Gnostics: that Jesus was not only a real historical character, but a truly and fully human being, psychologically as well as physiologically a son of his people and of his time.

2. It was a mistake to suppose, as many liberals did, that the possession of a clear portrait of the "Jesus of history" was sufficient in itself for religious purposes, and permitted one to shelve all vexatious Christological problems. Those who made this attempt often fell into a "sentimental Jesus-worship . . . a substitution of Jesus for the eternal God." [10] It has therefore been a good thing that Form Criticism has raised doubts about the clearness of the liberal portrait of Jesus, and Dialectical Theology has sharply revised the earlier judgment about the relative importance of the "Jesus of history" and the "Christ of faith." But the pendulum swing threatens to go too far when some (not all) Form Critics suggest that nothing definite can now be known concerning the life and teachings of Jesus himself, who is everywhere concealed behind the *kerygma* of the Primitive Church; and when some (not all) neo-orthodox theologians suggest that the life and teachings of Jesus are matters of no consequence to

[9] Baillie, *God Was in Christ*, pp. 11–20.
[10] *Ibid.*, p. 41.

one who believes in the exalted Lord. Here Baillie takes a firm stand against both the extremes between which recent theology tends to swing; and I believe that the common sense of all Christian churches will sustain him in this stand. He shows the inconclusiveness of the historical skepticism into which some Form Critics have fallen; and he shows conclusively that a Christian "orthodoxy" which tries to dispense altogether with the Jesus of history can never build a stable doctrine of the Incarnation.

3. Passing over the controversial and highly technical "Critique of Christologies" in Chapter IV (which only clears the ground) we arrive at Baillie's main positive thesis in Chapter V, "The Paradox of the Incarnation." Here as in the opening historical analysis, he steers a wise middle course between the liberal "Jesus of history" school, which found God too simply and unmysteriously revealed in the Man of Nazareth, and the neo-orthodox school, which often makes of the Incarnation a complete *"incognito"* or "absolute paradox" (Kierkegaard). Paradox there must be, when the eternal God presents himself in mortal man; but not paradox without analogy. In all God's dealings with men and things—even in Creation and general Providence —there is an apparent contradiction between a scientific, naturalistic account of these events and the viewpoint of Christian faith, which sees God working everywhere, *in and through* men and things. This general paradox of faith rises to a climax in the sanctuary of the Christian life, where it becomes the "paradox of grace": one and the same deed is ascribed to my own free decision, and to God's grace working in and through me. If Jesus the Christ came to share God's grace with me, then it is no impiety to recognize analogy as well as difference between the paradox of grace in the redeemed and in the Redeemer, or as St. Augustine said, "Every man, from the commencement of his

faith, becomes a Christian by the same grace by which *that* Man from His formation became Christ." [11] Baillie's own statement of this main thesis deserves quotation:

> This paradox in its fragmentary form in our own Christian lives is a reflection of that perfect union of God and man in the Incarnation on which our whole Christian life depends, and may therefore be our best clue to the understanding of it. In the New Testament we see the man in whom God was incarnate surpassing all other men in refusing to claim anything for Himself independently and ascribing all the goodness to God. We see Him also desiring to take up other men into His own close union with God. . . . And if these men, entering in some small measure through Him into that union, experience the paradox of grace . . . "It was not I but God," may not this be the clue to the understanding of that perfect life in which the paradox is complete and absolute, that life of Jesus which, being the perfection of humanity, is also, and even in a deeper and prior sense, the very life of God Himself? [12]

4. In his chapter on "The Incarnation and the Trinity" (Chap. VI), Baillie makes a secondary application of his main thesis. He notes the fact that there are two diverse lines of Trinitarian interpretation in contemporary theology, typified by Karl Barth and Leonard Hodgson. Barth describes the three persons of the Trinity as "modes of being"; Hodgson, as "distinct personal beings between whom there can be a 'social' relationship." [13] While Barth avoids the shoal of Sabellian modalism and Hodgson the shoal of tritheism, and while each can invoke a long line of precedents going back through St. Augustine on the one side and the Cappadocian Fathers on the other, neither can claim to state the Christian doctrine of the Trinity in a fully representative form. Whether we speak of "One Person in three modes

---

[11] St. Augustine, *De praedest. sanct.*, I, xv, quoted by Baillie, *ibid.*, p. 118.
[12] *God Was in Christ*, p. 117.     [13] *Ibid.*, p. 137.

of being" or of "three Persons in the highest kind of personal and social unity," we oversimplify a mystery and overrationalize a paradox.[14]

If, however, we accept the "paradox of grace" as our best clue to this doctrine, too, we may say that "the God of grace, who was revealed through the Incarnation and Pentecost as the One who paradoxically works in us what He demands of us, is the same from all eternity and for ever more."[15] Thus it means the same thing to say, "Not I, but the grace of God that was with me. Not I, but Christ who dwelleth in me. It is not we that speak, but the Spirit of our Father that speaketh in us."[16] Since grace sustains both the Christian person and the Christian community, we may add (as Baillie does not) that *both personal and social analogies for the Persons of the Trinity are legitimate,* provided that they are used as symbols of a mystery no finite analogies can exhaust.

There would probably be less agreement on Baillie's view of the Atonement (last two chapters) than on his view of the Incarnation and the Trinity. As he himself remarks, the "cosmic" element which is so prominent in Aulén's "classic" view of the Atonement is not very evident in the view that Jesus "went straight on as the 'friend of sinners,' and got deeper and deeper into trouble, until in the end He was condemned to death. . . . it was His love for them that brought Him to the Cross."[17]

We may say of this view what Baillie says of Barth's and Hodgson's views of the Trinity, that it is too one-sided and unparadoxical. Certainly no view of Christ's work which simply omits the idea of a cosmic struggle between "sin, death and the devil" and God's seemingly helpless but ultimately victorious

[14] *Ibid.,* pp. 140, 144.  [15] *Ibid.,* p. 147.
[16] *Ibid.,* p. 146.  [17] *Ibid.,* p. 183.

power in Christ, can adequately sum up the Christian consensus for a generation that has been deeply impressed by Aulén's rediscovery of this classic conception.[18] On the other hand, Aulén's attack upon Anselm's legalism has not persuaded most conservatives to give up their allegiance to the "satisfaction" theory, nor has his attack upon Abelard's subjectivism persuaded many liberals to give up the "moral" theory of the Atonement. The fact is that *no one theory of the Work of Christ has ever won its way to such general acceptance as the Nicene-Chalcedonian theory of the Person of Christ has received.* Neither the "classic" theory of a cosmic combat, nor Anselm's theory of a satisfaction of divine justice, nor Abelard's theory of a change of heart brought about in man by the divine self-sacrificing love revealed in Christ, can by itself sum up the great salvation which Christians believe God has brought to pass through Christ. St. Thomas Aquinas speaks more ecumenically than Anselm, Abelard or Aulén when he makes a long list of the benefits of Christ's work, and leaves the impression that the list could be still further extended without exhausting the joyful truth.[19]

Our best summary of the ecumenical consensus on Christ's work cannot therefore be drawn from either Baillie or Aulén—although Aulén struggles valiantly to make room in his favorite "classic" theory for valid elements in other theories—but from an Anglican theologian, the late Dr. Oliver Quick, who enumerates four persistent views of Christ's Atonement, and finds important truths in all of them—consistent and not conflicting with the truths in the other views.

---

[18] *Ibid.*, p. 200. Note. Aulén's view will be found not only in the opening and closing chapters of *Christus Victor*, but also in *The Faith of the Christian Church*, pp. 223–41.

[19] *Summa Theologica*, Part III, Q. XLVIII, "Of the Efficiency of Christ's Passion."

1. Quick places at the head of the list Abelard's "moral" or "subjective" theory that Christ "revealed God's fatherly love in a way which has stirred man's heart to fresh repentance." [20] (This we may remark has always been taught as an essential and primary part of the Gospel. Augustine, long before Abelard, advised catechizers of the uninstructed to begin with the text, "God commendeth His love unto us in that, while we were yet sinners, Christ died for us.") But this theory is incomplete by itself. *How* does Christ "reveal" God's love? In a mere gesture of affection, or in an "act of power"? [21]

2. The "classic" or "dramatic" theory supplies the lack in the moral theory at just this point, contending that God in Christ showed his love for man by fighting evil to the death, and at the cost of the life of his well-beloved Son, "has broken the power of the devil over man." But like the subjective theory, the dramatic theory is incomplete by itself. "We need to know more of what exactly Christ's victory was." [22] (Does not Aulén himself pass beyond the framework of dramatic combat when he speaks of God in Christ as both "Reconciler" and "Reconciled"?)

3. Anselm's "juridical" theory tackles the problem of reconciliation between a just God and a sinful mankind as the "dramatic" theory by itself could not do; yet as Quick points out, "There seems to be no reason in principle why Christ's vicarious suffering of the penalty for sin should not be regarded both as a demonstration of God's love for man, and as a means of his victory over sin and death." [23] It is the greatness of Anselm that he maintains (like a good Roman jurist) that "the law of justice still stands unshaken as a moral principle" even when it is transcended in divine forgiveness. This is surely true; but the scheme

[20] Quick, *op. cit.*, p. 221.
[22] *Ibid.*, p. 226.
[21] *Ibid.*, p. 224.
[23] *Idem.*

of substitution whereby Anselm tries to balance the claims of divine justice is artificial and unconvincing—largely, according to Quick, because he is confusing two essentially different conceptions of Christ's death—that of suffering a legal penalty *instead of us*, and that of suffering as a voluntary sacrifice *on our behalf*.[24]

4. This leads, finally, to the "sacrificial" theory of Christ's work—a theory fully worked out in the Epistle to the Hebrews, in clear independence of judicial concepts, but easily confused with the juridical theory by "the persistent mistake of supposing that sin offerings must somehow have been intended to propitiate God by the killing of a victim in the offerer's stead." [25] The real purpose of animal sacrifice was not propitiation of God's justice, but that the blood of an unblemished victim, representing a stainless life offered to God in death, might be applied so as to remove defilements caused by sin, in order that man might "draw near to God." [26] Christ is the perfect Sacrifice because unlike bulls and goats his purity is voluntary, his sacrifice is voluntary self-sacrifice, and the life he offers up represents real human life as it ought to be. Thus "Christ has actually opened for us a new way into heaven, and made available a new power to enable us to tread it" [27]—all this while upholding the moral law, breaking the power of evil, and revealing God's love.

It would be too much to claim that Dr. Quick's fourfold theory of the work of Christ would command universal assent, but it certainly points toward a synthesis of views that would win wider assent than any one theory has ever found. Another genuinely ecumenical feature of his view is that, unlike some other Anglicans, he does not set the doctrine of the Incarnation in po-

[24] *Ibid.*, p. 229.  
[26] *Ibid.*, p. 233.  
[25] *Ibid.*, p. 232.  
[27] *Ibid.*, p. 235.

lemical opposition to the Atonement, but sees the Johannine emphasis on Incarnation and the Pauline emphasis on Atonement as mutually consistent views.[28] Although the doctrines of the person and work of Christ have gone separate ways and had different fates, through much of the history of Christian thought, there is an emerging consensus in our time—found in theologians as diverse as Brunner, Aulén and Baillie—that affirms these two doctrines to be essentially one, and tries at all costs to hold them together.

If this trend goes on, the Nicene-Chalcedonian consensus on Christ's person may some day come to include an agreed consensus on Christ's work. Such a consensus would be bound to include more aspects of Christ's great salvation than can be seen from any one viewpoint.[29] It might take its departure from the fact that man's *need* of salvation is at least threefold: he is at odds with himself and his fellow men, a prisoner of the powers of evil, and alienated from God. If Christ is indeed the universal Savior, his saving work must at least make an inward change in man, free him from his external bondage, and reconcile him with God's holiness. All this and more, Christians believe, is really accomplished in Christ. A decisive beginning of this work was "once for all" made in the life and death and resurrection of Jesus; through the Holy Spirit in the Church, this work continues until God's Kingdom comes in its fullness.

[28] *Ibid.*, p. 189, "The Incarnation is seen as the method of the Atonement."
[29] A very brief and clear statement of a multiple-aspect view, close at some points to Canon Quick's, will be found in S. Paul Schilling's article, "How Does Jesus Save?" in *Religion in Life* (Spring, 1949).

SECTION 3. UNRESOLVED ISSUES CONCERNING JESUS CHRIST

It should not be surprising if there are many issues still unresolved concerning the One who is the very foundation and chief cornerstone of the Christian Church. The fact that all the divided Christian churches do consciously rest upon that same foundation is more important than any of the differences we shall discuss; but from a very early date, Christians resting together upon the same Christ have had diverse conceptions of his Person and Work. The Four Gospels, on which all conceptions of the Christ are fundamentally based, do not present a fully unified portrait. Each Evangelist follows a distinctive line of Church tradition; and between the Synoptics and the Fourth Gospel there is a wide difference of perspective. Despite the balance of the Prologue and its classic doctrine of the *"Word made flesh,"* there are many passages in the narrative and dialogue of the Fourth Gospel where Jesus is stripped of the genuinely human traits which are so evident in the Synoptics, and appears even in the "days of his Flesh" as though he were the divine Word *discarnate*, exercising the attributes of divine omniscience and omnipotence without restriction. Where the Synoptic Jesus says, "Why callest thou me good? There is none good but one, that is God," the Johannine Jesus says, "Before Abraham was, I am." (Mt. 10:18; Jn. 8:58.)

So long as the Gospel sources were uncritically accepted and mechanically harmonized, the best that could be done was to place the Synoptic Suffering Servant of God side by side, inconsistently, with the Johannine Word of God, whose supernal glory continually breaks forth as if the veil of flesh were too thin to conceal it. Docetic and monophysite conceptions of Jesus

Christ have their permanent basis in the Fourth Gospel; and so long as that Gospel is regarded as fully historical, the "end of docetism"—which D. M. Baillie proclaims as an already accomplished fact—will never really arrive.

It was a great achievement for the Council of Chalcedon to reject the monophysite views of Eutyches under these circumstances; but if the student will carefully examine the document which carried decisive weight at Chalcedon—Pope Leo the Great's letter to Flavian, popularly called "The Tome"[30]—he will see that it presents what might almost be called a "Dr. Jekyll and Mr. Hyde" account of the life of Jesus. From beginning to end, the life of our Lord is presented as *two lives*, not easily conceived as the lives of one person—one of them divine, and "sparkling with miracles," the other human, and "succumbing to injuries." Not exclusively but very largely, the first is Johannine and the second Synoptic. In the birth, the baptism, the ministry, the crucifixion of this allegedly single person, two opposite personalities or "natures" appear to dodge in and out, like the old man and woman in a Swiss weather box. When the human nature is out, the divine nature must be in, and vice versa. While most Christians accept the essential soundness of the Chalcedonian doctrine of "two natures in one person," those who have wrestled with historical criticism will differently narrate Christ's life, and differently interweave its divine and human aspects.

There is room, then, for serious debate among Christians as to the exact meaning of the common Christian faith that in Jesus the Christ "true man" and "true God" met and were one. Among the many unresolved issues in this field we select two for special attention, as living contemporary issues: Unitarianism, and the

[30] *Nicene and Post-Nicene Fathers*, Vol. XII, pp. 38-43 (Letter XXVIII).

Virgin Birth. The first of these issues lies on the liberal-conservative front; the second lies on the liberal-conservative and (through its connection with the veneration of the Blessed Virgin and the new dogma of her Bodily Assumption) on the catholic-protestant front. The conflict on both issues is keenest between churches not officially belonging to the Ecumenical Movement—the Unitarian to the left and the Roman Catholic to the right—but repercussions of the conflict are felt in many churches belonging to the World Council of Churches.

## A. *The Unitarian Issue*

The importance of the Unitarian issue far exceeds the numerical weight of the Unitarian and the Universalist churches which unite in the Unitarian view of Christ, and are very close to organic union with each other on this basis. Especially in America, Unitarian views are very widely held by liberal ministers and laymen in other denominations, such as the Society of Friends, the community churches, and others. Moreover, the Unitarian view of Christ is so close to that held by many liberal Jews that it raises an issue involving the very essence of Christianity: Can the New Testament revelation of God in Christ be regarded as the "fulfillment" of the Old Testament revelation, or does it fundamentally subvert and destroy Old Testament monotheism? Is the doctrine of the Trinity a reversion to pagan polytheism?

No conscientious Christian can be content to settle such issues by burning men like Servetus—Luther's remark about the futility of force against heresy still holds[31]—nor by simply excluding Unitarians from the Ecumenical Movement and thus hushing them up, nor by treating Jews as though their theological views were of no significance to Christians. While the Ecumenical

[31] "Heresy is a spiritual matter which no iron can strike, no fire burn, no water drown."

Movement has enough on its hands discussing issues arising among Christ-centered Christians, and would be very unwise to admit Jews or Unitarians to its membership, this by no means means that an ecumenical theology should be deaf to issues arising just outside this official boundary. There is every reason to believe that issues of this sort (arising just on the edge of the Christian consensus) can be reduced to more manageable proportions by the same methods of objective comparison and face-to-face discussion which have so considerably reduced the divisive power of issues arising between catholics and protestants, liberals and conservatives.

Let us take our objective statement of the Unitarian position from Channing's classic Baltimore sermon on "Unitarian Christianity." On the basis of loyalty to Scripture, and a confidence that there is nothing finally contradictory between Scripture and right reason, Channing asserts as the two fundamental theses of Unitarian Christianity *the Unity of God* and *the Unity of Christ*, who, though endowed with superhuman prerogatives elaborated to the point of "high Arianism" in other writings of Channing, is still clearly "distinct from the one God," God's servant and not God's embodiment. Channing complains that the three "persons" of the Trinity, as commonly interpreted by the orthodox, are hardly to be distinguished from three separate centers of consciousness, which converse with one another and have distinct functions and characteristics. This is tritheism, which subverts monotheism. He also complains that the "two natures" of Christ, as commonly interpreted by the orthodox, destroy the unity of his person, and tempt us to worship him instead of the one God to whom alone worship is due.[32]

[32] For a full report of the Baltimore sermon, and the response made to it by Moses Stuart and other champions of orthodoxy, see F. H. Foster, *History of the New England Theology*, pp. 283–315.

A first step in ecumenical conversation with this position might be for Trinitarian Christians to profess their allegiance to monotheism in the most unequivocal terms, and to disown any interpretations of the Trinity that are really inconsistent with this. So, for example, Dr. DeWolf in his *Theology of the Living Church* impressively insists that Christians have two great concerns in the doctrine of the Trinity: (1) to preserve the "rich, varied and tremendous new powers" which came into the world through Jesus and "produced the Christian Church" and (2) "to maintain the monotheistic faith." "For," he adds, "the Hebrew *Shema* belongs also to the Christians. 'The Lord our God, the Lord is one.' " [33] Once this confession has been made, it would be appropriate to add that some interpretations of the Trinity really must be disowned as tritheistic, and some interpretations of the Person of Christ make unreal that humble self-subordination to God, both in prayer and in conduct, which is so marked a feature of Jesus' character, *even in the Fourth Gospel*: "Truly, truly, I say to you, the Son can do nothing of his own accord, but only what he sees the Father doing" (John 5:19 R.S.V.). If we cling to the undoubted fact that Jesus lived by the *Shema*, and built upon it his First and Great Commandment to his disciples, we shall be in a position to talk more intelligibly with our Unitarian and Jewish friends.

After this initial clearing of the ground, perhaps the next step toward better understanding would be to point out that for those who believe that Jesus brought new light from God, new complexities are introduced into the idea of God, which cannot easily be handled on a strict Unitarian basis. As Canon Leonard Hodgson points out in his able book on *The Doctrine of the Trinity*, it is plainly misleading to suppose that the unity of God

[33] P. 276.

is comparable with the "mathematical unity" of a digit or point. If organic unity is more complex than mathematical unity, and psychological unity more complex than organic unity—thinking, feeling and willing "interpermeating" one another, though clearly distinguishable as separate activities of the same self— how much more complex is the unity we must ascribe to God. [34]

As already noted above, Hodgson goes on to suggest that not only the psychological unity of a self with three distinct functions, but the social unity of three selves in moral harmony, is a proper analogy to use in attempting to grasp the complex unity of God. Here he comes perilously close to tritheism, but is saved from it (as the Cappadocian Fathers were) by clear recognition that all earthly unities, whether psychological or social, are but "imperfect analogues" of the perfect though complex unity which belongs to God alone.[35] He is driven to this conclusion, not only by the increasing complexity of the "great chain of being," but still more by the complexity of the revelation of God in the New Testament. First in the life of Jesus and then by derivation in the life of the Church after Pentecost, God's presence is an inwardly abiding presence; while at the same time God on high remains the ultimate strength and reliance of those in whom God abides. To include the Father on high, the incarnate Son of God on earth and the Holy Spirit of God among the brethren in one conception of God, demanded the shattering of the simple mathematical idea of unity which had hitherto prevailed in Hebrew theology. The history of the great Trinitarian controversy in the Church is the history of a conflict between a complex revelation and an oversimple idea of divine unity: "one or the other, the unity or the revelation, had to give way." [36]

[34] Pp. 89 *et seq.*  [35] *Ibid.*, p. 96.
[36] *Ibid.*, p. 99.

But, the whole argument implies, to give up mathematical unity is not to give up monotheism.

A further step toward understanding might be to note the fact that the complexity of the Christian idea of God reveals itself even when the attempt is made, by Unitarians, to cling to mathematical unity. Aulén suggests this when he remarks that "Unitarian views" tend inevitably to become pantheistic or deistic.[37] Such, at any rate, has been the history of Anglo-American Unitarianism. It was at first very much under the influence of the eigtheenth-century Enlightenment, and tended to exalt God the Father in almost deistic transcendence. Then, under the influence of New England Transcendentalism, it rather suddenly reversed its emphasis, and stressed the indwelling of God's Spirit in all men and even in all nature, so that in Emerson's "Oversoul" doctrine this one-sided immanentism definitely became pantheistic. After this violent pendulum swing from the first to the third person of the Trinity, some Unitarian thought abandoned Christianity and theism altogether, and became humanistic; while the great British Unitarian, Martineau, became more sympathetic to Nicene Trinitarianism, and suggested that when Unitarians speak of God the Father they really mean what the Nicene doctrine means by God the Son: God coming forth from himself to reveal his nature in creative and redemptive action, above all in Christ.[38] Very few Unitarians would follow Martineau in this irenic solution of the issue, but it is impresssive that Unitarian thought has, so to speak, been forced by the complexity of the Christian idea of God to run through all three Persons of the Trinity successively in consequence of its refusal to assert them simultaneously.

[37] Aulén, *Faith of the Christian Church*, p. 258.
[38] See his essay, "A Way Out of the Trinitarian Controversy," in his *Essays, Reviews, and Addresses*, Vol. II.

If Trinitarian thought can firmly insist, with Aulén, that "the work of Christ is throughout the work of God, and the Spirit is not an independent being at the side of God, but . . . God's immediate and continuous activity."[39] it may maintain real monotheism better than Unitarianism, without tipping over into deistic or pantheistic extremes. If it can further insist with Baillie, that the "paradox of grace" (both in Christ and in the Christian) unites human activity with divine activity in one divine-human life, it may maintain the unity of Christ's person better than traditional Christian thought has done. Thus both Channing's theses, the unity of God and the unity of Christ, may be accepted by Trinitarians—which will not close the Unitarian controversy but may diminish the historic tension considerably.

## B. *The Virgin Birth and Mariology*

If the Unitarian doctrine of God as his own sole Mediator lies near one of the two poles of thought distinguished by Tillich, the pole of *ultimacy*, the Catholic doctrine of the Blessed Virgin as Mother of God, Queen of Heaven, Intercessor for sinners, lies at the opposite pole of *concreteness*. It looks to orthodox Protestants as close to idolatry and polytheism as the orthodox Protestant doctrines of the Incarnation and the Trinity look to Unitarians. The seriousness of the issue of the Virgin Birth hardly appears when the conflict between liberal and conservative Protestant thought is considered by itself; it is only when the consequences drawn from the Virgin Birth by Roman Catholics are added—Immaculate Conception, Perpetual Virginity, Bobily Assumption, Hyperdulia, and others yet perhaps—it is only then that this issue appears as the source of a "widening gulf" in the Christian community, already unbridgeable, and perhaps

[39] Aulén, *op. cit.*

eventually so broad that "even fraternal voices will scarcely be able to carry across it." [40] Let us consider the issue first in its milder form, as it arises on the liberal-conservative front, and then in its more acute form, on the catholic-protestant front.

The doctrine of the Virgin Birth was widely used during the Fundamentalist controversy as a touchstone of Protestant orthodoxy. One who denied it might be expected to deny all miraculous elements in the Bible, and all the essential mysteries of the faith, such as Incarnation, Atonement and Resurrection. A very little reflection upon theological positions actually held by various groups, would show that this doctrine is an extremely unreliable means of detecting departures from orthodoxy. On the one hand, there is the fact that Ebionites and Arians, Unitarians and even *Moslems* can and do profess belief in the Virgin Birth without accepting the orthodox Nicene-Chalcedonian doctrine of the Incarnation. On the other hand, there is the fact that neo-orthodox Christians like Brunner and Aulén express the most ardent and unwavering faith in the Incarnation, while remaining skeptical or unconcerned about the Virgin Birth.

How this can be, is perhaps best indicated in a passage already cited from Barth's *Dogmatics in Outline* (Chap. 14), where he distinguishes between the "Mystery of Christmas" (the Incarnation) and the "Miracle" (the Virgin Birth) whereby this Mystery is (not by necessity but by God's good pleasure) made known to us. He himself holds that the form and the matter of the Christmas story hang closely together, as the female passivity of Mary, and the absence of all male activity in the birth of Jesus present the essential condition for a real "hypostatic union" between God and man. He suspects that anyone who tries to

---

[40] Editorial on "The Widening Gulf," in *The Christian Century* (April 7, 1954), pp. 421–23.

"fly from the miracle" while accepting the mystery it enshrines must be under the influence of some rationalizing "natural theology." [41] But Barth's colleagues in neo-orthodoxy, Brunner and Aulén, who detest natural theology nearly if not quite as much as he, regard the miraculous form of the mystery as nonessential for faith in the Incarnation. Aulén goes so far as to condemn the Virgin Birth doctrine as an *illegitimate rationalization* of the unity of substance between God and man in Christ, which has nothing "physiological" about it, but simply means that we "possess the heart and will of the Father in Christ"—an affirmation only to be made in faith and essentially "inscrutable." [42] Clearly, the mystery of the Incarnation *is* independent of the miracle of the Virgin Birth, and does not stand or fall with the evidence for the latter.

That this is so is fortunate, because of the confused state of the evidence. If the New Testament's witness to the Virgin Birth were so clear and unequivocal as its witness to the fact of the Resurrection, C. S. Lewis' argument would have more force: that the Virgin Birth, after all, involves a less complete break with the natural order. But many Christian believers who admit the possibility of miracles, and who accept the miracle of the Resurrection, are honestly perplexed when they confront the testimony concerning the birth of Jesus: the silence of Paul, Mark and John; Matthew's genealogy traced through Joseph; Luke's reference to Joseph and Mary as Jesus' "parents"; the frequent allusions to "the carpenter's son." [43] Explanations of these discrepancies have often been offered in defense of orthodoxy; but a very solid contingent of leading Protestant thinkers now

[41] P. 100.

[42] Aulén, *Faith of the Christian Church*, pp. 221–23.

[43] For a good brief summary of these and other difficulties, see DeWolf, *Theology of the Living Church*, pp. 230–32.

accept the orthodox doctrine of the Incarnation while admitting their perplexity over the evidence for the Virgin Birth. Were this only an intra-Protestant issue, it might eventually be solved by thus demoting the doctrine of the Virgin Birth to an optional, second-rank position.

This, however, would never satisfy the Catholics. Not only the Roman Catholics who are continuing to accept a whole series of official dogmas concerning the Virgin as necessary to salvation, but the Eastern Orthodox and many Anglo-Catholics as well, who venerate the Mother of God as devoutly as the Romans —all these inhabit another world of piety, whose very basis is the doctrine of the Virgin Birth, and where the idea of demoting this doctrine to a second-rank status is simply unthinkable. Unless this whole world of popular piety should wither and die, as the Olympic gods died after the triumph of Christianity, no compromise is conceivable between Mariology[44] and *any* form of Protestant Christology, whether liberal or conservative. The best that is possible under the circumstances is an act of laborious comprehension on the part of Protestants, which may enable them to *tolerate* Mariology as a form of Christian thought, and an expression of Christian devotion, though they cannot heartily participate in it. (Cf. Skydsgaard, *One in Christ*, last chapter.)

Such an act of comprehension might begin by listening to Roman Catholic explanations of the recently promulgated dogma of the Assumption. A Catholic writer on the "Theology of the Assumption"[45] begins with a candid admission that there is no direct *Scriptural* basis for this dogma, that there is no clear *traditional* basis for it, and that certain *apocryphal* foundations for it

[44] We are avoiding the term "Mariolatry," which implies that Catholics really "worship" Mary (*latria*). Highest veneration (*hyperdulia*) is all they claim to offer her. A few Protestants do show traces of such veneration.

[45] Dom Bernard Capelle, o.s.b., *op. cit.* (See Chapter II, *supra*.)

have always been doubted by the Church. Since there is so conspicuous a lack of authentic texts or traditions (*auctoritates*) on which to ground this dogma, it necessarily rests upon logical arguments (*rationes*) that connect it with Scripture and Tradition. There are three principal arguments: (1) Mary is the Second Eve, as her Blessed Son is the Second Adam. She must therefore escape the malediction ("dust thou art") pronounced upon Adam and Eve. Since she has already been declared sinless in the dogma of the Immaculate Conception, it is logical to believe that she escaped bodily death, the wages of sin. (2) The sacred body that bore our Lord cannot see corruption. Since her body has always been regarded by the Catholic Church as "perpetually virgin," even after the birth of her Son, the logical consequence of the stainlessness of her body is—Bodily Assumption. (3) The Blessed Virgin is so joined to her divine Son that she has a privileged status only His Mother could have. Since her saintliness exceeds that of the greatest saints she is worthy of the special privilege of direct entrance into heaven, where she joins her intercessions with those of her Son. There is in all this a logical "development" (Newman) of early Catholic beliefs. The Church and her infallible Pontiff have the authority to sift Tradition and interpret Scripture in this way, setting aside false interpretations and developing the true ones.

Logical connections certainly do exist between the new dogma and long-established Catholic belief and practice. On the basis of these logical connections, the doctrine of the Assumption was already being taught in Catholic theology before it became a dogma. In the Rudloff-Muller *Dogmatic Theology* for Catholic laymen, which received the Imprimatur in Paris, 1937, we find a skeleton outline of the development of Mariology in logical stages, with each proposition labeled D (dogma), C (certain;

admitted by all theologians), Com (commonly admitted by theologians) or Prob (probable; taught by some respected theologians). Note the place accorded to the doctrine of the Assumption in advance of its *ex cathedra* promulgation, and note also the high probability that Mary will presently be declared Mediatrix:

Christ was born of the Virgin Mary—D (Apostles' Creed)
Mary is "Mother of God"—D (Ephesus)
Mary remained perpetually virgin—D (common teaching of Church)
Mary was conceived without sin—D (Pius IX, 1854)
Mary was received bodily into heaven—C
Mary is Mediatrix of divine graces
  (a) in that she gave us Christ—D (common teaching)
  (b) in that she has *the power* to obtain by her intercession full peace for all men—C
  (c) because every grace is *in fact* attained through her intercession—Prob
  (d) Mary is the object of a special cult ("hyperdulia")—D (common teaching of the Church) [46]

For most Protestants, the indubitable logic of this sequence of beliefs will not be persuasive, because it moves in an unfamiliar world of devotion, and toward a goal that seems idolatrous: the enthronement of Mary at the side of her Son, as co-Mediatrix of the world's salvation. If the uniqueness of Christ's Saviorhood and Mediatorship is thus to be infringed in favor of the Blessed Virgin, what (Protestants will ask) is to prevent Mary's eventually becoming a fourth Person in the Blessed Trinity— and much the most important. In fairness to Catholic thought it should be said that Mary's role in our salvation is always connected with and subordinated to that of her Son: she is our

[46] Rudloff and Muller, *op. cit.*, p. 191. Cf. English version, cited on p. 275.

Mother, as she was His, "since we are members of Christ's mystical body"; she is our *suppliant* Mediatrix, "for the one true Mediator between God and man is Christ, and no one could be placed between our souls and Him"—except as a kind, suppliant intercessor.[47]

What must be understood if this doctrine is not to be unfairly misinterpreted, is the Catholic doctrine of the Communion of Saints. The Eastern Orthodox Churches, which take their Mariology more mystically and less logically than Rome, are accustomed to pray for St. Mary and ask her to pray for us, just as they do with all the great saints but, so to speak, on the highest level below Christ. The issue here is not whether Christ's saving Mediatorship is unique, but whether there is a place below Christ for other mediators, who mediate Christ's grace and presence as Christ mediates God's. In Protestant *practice*, do not men like Luther and Wesley mediate Christ to the churches they founded, and does not each generation of Christian parents and teachers mediate Christ to the next? And is there not a psychological analogue to the cult of the Blessed Mother in that cult of "Home and Mother" which plays such a role in revivalistic hymn books?

It is of course unlikely that interpretations and comparisons of this sort will ever bring Catholics and Protestants together on this crucially divisive issue; but to confront the other party—perhaps through the Orthodox and Anglo-Catholics who occupy intermediate positions—may be a salutary source of self-knowledge and corrective self-criticism for both parties. If Catholics need to be made aware of the danger of idolatry in the veneration of the Virgin and the Saints, Protestants need to be made aware of the danger of reverting, through fear of idolatry, to a

[47] *Ibid.*, p. 84.

bare, austere Old Testament piety, in which the joyful New Testament sense of "God *with* us" would be lost.

Protestants commonly object to Unitarians for losing the distinctive Christian revelation in an abstract devotion to "mathematical unity"; but they should realize that they seem to Catholics to fall just short of Unitarianism in their failure to recognize the Communion of Saints and the place of the Virgin Mother at the head of the saints. Vigorous, concrete faith in God thinks of the Deity as *supreme but not solitary*, surrounded by messengers and blessed ones who live in the divine light. If even Judaism did not wholly reject the idea of subordinate messengers (angels) and mediators, why should Protestantism try to confine itself exclusively to the One Mediator?

As a matter of fact, as we shall see in Chapter VII, *every* Christian denomination recognizes the principle of subordinate mediatorship in its conception of the Church itself as Christ's Body, and of the various "means of grace" as specific media for conveying Christ's presence and power from generation to generation. The schism and dissension that plague the Protestant Church are largely due to the fact that each denomination tends to fasten on some favorite means of grace, and (living for long years apart from other denominations) tends to conclude at last that God's saving grace simply cannot flow except through this one favorite channel. If there is idolatry in Catholic Mariology, there is a worse idolatry here, at the root of Protestant sectarianism.[48]

[48] There is a close relation between the idolatry described here and the root evil which Charles Clayton Morrison in *The Unfinished Reformation* (Harper, 1953) calls "the churchism of the denominations."

# VII

## THE CHURCH AND THE MEANS OF GRACE

### SECTION 1. THE UNIVERSAL NEED FOR FELLOWSHIP AND INSPIRATION

IN all historic religions, there is something analogous to the Christian Church, which meets the universal human need for fellowship and inspiration. In terms of our triangular diagram, this need lies in the middle of the horizontal line, between the point of intersection (mediator, savior, way-shower) and the right-hand end (final goal). There is no likelihood that a religious movement will reach its goal, or even approach it, unless the work of its founder or its tutelary deity is perpetuated and constantly renewed in an inspiring fellowship.

A religion that is only a teaching or a way of life, to be studied and practiced by individuals, is a philosophy or theosophy rather than a full-fledged religion. The theosophical and anthroposophical movements are more than philosophies, since they are not only schools of thought, but also *societies*, practicing *common worship*. Buddhism, despite its dryly philosophical beginnings, has become a great religious movement through the spread of its *sects* and *orders*, which have taken the place occupied by *castes* in the Hindu system from which it sprang. In making his profession of faith, a Buddhistic monk declares that he "takes his refuge" in the *Buddha* and his *Dharma* (teaching), but also in the *Sangha*—the inspiring religious fellowship which he joins.

The same need expressed in these historic religious fellowships can be discerned in modern "nonreligious" or "antireligious" movements that react against the Christian Church and try to by-pass it. D. R. Davies, in his little book on Reinhold Niebuhr, expresses surprise that Niebuhr has given so little attention to the idea of the Church, when he is so good a student of Marxism. [1] What in fact would Marxian Communism be without its local "cells," its national "parties," its international "Comintern" or "Cominform," and its supreme Pontiff in the Kremlin? Analogies of all sorts leap to the eye. What the clergy is to the laity, or what the *ecclesiola* is to the *ecclesia*, the Communist party members are to the whole Communist movement and its "fellow travelers." This is certainly not the result of conscious imitation, but of a necessity for comradeship and stimulation that imposes itself upon every movement seeking to save mankind.

A particularly instructive example of the spontaneous generation of a Church substitute may be found in a book called *The Open Conspiracy* (1928) by the late H. G. Wells. Wells was a bitter critic of the Church, but a devoted champion of socialist reform and international fraternity. Having noticed how easily social reformers become discouraged and confused,[2] overcome by a certain "everydayness" that dulls their dreams and blunts their first resolutions, he sets himself in this book to provide a remedy for this peril in the shape of an inspiring fellowship, open to all good "conspirators" seeking the Good Society. Looking only to the peril and the remedy, he finds himself recommending to his conspirators so many methods analogous to the

---

[1] Davies, *Reinhold Niebuhr: Prophet from America,* London: Clarke, 1945.
[2] Wells himself fell into despair in his last days.

historic "means of grace" employed by the Church—inspirational meetings and inspirational reading, for example—that he apologizes for the resemblance. Evidently, if the Church did not exist, she would have to be invented.

While the pressure of need, given time enough, is sure to create some sort of Church substitute—especially in a depersonalized, mechanized society where men are hungry for fellowship —it cannot be a matter of indifference to *what sort* of fellowship one is devoted. Psychologically, of course, any fellowship is better than none for the lonely individual; and devotion to the Masonic Order, or the League of Women Voters, or the American Legion, or any social movement whatsoever, may help him to clear up his unresolved mental conflicts. Yet in the long run, no partial or limited fellowship can meet his need. What he half-consciously seeks is central participation in the true destiny of mankind, such as the Church at its best really offers; so to make a Church of his lodge or his luncheon club turns out at last to be as frustrating an experience as to make a god of his wife. It is a great tragedy when failure of true fellowship in the Church drives men to seek inspiration in such unsatisfactory substitutes —or in truly diabolic alternatives such as frenzied nationalism or racism.

In the welter of alternative loyalties that beckon to the modern man and solicit his full commitment, an ancient contrast is still basic, between the sort of fellowship proper to *mystical* religion and to *prophetic* religion. Mystical fellowships seek to elevate their members above the world, gathering them into esoteric bands of Enlightened Ones who practice the life of heaven on earth while they await the call to come up higher. Prophetic fellowships unite their members in dedication to a cause or purpose, and train them for more effective service. In contemporary religious movements, this ancient contrast sometimes expresses itself quite violently, in mystical cults which have no social concern, and in ethical cults which have no concern for worship, or for metaphysical ultimates. The issues of life are decided in radically different ways, if one takes the left-hand or right-hand path at this great crossroads. It cannot be a matter of indifference which turn is taken. We shall see that Christianity's specific answer decisively takes the prophetic turn, but in a manner as unique as the Person on whom the Christian fellowship is based—a Person with whom the fellowship is mystically united, while at the same time it is prophetically led by the same Person.

## Section 2. The Christian Consensus Concerning the Church and the Means of Grace

It may seem presumptuous to speak of any "Christian Consensus" concerning the Church and the Means of Grace. Here, above all, Christians are divided, not only into schools of thought but into separate bodies, between which there is no full and free communion. At all three of the world conferences on Faith and Order—Lausanne, Edinburgh, Lund—it was discovered that the major differences holding the Christian churches apart clustered around the doctrine of the nature of the Church itself, more especially around the doctrines of the Ministry and the Sacraments. It will be the task of Section 3 in this chapter to look at these differences realistically, and consider the prospects for their eventual resolution. There is, frankly, no *immediate* hope whatsoever of their being resolved. Yet it is the central paradox of the Ecumenical Movement that in the very act of noting these deep and seemingly insoluble differences, we have become aware of a "given unity" that underlies them, and holds us together in spite of them.[3] And as William Nicholls puts it, "We must certainly say without hesitation that this reality in which we all cohere, the basis of this given unity, is in some sense the Church. . . . The whole difficulty is to say in *what* sense we are together in the Church."[4] In this section, we shall try to articulate the agreements about the Church which are implicit in this paradoxical situation, and hold Christians together in one Church despite their divisions. Needless to say, the Christian fellowship will have little appeal as an alternative to its secular rivals unless it can be made clear that it is sober truth and not just inflated advertising, when Christians sing, "We are not divided, all one body we."

The doctrine of the Church has, strangely enough, never been as well articulated as other Christian doctrines. After getting into the Apostles' and Nicene Creeds, after being set in majestic historical perspective by St. Augustine in his *City of God*, the doctrine of the Church suffered something like a total eclipse in medieval scholasticism. In St. Thomas' vast *Summa*, all one finds on the Church is a discussion of Christ or the Pope as its Head, and a long treatise on the Sacraments.[5] "The impression usually accepted without investigation," says T. O. Wedel,

---

[3] Cf. the report of Section I at the Amsterdam Assembly: "Although we cannot fully meet, our Lord will not allow us to turn away from one another." Amsterdam *Official Report* (Harper, 1949), pp. 54, 55.

[4] *Ecumenism and Catholicity* (London: S.C.M. Press, 1952), p. 33.

[5] Father Yves Congar has written a fine essay on "The Thomistic Idea of the Church" in his *Esquisses du Mystère de l'Eglise* (Paris, Cerf, 1953). He maintains (p. 61) that "ecclesiological texts are numerous in St. Thomas," and the whole of Part IIa of the *Summa*, on "the movement of the rational creature toward God," implicitly involves a doctrine of the Church. The fact remains, as Congar admits, that except for a few remarks in his *Exposition of the Apostles' Creed*, St. Thomas never wrote a formal treatise on the Church.

"that Catholic dogma is rich in doctrines of the Church is simply an illusion. But a vacuum exists in Protestant theological thinking on the Church also. To work out a doctrine of the Church may have been the task assigned precisely to our era in Christian history." [6] The Ecumenical Movement has addressed itself specifically to this task in recent years, and it is upon ecumenical documents that we shall mainly base our account of the Christian consensus concerning the Church.

To begin with, *all Christians are agreed in tracing the origin of the Church back to God's calling of a Chosen People under the Old Covenant.* The Greek word *ekklesia* translates the Hebrew *Qahal*, "which expressed the religious unity of the Jews as the one people of God . . . of God's own choosing," of whom "at least a remnant would be saved," [7] despite their many apostasies. The New Israel is, to be sure, not limited to one nation or bound to one law code—hence some object to the term— but the newness of the new Covenant certainly does not dissolve all connection with the Jewish heritage. The New Testament Church was deeply conscious of its continuity with the ancient People of God; it thought of itself as the saving remnant of that People, the true "Israel of God," the real "seed of Abraham." Its Twelve Apostles were appointed to judge the Twelve Tribes of Israel. The American Theological Committee points out in its Report that "a broad and universal agreement lies in the very idea of the Church itself as the People of God. . . . All acknowledge one God as Founder of the Church. They recognize a covenant between a God who is faithful and a people whose faithlessness is ever overcome by Him 'whose

[6] Wedel, *The Coming Great Church* (Macmillan, 1945), p. 49.
[7] Report of the American Theological Committee on "The Nature of the Church," reprinted in *The Nature of the Church* (Lund preparatory volume), ed. by R. Newton Flew (Harper, 1952), p. 235.

mercy endureth forever.' This Church has been brought together by the revealing, redeeming act of God in Christ, whose
purpose has its consummation in a redeemed people." [8] To join
the Church is to join the sequence of events, the succession of
people, that gives divine meaning to human history.

The act of God in Christ is therefore not the *first* in the long
series of revealing, redeeming acts on which the Church is
founded. The call of Abraham, the Mosaic covenant, and Jere-
miah's prophecy of a New Covenant written in the heart, come
earlier in the series. *Yet all Christians are agreed that the decisive
act of God in the forming of the Church, was accomplished in
the death and resurrection of Jesus Christ, and the Church is in
some sense the prolongation of this act.* Hence we sing, "The
Church's *one foundation* is Jesus Christ her Lord; she is his *new
creation* by water and the Word"—not that nothing was there
before Christ came, but what was there was decisively rebuilt
and re-created through him. This decisive and determinative
relationship between Christ and the Church is expressed in many
New Testament figures: the foundation and the superstructure
of a temple (I Cor. 3), the vine and the branches (John 15),
the bridegroom and the bride (Rev. 19:7-9), and most influential of all, the head and members of one body (I Cor. 12).
Every ecumenical gathering has borne witness to the fact that
all unity in the Church, actual or potential, roots in the universal
Christian acknowledgment of one Lord and Savior as the supreme Head of the Church. Out of many recent statements of
this universal acknowledgment, we select the following from
the report of Section I at the Amsterdam Assembly:

God's redeeming activity in the world has been carried out
through His calling a People to be his own chosen People. The old

[8] *Ibid.,* pp. 249, 250.

covenant was fulfilled in the new when Jesus Christ, the Son of God incarnate, died and was raised from the dead, ascended into heaven and gave the Holy Ghost to dwell in His Body, the Church. It is our common concern for that Church which draws us together, and in that concern we discover our unity in relation to her Lord and Head.[9]

In this statement there is a reference to a third element in the nature of the Church, on which there is universal agreement. *The Church is not only the People of God and the Body of Christ; it is also the Community of the Holy Spirit.* The gift of the Spirit, at Pentecost and after, is a further act of God which, dependent as it is upon the central and decisive act in Christ, may nevertheless be considered as the *final* act that created the new People of God out of the old; hence Pentecost is often called "the birthday of the Church." It is no accident that the Apostles' Creed links faith in the Holy Ghost and faith in the Holy Catholic Church closely together; the Holy Spirit and the true Church are in fact correlatives, inseparable from each other. Robert Nelson, pointing to the fact that in the New Testament a baptism of the Spirit is closely connected with baptismal incorporation into the Christian community, declares that "Baptism, the gift of the Holy Spirit, and incorporation into the Church—none of these three stands isolated from or opposed to the other two." [10] Besides this initial act of incorporation into the community, Nelson finds in the New Testament four "major contributions" of the Spirit to the Church: "He makes the presence of the glorified Christ a reality to men in all generations. He calls men to faith and leads them in life as sons

[9] Amsterdam *Official Report*, p. 51.
[10] J. R. Nelson, *The Realm of Redemption: Studies in the Doctrine of the Nature of the Church in Contemporary Protestant Theology* (London: Epworth Press, 1951), p. 47.

of God. He gives them the 'fruit' of Christ-like character. And he binds them together in their sharing of the life of *koinonia*." [11]

The Church as thus far described is emphatically a divine institution, founded upon God's covenant with Israel, refounded by Christ's sacrificial life and death, indwelt by the Spirit of Holiness. Were we to stop at this point, secularists would be entitled to jeer at the inconsistency between the Church as she represents herself and the Church as she actually appears on the corner of Main Street, Middletown. But there is a misunderstanding here; *Christians are universally agreed that the Church is a human as well as a divine institution.* Not only is she composed of human beings—Christ, too, was a human being—but of *all too human* beings who, despite the forgiving and transforming grace of Christ, lapse repeatedly into sin and so deny their Lord. As Lesslie Newbigin reminds us,[12] the Apostle Paul sees in the New Testament churches not only embodiments of Christ, human fellowships indwelt by the Holy Spirit; he also sees in them a "carnal" nature, a manifestation of the insurgent "flesh" which he constantly has to rebuke. So it has been ever since. The miracle is that the divine nature of the Church is not altogether obscured by the all too human nature of her members. The traditional "marks of the true Church"—that she is One, Holy, Catholic and Apostolic—can to some extent be *seen* in our actual, "visible" churches, in spite of the quarrels, sins, provincialisms and complacencies of their members.

There is more agreement here than disputed terms would indicate: Protestants agree that the Church is composed of vis-

---

[11] *Ibid.*, p. 58. Dr. Nelson is secretary of Faith and Order in the World Council of Churches. His book surveys agreements and differences concerning the Church in a vast cross section of current theological discussion.

[12] *The Reunion of the Church* (Harper, 1948), Chap. IV, "The Spirit, the Body and the Flesh."

ible, human members; though the true Church is often so hard to see in those members that they are driven to define it as "invisible." Catholics agree that the *members* of the Church can and do fall into sin; though they define the true Church as the divine, sinless element in the Church—Christ himself, living and working in the Church as the Savior from sin and the Victor over all evil. In practical effect, all agree that the Church has divine, human, and all-too-human aspects; that her unity, holiness, catholicity and apostolicity are seen even by her own members "through a glass darkly," by faith and not by clear ocular evidence; that she is a communion of saints in the making, not yet perfected in holiness and often needing forgiveness.

The paradox just discussed is closely connected with a further and final element in the Church's nature: her positive and negative relationship to the Kingdom of God. *All Christians are agreed that the Church is positively related to the Kingdom of God, but they are also agreed that she is not the Kingdom of God without qualification.* It was in view of establishing his Kingdom among men that God called Abraham, gave the Law to Moses, sent the prophets, became incarnate in Christ, and poured out the Holy Spirit on the Church. The gift of the Spirit to the Church is in itself an *arrhabon*, a down payment on the Kingdom, a partial realization of it in the present— "realized eschatology." Some churches emphasize this present realization of the Kingdom in the Church more than others; and therefore they are suspected of completely identifying the Church with the Kingdom. Yet the clear consensus which Robert Nelson finds among Protestant theologians, "that the Church is not the completed Kingdom of God," [13] most cer-

---

[13] *Op. cit.*, p. 234.

tainly includes Catholics, too. From New Testament times until now, the Church has always been what Rudolf Bultmann calls an "eschatological community," preaching the coming of God's Kingdom partly by what she *is and does*, partly by what she *hopes and prays*. T. O. Wedel, commenting on the Pauline comparison of the Church to a "colony of heaven," puts the positive and negative sides of the Church's relation to the Kingdom very clearly:

> Is not this the life of the people of God in the World? We, too, are only a colony of heaven. We are not the homeland of the final Communion of Saints, but even less are we the alien world which has not been won to membership in the Family of Christ. Our life is tension, and even compromise. To escape from tension is a denial of our mission in historic existence. . . . For the Church of God is the Kingdom after Pentecost but before the Final Judgment. It is the Kingdom *in history*.[14]

We may summarize the entire doctrine of the nature of the Church, as commonly agreed among Christians, in the words of the pre-Lund Commission on the Nature of the Church:

> Every communion holds that the Church is not a human contrivance, but God's gift for the salvation of the world; that the saving acts of God in Christ brought it into being, that it persists in continuity in history by the presence and power of the Holy Spirit. Every communion likewise believes that the Church has a vocation to worship God in His holiness and to proclaim the Gospel to every creature, and that she is equipped by God with the various gifts of the Spirit for the building up of the Body of Christ. And every communion believes that the Church is composed of forgiven sinners, yet through faith already partakes in the eternal life of the Kingdom of God. These agreements cover the Church's origin, the mystery

---

[14] *Op. cit.*, pp. 76, 77. Some, of course, might wish to include *more than the Church* in the historic Kingdom.

of the Church's present being, and the Church's goal. They ascribe to the Church both a divine and a human element, both a possession and an anticipation of the age to come. They imply an insistence upon the holiness of the Church without any identification of this with a mere human moralism; an insistence upon the visibility of the Church without obscuring the tension between the Church as it is now, and the Church as it is destined to become.[15]

We submit that this sequence of agreements constitutes a real, intelligible body of doctrine concerning the Church's nature, and no mere Least Common Denominator abstracted from a series of incompatible denominational positions. The "given unity" of Christians is at this point something more than a vague feeling of kinship through common loyalty to one Head; it is capable of clear and convincing articulation—a firm basis for the common evangelistic appeals in which Christians of different communions have quite often (and quite logically) found it possible to join. There is even one sentence in this statement of agreements, concerning the Church's "vocation" and spiritual "gifts," which lays a foundation for the much more difficult and disputed doctrine of the ministry, the sacraments, and the other "means of grace" committed to the Church, to which we now turn. Here it must be confessed that the difficulties increase at every step, and the agreements sometimes diminish to the point of bare abstraction; but this does not mean that *no* ecumenical statement is possible.

We may start with the common Christian conviction that *the Church is charged by its Lord with a mission and a ministry in which all Church members are included and each is commissioned to some unique form of service.* One of the implications of the common faith that the Church is the "Body" of Christ, is

[15] Faith and Order Commission Papers No. 7, *The Church*, p. 13.

that she is the chief instrumentality through which he continues his saving work. The Head lays upon all his members a world-wide mission of stupendous scope, to "preach the gospel to every creature," and promises to stay with them forever as an inward source of grace. (Mk. 16:15; Mt. 28:20.) This Great Commission gives to the Church a double function: *within* the fellowship, to maintain vital connection between Head and members by the preaching of the Word, by sacramental rites, by worship, education, pastoral guidance, or by other "means of grace"; *beyond* the fellowship, to spread the knowledge of the Gospel to all mankind, apply its principles to every aspect of life and so promote the growth of God's Kingdom on earth. All Christians without exception are called to be ministers of Christ's grace to one another, and ambassadors of his mission of mercy to the world. While there are serious differences about what constitutes a "valid" ministry for the preaching of the Word, and the administering of the Sacraments, there is agreement about the twofold mission of the Church just described, and the vocation of every Christian to participate in it. The Edinburgh Report expressed this agreement in these terms:

It is the function of the Church to glorify God in its life and worship, to proclaim the Gospel to every creature, and to build up in the fellowship and life of the Spirit all believing people, of every race and nation. To this end God bestows His grace in the Church on its members through His Word and Sacraments, and in the abiding presence of the Holy Spirit, [p. 6]

I. The ministry was instituted by Jesus Christ, the Head of the Church, "for the perfecting of the Saints. . . . the upbuilding of the Body of Christ," and is a gift of God to the Church in the service of the Word and Sacraments.

II. This ministry does not exclude but presupposes the "royal priesthood" to which all Christians are called as the redeemed of Jesus Christ.[16] [pp. 23, 24]

"There are diversities of gifts, but the same spirit" (I Cor. 12:4). In the recognized forms of ministry, and in the preferred means of Grace, there are wide diversities among Christian churches; yet this in itself is not necessarily a cause of dissension or confusion. The Apostle Paul's ideal picture of the Body of Christ makes room for wide diversities of operation among its various organs, which enrich and do not divide the organism. All churches have recognized special ministries of various sorts— from the Quaker custom of inviting certain "weighty Friends" to sit on the "facing-bench" to the Catholic recognition of monastic orders of many types—but this need not oppose one form of ministry to another, nor deny the universal ministry of all Christians. All churches have differing preferences concerning the means of grace—catechetical or "child-centered" teaching, liturgical or "free" worship, emphasis on the Word or on the Sacraments—but such varieties need not split the Church. The Edinburgh Report says: "In the non-sacramental worship of God the Father, Son and Holy Spirit, we are agreed that there is little remaining occasion for maintaining the existing divisions between our churches, and much common ground already exists

---

[16] Report of the Second World Conference on Faith and Order, Edinburgh, 1937 (Faith and Order Pamphlet No. 90). Cf. the Tambaram (Madras) Report on "The World Mission of the Church," 1938. Bell, *op. cit.*, includes these reports.

It is important for Protestants to understand that the doctrine of the "priesthood of all believers," properly interpreted, is not a peculiar badge of non-Catholics, but a universal Christian idea. The Edinburgh statement just quoted was accepted by Anglo-Catholics and Eastern Orthodox. At the Madras meeting of the International Missionary Council, the year after Edinburgh, it was an Anglican bishop who insisted that the training of an indigenous ministry in a new field had to begin with the universal ministry, and only gradually develop a specially trained and ordained ministry.

for further unity." [17] Even in sacramental worship, there is much unity in the midst of division. All agree that it is the one indivisible "grace of the Lord Jesus Christ" that operates in the preached Word and the acted sacraments, and that "God's gracious action is not limited by His sacraments." [18] Most churches celebrate the two central sacraments of initiation into Christ's body (Baptism) and deepening fellowship with Christ and all his members (Holy Communion). The Society of Friends and the Salvation Army, which have no formal sacraments at all, have informal ways of performing the same two essential functions.

Thus in the midst of the divisions of Christendom, there is common agreement that the Church is constituted by the living presence of Christ—*ubi Christus, ibi ecclesia*—and kept vital by various means of grace which maintain close connection between Christ and his members, when actively appropriated by those members. The "marks of the true Church" insisted upon by the Protestant Reformers—"where the Word is rightly preached and the Sacraments rightly administered"—are not a divisive criterion. Like the classical Catholic "notes" of Unity, Holiness, Catholicity, Apostolicity, they express an ideal of the Church which is common to all, though variously interpreted.

SECTION 3. UNRESOLVED ISSUES CONCERNING THE CHURCH AND THE MEANS OF GRACE

A. *The Main Issues and the "Deepest Difference"*

Unresolved issues concerning the Church and the Means of Grace are so numerous and various that they have to be grouped

[17] *Ibid.*, p. 32.          [18] *Ibid.*, pp. 6, 19.

and classified in order to be discussed. Infant and adult baptism, open and close communion, apostolic succession, possibility of salvation outside the Church, possibility of more than one organized Church, necessity of having bishops, necessity of having seven sacraments, foot-washing as an additional rite, unimportance or basic importance of correct church government and church discipline—to discuss such issues one by one would lead to hopeless complexity and confusion. At all these points, churches have actually already broken off fellowship with other churches; but the meaning of each such conflict remains obscure until it is related to a larger issue of which it is only a local manifestation. C. T. Craig in his book on *The One Church* very helpfully grouped the "major disagreements which keep us apart" into three main issues: "(1) What are the limits of this one Church which alone can exist? (2) Is there a prescribed form for the Church? (3) How is continuity to be maintained within this Church?"[19] Detailed disagreements over such matters as Baptism and the Lord's Supper are simply nondiscussible until these larger issues are confronted.

On the first main issue, there are three chief positions: First, "We are the Church." The Roman Catholic Church and the Eastern Orthodox Church explicitly claim to *be* the only true Church, beyond whose limits there may be some *Christians* (unofficial Catholics, bound to the true Church by valid baptism or by God's uncovenanted mercies) but there is no real Church. Some strongly separatistic Protestant churches implicitly take up a similar position, as do some Anglicans (less consistently) with their theory that the one true Church exists in

[19] Abingdon Press, 1951, p. 27. Cf. the analysis of issues in Faith and Order Commission Papers No. 7, *The Church*, on which Craig's analysis is partly based. The following three paragraphs are a free summary and commentary on the three chapters in which Craig develops these issues.

several "branches," certainly including an Anglican and an Orthodox branch and perhaps a Roman and a Swedish Lutheran —but no nonepiscopal branches. A second position, possible by way of reaction against the first, is that the Church "does not exist" at all, since unity is an essential mark of the Church. The Ecumenical Movement by its very existence rejects this position, since it constantly rediscovers a "given unity" in the midst of all divisions. (On the first position, the Ecumenical Movement refuses to take sides, since it has found fruitful conversation possible between those who do and do not claim to be the one true Church.) It would be fair to say, however, that the great majority of churches participating in the Ecumenical Movement assume something like Craig's third position, that "the one Church is found wherever God's saving grace in Christ is operative." This implies that the true Church is "by schisms rent asunder, by heresies perplexed," without ceasing to exist.

On the second main issue, concerning the *form* of the Church, some denominations hold that there is one "obligatory form" of Church order, episcopal or presbyterial or congregational, usually on the ground that this form is prescribed in the New Testament; while other denominations hold that Church orders are "determined by historical development and therefore subject to change under new circumstances." It is evident that churches of the second type can easily unite with churches of a different polity, whereas those of the first type cannot. The First World Conference on Faith and Order, at Lausanne in 1927, came to an important decision on this issue: that in view of the presence of "the episcopate, the council of presbyters, and the congregation of the faithful" in the early Church, and their persistence in great Christian communions today, "these several elements must all, under conditions which require further study, have an appropriate place in the order of life of a reunited Church." [20] The Church of South India has followed this recipe precisely, and adopted a polity in which all these elements are present.

On the third issue, concerning *continuity* in the Church, the great touchstone is the doctrine of Apostolic Succession. Catholics, Orthodox and Anglicans who hold this doctrine maintain that saving grace and authority to teach and govern were imparted by Christ to his Apostles, and by them to their successors, the first bishops; so that any breach of continuity in the line of episcopal succession destroys the validity of ministerial ordination and the validity of all sacraments performed under such ordination. Protestants have generally laid less stress on the need of unbroken "horizontal" continuity, and more stress on what has been called "vertical" continuity in the Church's life. So long as the right preaching of the Word continues to connect the Church with her living Lord, and the free Spirit continues to guide and inspire her, she is truly connected with her Head, despite "horizontal" breaks in geographic or historical continuity. Here is the place where the Amsterdam Assembly saw the "deepest difference" between its member churches, a difference systematically dividing the more "catholic" from the more "protestant" communions, along a line running from Orthodoxy and Anglo-Catholicism at one end, through Lutheranism and Calvinism in the middle, to the "free churches" at the opposite end.

The Amsterdam Assembly was probably correct in calling attention to a single main division running through all the particular divisions among the Christian churches, and in relating this main division somehow to the "catholic-protestant" issue. The Edinburgh Conference of 1937 had already been led to "the conclusion that behind all particular statements of the problem

---

[20] *Faith and Order: Proceedings of the World Conference, Lausanne,* p. 469.

of corporate union lie deeply divergent conceptions of the Church." [21] Plainly, it would shed light on all specific differences if this main difference could be clarified. Edinburgh was sure that it was not just "the antithesis of episcopal and non-episcopal orders," but the basic contrast between (1) "authoritarian" churches, insisting upon "a divine givenness in the Scriptures, in orders, in creeds, in worship," and (2) "personal" churches, insisting upon "the individual experience of Divine grace, as the ruling principle of the 'gathered' Church." [22] Amsterdam was obviously pointing to the same contrast when it distinguished "catholic" churches, insisting upon "the visible continuity of the Church" from "protestant" churches, emphasizing "the initiative of the Word of God and the response of faith." [23] Subsequent discussion has tended to be critical of the terms "catholic" and "protestant," even when spelled with small letters, because no proposed definition of this basic contrast satisfied either the Catholics or the Protestants. Whether or not the terms are abandoned in later ecumenical conventions, they have led to some very fruitful exchanges between Roman Catholics, High and Low Anglicans, free churchmen and other Protestants, which have helped to define the catholic-protestant issue, and tend to prove that the main differences concerning the doctrine of the Church and the Means of Grace are indeed on what we have been calling the "catholic-protestant front," rather than on the "conservative-liberal front." One of the most impressive contributions to this exchange of views has been made by Father W. H. Van de Pol, a Dutch Roman Catholic who was formerly a Protestant. In his book, *The Christian Dilemma* (*Catholic Church-Reformation*), we find in the midst of definitely appreciative comments on the

[21] Edinburgh Report, p. 34.      [22] *Ibid.*, pp. 34, 35.
[23] Amsterdam Report, I, p. 15.

deep agreements of the two faiths, and the nonessential "psychological obstacles" that keep them apart, a striking definition of their "cardinal differences," which is that "according to the Catholic Church revelation is a reality-revelation, according to the Reformation it is a word-revelation." [24] The author is at pains to explain that the Protestant like the Catholic meets "reality" through the Word, and a reality which has entered history in Christ; but the Catholic adds to this, above all in the mystery of the Eucharist, a conviction of Christ's continued incarnation in the Church, which makes Him

a full and true reality in the present. . . . Holy Church is His Body; the authoritative preaching of the Church is still infallibly His preaching; the species of Bread and Wine in the Holy Eucharist are the outward signs of His real Body and Blood and of His Real Presence. . . . the "being in Christ" is not only a relation by faith, but signifies a real supernatural, regenerating union with Him and in Him, with all the saints; the Communion of Saints is a real supernatural union whereby we are, here on earth, already in a certain sense in heaven.[25]

Father Van de Pol's distinction, careful and sympathetic as his personal knowledge of Protestantism permits him to be, suffers from a difficulty that affects all other attempts to distinguish Catholicism from Protestantism: the distinction is not clear-cut, for it is only a difference of degree or of emphasis. *All* Christians, compared with Jews, believe that salvation is real *now*, and not just a promised future event. Quakers as well as Catholics believe in the Real Presence of Christ in their meetings; Evangelical Protestants would gladly agree with Van de Pol that "the 'being in Christ' is not only a relation of faith, but . . . a real, supernatural union." The moderator of the International

[24] Philosophical Library, 1952, p. 133.
[25] *Ibid.*, p. 136.

Congregational Council recently described a Congregational Church as a "door open into heaven."[26]

When the Anglo-Catholics responded to four questions from Archbishop Fisher concerning the catholic-protestant contrast, with a Report called *Catholicity*,[27] the British Free Churchmen answered it in a Report called *The Catholicity of Protestantism*.[28] The major criticism they offer is one that constantly recurs in such discussions: that in defining the antithesis between Catholicism and Protestantism, the Anglo-Catholics make Protestants say what they actually do not say. To define the distinction between orthodox and liberal Protestants, the Anglo-Catholics put conceptions in opposite columns—"God transcendent" versus "God immanent"—which are in fact both held in various degrees by both parties;[29] so in order to distinguish Protestantism from Catholicism, they rob all Protestants of the "Catholicity" which for this group of Free Churchmen is of the essence of their faith.

A vigorous attempt to define and resolve the catholic-protestant issue from the Protestant side has been made by Emil Brunner in his book on *The Misunderstanding of the Church*. Commenting on Calvin's double definition of the Church as, on the one hand, the invisible "number of the elect," known only to God, and on the other hand, the visible institution which is an "external help to faith" (*externum subsidium fidei*) through its teachings and ministries, he finds that both definitions fail to describe the New Testament *Ecclesia* as it really was. It was no mere roll call of individuals whose names were in the invisible Book of Life; it was a visible *koinonia* or community. On the

[26] *The Christian World* (London, June 25, 1953) prints Dr. Douglas Horton's moderator's address, "A Church Free and Catholic."
[27] Dacre Press, 1947.          [28] Lutterworth Press, 1950.
[29] *Ibid.*, p. 38.

other hand, it was not a formal institution, serving as the "external means" to some worthy end; its fellowship in Christ and the Spirit was warmly intimate, and an end in itself. "The Catholics are right: the *Ecclesia* of the New Testament is no *externum subsidium fidei*, but the real thing. The Protestants are right: What the Church has become as a matter of historical fact is not the real thing, but something which may very fittingly be understood as a "means to an end." [30]

How did the New Testament *Ecclesia* become the churches as we know them today? "The Christian community," says Brunner, "is the great miracle of history, and history is the proof that the gates of hell shall not prevail against it." [31] The Christian churches are the external "shell" in which this "precious kernel" has been preserved. From the struggle with Gnosticism to the recent struggle with Hitlerism, the official churches have often proved a powerful *externum subsidium* to the Christian *Ecclesia*; but when they are identified with the *Ecclesia* (to which alone the promise of eternal durability was given), they become its worst enemies. "Not the hostility of the unbelieving world, but clerical parsonic ecclesiasticism has ever been the greatest enemy of the Christian message and of the brotherhood rooted in Christ." [32] A line of development connecting the New Testament *Ecclesia* with the modern Roman Church by way of the Early and Eastern Church may appear (as Catholic theory says) simply "to realize the implicit promise of Christian beginnings"; but in spite of unbroken continuity and legal apostolic succession, it is actually (according to Brunner) a line of progressive apostasy. Institutionalism grows as the Spirit declines. *Sacramentalism* marks the apostasy that divides the Eastern

---

[30] Westminster Press, 1952, p. 10.
[31] *Ibid.*, p. 116.     [32] *Ibid.*, p. 117.

Church from the New Testament as early as Ignatius of Antioch; *canon law* marks the apostasy that divides the Roman Catholic from the Eastern Church, and turns it into an almost purely institutional and organizational affair.

The Protestant Reformation represents the still abortive effort of the Christian movement to recover the New Testament fellowship—an attempt in which the Western Church has been shattered into a multitude of sects. The Ecumenical Movement is right in its aspiration to recover the *unity* of the broken Body of Christ; but if it tries to do so by merging the existing church institutions in one great institution, it will repeat the error of Rome and miss its mark completely. The real *Ecclesia* is not an institution at all, but a free fellowship serving God and men as prompted by the Spirit of Christ. The Y.M.C.A. and the "non-church movement" in Japan[33] may come closer to the real *Ecclesia* than any ecclesiastical institution. An age "when men are hungering and thirsting after fellowship as never before"[34] senses this, and persists in preferring the less formal expressions of Christianity to its more stately institutional expressions—unless indeed it seeks refuge in Christian collectivism for the same reason that it does in the totalitarian state.

Brunner's trenchant analysis certainly pierces deep into the causes of catholic-protestant tension, as well as into the causes of sectarian divisions within Protestantism—each sect aspiring to "imitate the New Testament *koinonia*," but failing to escape the influence of its particular institutional environment. Yet it seems doubtful whether Brunner has fully defined, much less resolved, the catholic-protestant issue. In spite of his irenic beginning, and occasional appreciative remarks about Catholicism, he has come out (like Karl Barth in his later period) at an extreme Free

[33] *Ibid.*, p. 111, 131.      [34] *Ibid.*, p. 105.

Church position from which it is hard to see truth or value in any Church institution, Catholic or Protestant. Even Free Churchmen have criticized this position. Principal H. Cunliffe-Jones, reviewing Brunner's book in the *Congregational Quarterly*, finds its position "quite incredible," because "a fellowship completely devoid of all elements of institutional life is not a historic entity at all." [35] It may not be fair to summarize Brunner's position in such sweeping anti-institutional terms, but he himself has described Catholicism in too purely institutional terms. After all, the Pope himself has defined the Church as Christ's "mystical Body," and it is outside of this divine-human *fellowship*, not outside of the Catholic Church as an *institution*, that there is "no salvation" in the eyes of Rome.[36] It is the main purpose of Pius XII's Encyclical of 1943, *Mystici Corporis Christi*, not to maintain a purely or even predominantly institutional view of the Church, but to reject two extreme views with equal firmness: one that defines the Church as "a human institution with a certain body of doctrine and external rites," and one that defines it as a "sort of society formed and maintained by love," devoid of all "judicial" or "social" features such as a "perfect society," that is to perpetuate the redemptive work of Christ, must possess.[37]

It will not do, then, to draw the "catholic-protestant" line between the Church as "institution" and the Church as "fellowship," any more than it will do to draw it between "reality-revelation" and "word-revelation," with Father Van de Pol.

[35] Vol. XXXI (April, 1953), p. 179.

[36] DeWolf, in his *Theology of the Living Church*, pp. 323, 327, from a perspective similar to Brunner's, attributes to Rome a denial that there are members of the Body of Christ outside the institutional bounds of the Roman Catholic Church. But Father Leonard Feeney, in the "Boston College Case," was reprimanded and finally excommunicated for teaching just this. Congar, *Divided Christendom*, pp. 222-24, states the commoner view.

[37] Encyc. *Mystici Corporis Christi* (Bonne Presse Edition), p. 35, section on "The Juridical Church and the Church of Love."

The fact is, that the differences between the Catholic and Protestant Churches are not reducible to any one clean-cut difference of general principle—at least, none so far proposed. Every proposed definition of that "deepest difference" between Christians discovered at Amsterdam, finds Catholics and Protestants affirming *both* sides of the alleged disjunction, with somewhat differing emphasis. Both are concerned to keep "vertical," mystical continuity with the living Lord and Spirit, *and* to keep "horizontal," historical continuity with Jesus of Nazareth, and with the "saints, apostles, prophets, martyrs" who have carried the Christian movement through the centuries.[38] Both value "word-revelation" *and* "reality-revelation"; both cherish the Christian fellowship *and* certain institutional forms which help to preserve and extend it.

Theologically, this impossibility of defining the difference in general terms is baffling and disappointing; practically, it is encouraging. If Catholicism and Protestantism do not differ absolutely in principle, but only in emphasis, there is hope of their ultimate reconciliation. Meanwhile, we must acknowledge that there are particular differences concerning the Church and the Means of Grace which flatly prevent organic union between more catholic and more protestant churches at the present date. A church which believes itself to be the One True Church can never unite with another church except by destroying it and absorbing its members. A church which believes that unbroken "apostolic succession" is necessary to guarantee the validity of ministerial ordination can never unite with any nonepiscopal

---

[38] In one of the sections at the Lund Conference, the Anglican secretary defined Free Church Protestantism as wholly unconcerned with historic "succession" of any sort. A Congregationalist and a Quaker at once protested. It finally appeared that all those present—even if they rejected "apostolic succession"—believed that each Christian generation has an "apostolic function" to transmit the Christian message and movement to the next generation.

church without reordaining its whole ministry. A church which holds that the bread and wine of the Eucharist are literally turned into the broken body and shed blood of Christ, in such a sense that they must be reverently reserved as sacred objects, when the sacrament is over, can never have "altar fellowship" with a church that holds a less realistic view. (Indeed, it cannot regard other "altars" as real altars at all.) A church which holds that the local congregation is literally and absolutely "autonomous" cannot unite—except for momentary acts of local co-operation —with any other body whatsoever.

While such particular points of difference hold the Christian churches apart, a *complete* doctrine of the Church and the Means of Grace cannot be stated in ecumenical terms. In order to state the whole doctrine of the Church, one must either revert to denominational bias, or—the expedient here to be adopted— group churches in types or families, each with its characteristic insistences and emphases. For our purposes, it will be sufficient to consider three main types or families: the Catholic, the classic Protestant, and the free-church Protestant. In Europe, the most difficult ecumenical issues arise on the boundary between the Catholic and the classic Protestant families of churches—a boundary which runs straight through the middle of the Church of England. In America, the hottest discussions arise on the boundary between the classic Protestant and free-church families, with Methodism instead of Anglicanism in a mediating position between them. At Amsterdam, American free-church-men insisted on a threefold division of the main types of church-manship, when a twofold division would have satisfied the Europeans. It is one of the many merits of Bishop Angus Dun's Hoover Lectures, *Prospecting for a United Church*, that they are based on a threefold analysis of Church types, and so really face the American situation squarely. We shall follow Dun's order, while citing freely from other sources.

## B. *The Catholic Idea*

The Catholic idea of the Church, according to Dun, is that "the Church is the great society, with its essential institutions, established on the earth by God to bring men into right relations with himself and with one another under him."[39] Roman Catholic definitions of the Church lay special stress on its societal, institutional character, while at the same time (as we have seen) implying its "mystical" character. So, for example, Cardinal Bellarmine's definition: "A body of men united together by the profession of the same Christian Faith, and by participation in the same sacraments, under the governance of lawful pastors, more especially the Roman Pontiff, the sole vicar of Christ on earth."[40] All expositions of the Roman Catholic doctrine of the Church single out these three great "powers," vested by Christ in the divine-human Society which continues his prophetic, priestly and kingly work: prophetic power to teach the faith infallibly, priestly power to impart saving grace through sacramental rites, kingly power to rule and discipline the faithful in matters of faith and morals, and ultimately to rule the world. The three powers are finally one, since they are derived from one Lord, but not simply reducible to one another—though theologians have debated which is the most fundamental. The Roman Catholic Church recognizes the validity of the powers of the Eastern Orthodox clergy, despite their long separation from the See of Rome.

---

[39] Dun, *op. cit.*, Harper, 1948, p. 46. A similar threefold analysis runs through Bishop Newbigin's *Household of Faith*, S.C.M. Press, 1953.
[40] Cited in *Cath. Encyc.*, Art. "Church." Cf. *Dict. de Théol. Cath.*, IV, 2110.

As custodian of these three divine powers, given her by Christ, the Catholic Church claims to be irreformable in doctrine, holy and sinless in her essential nature (whatever sins her human members and leaders may be guilty of), and worthy of absolute, unquestioning obedience. She is the holy Mother to whom the faithful look up trustfully, like little children, for all the essential needs of their souls. "Which is to say that the Church in its visible, institutional character—its teachings formulated in dogma, its priesthood and hierarchy of ministers and governors, its rites and ceremonies, its laws—partakes of the quality of God. God's saving presence and saving action among men are mediated through all of these. . . . Priests are failing men, but the priesthood is unblemished. The Church in its ideal character is not under judgment." [41] Father Van de Pol remarks, "Whenever the Catholic hears the Protestant maintain that the Church is guilty and must humble herself and be converted, he feels this is an insult offered to Christ Himself. Though anything may be said against the members of the Church, even against priests, bishops, and popes, one must not touch the Holy Church itself, the Body of Christ, the Mother of the faithful." [42] There are human elements in the Church that are open to criticism and modification —"the science of theology, devotions and customs, Orders and Congregations," and the like.[43] But when the Roman Catholic says "Church," his mind passes beyond these "accidents" to the Pope and the hierarchy defining the unchangeable faith, the real Presence in the Mass, the saints above glistening with heavenly glory, and at their head, Christ Himself and His Blessed Mother.

Among the Means of Grace, the Sacraments have the pre-

---

[41] Dun, *op. cit.*, p. 51.  [42] Van de Pol, *op. cit.*, p. 79.
[43] *Ibid.*, p. 77.

eminence for Catholics. Not that the preaching of the Word is despised, nor discipline, nor prayer, nor even Bible reading in these recent years; but the good Catholic principally attributes his growth in grace to the visible, tangible nutriment he receives through the seven sacraments. "Catholicism is sacramental through and through. Its worship is most characteristically a holy action of the Church. . . . The Church does not talk to people chiefly; it acts upon them or for them. It takes them up into its life."[44] This process begins with the Baptism of the Catholic child and his Confirmation in adolescence; continues through the blessing of his vocation (whether it involves Matrimony or Holy Orders) and through his restoration in Penance as often as he falls into sin; concludes with the solemn act of Extreme Unction at his life's last hour. But more sacred than all the other six is the supreme sacrament of the Mass or Eucharist, which offers him Christ's Body and Blood as his Bread of Life throughout his earthly pilgrimage. Here, in the repeated sacrifice of the "saving Victim" upon the altar, and the receiving of His merits, His grace, and His very self by the communicant, the Catholic system reaches its climax. After Mass, the consecrated wafer is reserved and venerated; Christ is still in it.

The validity of the Sacraments is guaranteed by the Catholic priesthood and hierarchy. "This priesthood is a gift of God to his Church. Its authority comes from above. Its origins are seen in Christ's empowering and commissioning of his apostles as his plenipotentiaries. The Church's bishops are the bearers of the authority and sacramental power in apostolic succession. To be without them is to lack the ministry which God in Christ has given to his Church."[45] This may seem to give the laity a purely

---

[44] Dun, *op. cit.*, p. 52.
[45] *Ibid.*, p. 54.

passive and receptive role in the Church. As a matter of fact, the idea of an active "lay apostolate," which takes the lead in Catholic Action movements, thus performing a function in Christ's Body which no unworldly cleric could so well perform, is a rapidly growing idea in contemporary Catholicism.[46] In the Liturgical Movement, a similar trend is visible, to give the laity a more active part in public worship.[47]

Here as elsewhere, time is modifying the logical antithesis between Catholicism and Protestantism. Yet the dominant emphasis of the whole Catholic system is still upon what is *objectively done* to and for the believer through the clergy in the sacraments, dogmas, laws given to him by the Church, rather than what he subjectively feels, thinks and does. If this emphasis were literally all-controlling, the sacraments would become magic, the dogmas meaningless and the laws tyrannous. Actually, the subjective role of the believer is sufficiently stressed to prevent this awful outcome; but in all Catholicism, including Anglo-Catholicism and Eastern Orthodoxy, the balance is on the other side. All Catholics stress the apostolic authority of the hierarchy, and its commissioning from above, whether or not they accept the primacy of Peter and the Pope; all stress the literal identity of the consecrated Bread and Wine with Christ's Body and Blood, whether or not they accept the scholastic doctrine of transubstantiation; all stress "*the* faith" of the Church rather than the "faith" of the believer, whether or not they accept the infallibility of the Pope as final interpreter of the faith. In all its forms, Catholicism is a complete social system, objectively given, to be obediently and humbly received.

[46] As an expression of the theory behind this development, Cardinal Suhard's pamphlet, "Priests among Men," is very representative.
[47] See Pius XII's Encyclical, *Mediator Dei et Hominum* (1947), in which this movement is at once recognized and regulated.

## C. *The Classic Protestant Idea*

The classic Protestant churches are the Lutheran and the Reformed (Calvinist) churches, the offspring of the German and Swiss Reformations. The problem of Protestant unity in Continental Europe is still mainly one of the relationship of these two groups of churches. From the beginning, they felt deep kinship, which fell just short of full unity. Failing to agree upon the Lord's Supper at the Marburg Colloquy, the Lutheran and Reformed churches were nevertheless so close to each other in most of their teachings that Martin Bucer of Strasbourg never ceased to go back and forth between them in hope of reconciling them. A modern Strasbourg theologian, Henri Strohl, has made a comprehensive survey of the agreements between the Reformers, and found that they extend into every major topic of theology, *including* the Lord's Supper.[48] It is not surprising, then, that organic unions should have been consummated in modern times between Lutheran and Reformed churches in Germany and America, nor that they should frequently find themselves taking common ground in ecumenical discussions with other churches.[49] While there is undoubtedly a resurgence of "strict confessionalism" in both camps since World War II,[50] there is good ground for treating Lutheran and Reformed churches as one type or family of churches, the "classic Protestant," with two main branches eventually destined to be united.

[48] H. Strohl, *La pensée de la réforme* (Neuchâtel, 1951).

[49] In the pre-Lund Commission on the Nature of the Church, the secretary at one time saw so many similarities between the Lutheran and Reformed positions that he asked these groups to hold a joint session to study their agreements and differences. They came back the next day with the news that they had resolved *all* their differences and were ready to make a joint report. A prophetic incident.

[50] See Edmund Schlink's description of the German situation in *The Nature of the Church* (pre-Lund volume), pp. 54-58.

The fundamental Protestant idea is that the Church is not above judgment, inerrant and "self-authenticating" as though she were God himself; she is *the servant of God's Word*, and must perpetually be judged by her degree of conformity to that Word. The Reformers "put into the hands of their members a Book by whose standard even the Church may be weighed and judged. . . . 'the Word had its being before the Church and is the foundation of it'; '*There* may be found the sure and infallible rule whereby may be tried whether the Church doth stagger or err, and whereunto all ecclesiastical doctrines have to be called to account.' " [51] Whereas the Catholic Church is in her essential structure "irreformable," [52] the Protestant slogan is, *"Ecclesia reformata semper reformanda"*—the Church is to be reformed not just once but continually, by constant comparison with God's Word.

There was and is some confusion among Protestants as to how the Bible is related to "God's Word," and how it is to be used as an instrument of judgment and reform in the Church. Luther was less literal than Calvin in his use of the Scripture, and more conservative in his judgments upon the Catholic system—changing only what he considered *contrary* to Scripture, whereas the Swiss Reformers looked askance at anything not clearly commanded in Scripture. In subsequent centuries, some Protestants have identified the Word of God with the verbally inspired text of the Scriptures, while others have preferred to say that the Bible "contains" or "records" the revelation of God's Word.

[51] Dun, *op. cit.*, p. 65.
[52] Father Yves Congar, the leading Roman Catholic authority on ecumenical problems, has, to be sure, distinguished between "True and False Reform," but his book with that title has been judged overbold in its demand for structural reforms, and subjected to mild disciplinary action (first edition not to be reprinted, and a corrected new edition to be prepared).

Robert Nelson points out that a very considerable consensus has been reached on this topic in contemporary Protestant theology, stimulated by Karl Barth's "theology of the Word." The *primary* meaning of "God's Word" is Christ himself, the living Word; the *secondary* meaning is the Bible, which testifies uniquely to Christ; the *tertiary* meaning is preaching, which applies this testimony to the condition of each generation, under the guidance of the Holy Spirit.[53] Leaving aside the third meaning for the moment, it is important to note that Protestants and Catholics were able to agree at Edinburgh (1937) in granting the priority of the Word over the Church in the *first* sense, while acknowledging that the Church (which existed prior to the New Testament) has always given the Scriptures a unique place of authority in its life:

A testimony in *words* is by divine ordering provided for the revelation uttered by the *Word*. This testimony is given in Holy Scripture, which thus affords the primary norm for the Church's teaching, worship and life.[54]

The classic Protestant churches give to the preaching of the Word a primacy among the means of grace corresponding to the primacy of the Bible as norm of the Church's life. Luther and Calvin agreed on two great tests of the true Church—"where the Word is rightly preached and the Sacraments rightly administered." It is significant that they mentioned the Word first, and often interpreted the sacraments in St. Augustine's sense, as *verbum visibile*, the "word made visible." Bishop Dun does not exaggerate the main emphasis in classic Protestantism:

[53] Nelson, *op. cit.*, Chap. 4, "The Word of God As the Church's Authority."
[54] Edinburgh Report, III, ii.

When we enter a church which stands clearly within the inheritance of classical Protestantism, the Bible is in the center—often the book itself. The Word is read, not in any ancient unknown tongue, not as a ritual, but read to be understood. And the Word is interpreted in the words of a living and contemporary man, who because he is presumed to know the Word and to know the people may be expected to make the Word live for the people. Song and prayer are the people's answer to the Word.[55]

Having reduced the sacraments to the two primary ones, Baptism and the Lord's Supper, it was tragic that the Lutheran and Reformed Churches should have fallen out over one of these. Even in Reformation times, Calvin amended Zwingli's too purely commemorative and symbolic interpretation of the Lord's Supper, so as to acknowledge Christ's Real Spiritual Presence in this sacrament. How near to agreement some modern Lutheran and Calvinist theologians have come, may be judged from Aulén's irenic treatment of this moot question. Rejecting the scholastic arguments by which Lutheran and Calvinist theologians formerly defended their positions—"ubiquity" of the glorified body of Christ *vs.* its simple location at God's right hand in heaven—Aulén interprets Luther's real motive to have been, *not* to maintain a "realistic" view of the sacrament in a sense utterly opposed to the "symbolic" view, which would have implied a "sensuous mechanization of sacramental grace," but only to maintain the ancient Church's view of "the sacramental act as at the same time, a symbolic act and a deed of God,"[56] against Zwingli's purely symbolic and subjective view. In some such position as this, there is reason to hope that modern Lutherans and Calvinists may come to agree. There is even (as Aulén

[55] Dun, *op. cit.,* p. 67.
[56] Aulén, *Faith of the Christian Church,* p. 378.

hints) a tradition in ancient *Catholic* thought—common in the East, and in the West through St. Augustine—which would concur in the same consensus. As "the sacrament of prevenient love" and "the sacrament of suffering and victorious love" (Aulén's phrases) Baptism and the Lord's Supper preach the Word of the Gospel in concentrated form, and convey the saving grace of the Gospel as only acts and deeds can do.

We noted that Catholicism does not exclude the personal and subjective side of religion, but lays primary emphasis on something objectively given to the believer through the Church. In classic Protestantism, the doctrine of "justification by faith" contains the same two elements, but in inverse proportion. The gracious act of God in Christ, forgiving our sins, is the objective ground of our salvation; but since this is already done once for all, and not repeated in the Mass, the main emphasis now falls on the individual Christian's act of faith (trust) which seizes hold of this assurance, feels gratitude and penitence commensurate with the grace received, and finally brings forth fruit "meet for repentance," but does not consider these "good works" as any essential part of the process of salvation. Catholics, too, agree that God's grace (in the sacraments, for example) cannot be rightly received when man opposes to its working the obstacle of unbelief; but the doctrines of faith and repentance, justification and sanctification received a development in the classic Protestant creeds (e.g., the Augsburg and Westminster Confessions) such as they never had undergone in Catholic thought—except in St. Augustine, whom both Luther and Calvin regarded as the greatest of the Fathers. The Christian's own faith and prayer came now to be numbered among the decisive means of grace, alongside of the Word, the sacraments and—as the Calvinists would add—Church discipline.

## D. *The "Free Church" Idea*

The term "free church" is not easy to define. It does not simply mean "self-supporting" as against "state-supported"; though this group of churches traditionally favors the separation of Church and State. It does not mean "liberal" in theology —which certainly would not apply to those ardent free churchmen, the Southern Baptists—though this group traditionally opposes the use of written, man-made creeds as tests of faith. It does not mean "free from all overhead control"; though congregationalism is the prevailing form of church polity among free churchmen, and the wide prevalence of this polity in the United States makes this a typically free-church country. (As Edmund Burke noted long ago, American Christianity represents "the dissidence of dissent, the Protestantism of the Protestant religion," which fled from Europe in search of greater independence than classical Protestantism allowed.) The variety to which freedom from the State, from written creeds, and from ecclesiastical oversight has led, makes it hard to find a single, simple definition that will cover all such bodies as the Quakers, the Brethren, the Mennonites, the Baptists, the Congregationalists, the Disciples, the Methodists, and their numerous relatives in this large but scattered family of churches. Nevertheless, it is possible to state a view of the Church and the Means of Grace which runs widely through the free churches, and constitutes their deepest bond of kinship.

We have already encountered this view in Emil Brunner, who shows marked free-church leanings, though a member and leader of a classic Protestant body, the Swiss National Church (Reformed, Calvinistic). It is the view that in its real, New Testament form, the Church is "a fellowship, not an institution."

Not just a man-made fellowship, of course, but what Bishop Dun describes as "The Fellowship of the Spirit or the Community of the Perfect Way"—a fellowship whose freedom is under Christ and in the Spirit, whose ways are emphatically *not* the ways of the world. No one belongs to such a fellowship by being baptized in infancy and getting his name on the parish roll; only converted believers really belong.

The faithful, the converted, the saints, the Spirit-led, draw together; they delight to congregate. In the meeting of the faithful they can share their testimony, their spontaneous prayers, their concern. They find this fellowship in the face-to-face meeting of the congregation within the meetinghouse. There in the congregation of the faithful the Church is really found. For where Christ is, there is the Church, and the focus of his presence in the Spirit is now found, certainly not in the sacrament of the altar, not even so vividly in the Word, but in the gathered fellowship itself.[57]

Here a new conception of the means of grace is clearly implied, less objective and more personal than the classic Protestant conception. The *Word* is still important, but not as formally taught and preached in catechisms, creeds and sermons. The Word of power is what rises in the believer's heart, through the inspiration of the Spirit, as he reads, listens or meditates; what he testifies to his brethren in the prayer meeting; what he witnesses to the world in words and deeds that bring the Gospel into everyday life. "The sacraments become ordinances or disappear. Baptism . . . is primarily an act of faithful obedience on the part of the believer, wherein he testifies publicly to his faith and to the gift of the new life he has already received. The Lord's Supper is primarily an act of fellowship in which the congregation of believers testifies together in act to that com-

[57] Dun, *op. cit.*, p. 81.

munion in the Spirit which is already theirs." [58] What need of sacraments to communicate grace objectively to the members of such a Church, when the Fellowship itself is already full of grace? What need of an apostolic ministry, divinely commissioned and sent to lead such a Church, when the Fellowship is already Spirit-led, and every member is ordained to some special form of ministry by the divine Leader of all?

The radical implications of this third conception of the Church and the Means of Grace are best seen in the Society of Friends, which in most of its branches has no formal sacraments and no ordained ministry, but only a Spirit-led fellowship which more than makes up for the lack of all else. In free churches which have grown to a large size through the evangelistic outthrust characteristic of this group, the pattern is not so clear and simple. As they become nation-wide and world-wide fellowships, the intimacy, purity and power of the local fellowship tend to diminish, and the institutional framework tends to grow by leaps and bounds. Thus they gradually approximate to the classic Protestant type, and can logically unite or co-operate with churches of that type. This can be seen in the development of the Baptist and Congregational churches, but perhaps most clearly in that of the Methodist churches, whose original societies and class meetings perfectly expressed the free-church idea, but whose powerful world-wide organization has given them a more and more central place in negotiations between the free churches and the classic Protestant churches.

The existence of the Anglican and Methodist churches is proof that the three ideas of the Church we have been describing are not utterly incompatible with one another, since at least two of them can be held in the same body without splitting it. The

[58] *Ibid.*, p. 85.

241

Church of South India includes all three ideas in one body—
without fully satisfying the Anglo-Catholics as yet. Because of
this remarkable practical achievement, great weight attaches to
the views of one of its bishops, Lesslie Newbigin, on *The Reunion of the Church.* In his opinion, and that of many others, the
one great question to be settled, if institutional reunion of the
Christian churches is to be achieved, is "whether non-episcopal
ministries are real ministries." [59] It should be pointed out, however, that the ideal of *reunion in one universal church organization* is not an ideal universally held by Christian churches, even
within the Ecumenical Movement. The Catholic churches hold
it; the free churches generally reject it. Many Christians, of
many different communions, would find their imaginations
kindled by the figure of speech in which Bishop Dun expresses
his own ideal of the united church of the future: not a disem-
bodied "spiritual unity," nor on the other hand one all-embracing
structure, with one great overarching "roof," but *a series of
structures of diverse architecture, tied together with colon-
nades.*[60]

While we await the outcome of continued ecumenical conversation among churches of these different families and types,
we must not ignore the relationship between these discussions
and the deep hunger of the modern man for fellowship and
inspiration (Section 1). A Church whose segments are not only
divided but hostile to one another, mocks all his hopes and long-
ings and contradicts the Gospel itself. The Roman Catholic
Church attracts him by its world-wide scope, its powerful organization, its calm certainty, but repels him by its authoritarian

[59] P. 186.
[60] Dun, *op. cit.,* p. 109: "a central structure with other structures gathered
around it, all forming a unity and with the internal channels of communication
wide open."

discipline. The classic Protestant churches attract him by their clear and emphatic Biblical doctrine, but do not often convince him that their doctrine is practicable in modern life. The free-church type of fellowship has a great missionary appeal, as the Laymen's Report on *Re-Thinking Missions* [61] rightly pointed out; but if all the world's churches had been reduced to free, undogmatic fellowships, like those proposed by this Report, they would not have met the test of Hitlerism as they did. None of the three main types of Christian Church by itself gives Christ an adequate Body, or the modern man an adequate answer to his quest of fellowship and inspiration. Only an organization, or a series of co-operating organizations, which made room for the values in all three types, would answer to those requirements. We must pray that the growth and influence of the Ecumenical Movement may steadily make more room in all of our churches for the values represented by our divided brethren.

[61] Edited by William Ernest Hocking, Harper, 1932, Chap. V.

# VIII

## *THE CHRISTIAN HOPE*

### SECTION 1. THE UNIVERSAL NEED FOR HOPE

Hope of some kind is implied or stated in every livable faith, every consistent philosophy of life, whether Christian or non-Christian. When the Apostles' and Nicene Creeds conclude their third and last sections with an affirmation of hope in "the life everlasting" or "the life of the world to come," they do what every creed must do, in one way or another. The triangle of faith inevitably terminates in an act of hope—or else loses its capacity to guide and inspire. Without any goal of hope and of endeavor, life becomes confused and melancholy. Animals, led by instinct, may live without conscious goals; but human beings, who "look before and after, and pine for what is not," cannot live without them. A human life without hope is a meaningless, unendurable treadmill. Emil Brunner describes the human situation very graphically and very truly when he says,

What oxygen is for the lungs, such is hope for the meaning of human life. Take oxygen away and death occurs through suffocation, take hope away and humanity is constricted through lack of breath; despair supervenes, spelling the paralysis of intellectual and spiritual powers by a feeling of the senselessness and purposelessness of existence. . . . No work of man, not even the plainest, can be successfully performed without hope. The farmer sows, the mother nurses and rears her child, the responsible statesman guides and achieves—on the foundations of hope. . . . No spade, no needle, no chisel, no saw would be taken in hand if it were not permissible to believe that something good would come out of it. The picture of the future sets in motion the powers of the present, but can have this effect only through hope.[1]

It is true, as Brunner admits, that hope in the "limited sense," hope "closely bound up with the present," is more obviously necessary to human life than hope in the ultimate sense, "gathering up the whole of life and the life of all far-reaching aims," as in the great religions. Yet he is surely right in his contention that when ultimate hope dies, it becomes harder and harder for immediate hope to survive. How can "partial aims" be maintained "when the sense of the totality, the universal, is lost," or "tiny personal hopes" be "nourished in an atmosphere of general hopelessness"? [2]

The logic of hope to which Brunner here appeals is very similar to the logic of monotheism, which was analyzed in the introductory sections of Chapters II and III. There is a slow but inexorable push toward an *"ultimate Object of trust and devotion"*, which makes men tire quickly of little finite idols—unless they can be seen as partial revelations of a more ultimate Deity. There is a similar push toward an *"ultimate Goal of hope and endeavor,"* which makes men tire of little plans and projects, unless they can be seen to serve some Chief End or Highest Good. Every decision between possible lines of action is made in terms of some implied scale of values; and every scale of values involves some Chief End or Highest Good that determines what values

---

[1] Brunner, *Eternal Hope* (Westminster Press, 1954), pp. 7, 12.
[2] *Ibid.*, pp. 12, 13.

are primary, what secondary. Without some at least tentative notion of an ultimate end or goal, life bogs down in indecision, and no longer makes sense. Why eat and sleep, why get up in the morning, if it is all to no known end? The question, "To what end?" is thus an inescapable human question, which men answer implicitly by their decisions and indecisions, even when they reject all formal definitions of their final destiny.

The thesis here maintained, that hope is a universal and inescapable human necessity, may seem to be in contradiction to John Baillie's thesis, in *The Belief in Progress* (1951), that hope is a purely Western phenomenon, derived from the Hebrew-Christian tradition, and all religions not derived from this tradition are religions without hope. It is true, and very important, that in ancient Greco-Roman and modern Oriental religions, the cyclic view of time reigns supreme, and history is not believed capable of reaching any significant goal. As Ecclesiastes, the least Hebraic book in the Bible, puts it, "What has been is what shall be . . . . and there is nothing new under the sun" (1:9, Moffatt). This fact leads Baillie to deny that hope exists at all, where this ancient cyclic view prevails. From the point of view we have adopted, it seems preferable to say that hope, in the broad sense of a goal of aspiration or a notion of the Highest Good, appears in the Greek and Hindu and Chinese traditions as it appears in every livable faith whatsoever; but, so to speak, in these non-Hebraic faiths the indicator of hope points vertically upward toward eternity, toward a way of escape from the revolving wheel of time and change, instead of pointing horizontally ahead toward some great Consummation of History.

The acuteness of the crisis of hope in the second half of the twentieth century springs from the fact that the cyclic view of nature and history has been as decisively shattered in the modern

Orient by influences from the West as it was shattered in the ancient Greco-Roman world by the advent of Christianity, while at the same time the West has become disillusioned about the great hope which has guided and inspired it throughout the modern era—a hope ultimately derived from Hebrew-Christian sources but finally estranged from its sources by a long process of secularization—the hope of Progress.

The "revolution" in Asia (incipient also in Africa and other regions remote from the West) of which all political commentators now talk, is partly due to nontheological factors such as the penetration of Western technology and the revolt against Western imperialism; but one of its profoundest and most powerful causes is the awakening of new temporal hopes (inspired by contact with the West) in vast populations hitherto chained to the conviction that nature and history move forever in unalterable cycles. Where this conviction prevails, it is folly to look forward to a better state of affairs on earth, and wisdom to accept poverty, injustice and all the woes of mortal flesh with passive resignation, looking solely to eternity to heal the wounds of time. Yet today, under Nationalist or under Marxist auspices, millions of people in the "passive" East are actively hoping for a better standard of living and a juster social order than has ever been known before in their countries. Hinduism and Buddhism are warning, not without reason, against the spiritual perils of this Western materialism, and experiencing something of a revival in the act of protest; but once the East has seen how the supposedly unalterable framework of this temporal world can be rendered malleable to human desires, no orthodox revival of eternalism can check the passionate wave of temporal, futuristic hope that is now sweeping over the East.

It is ironical that the very sort of hope that the West has kindled in the East is now turning into despair in the West. In order to understand this situation, we need to comprehend the historical process by which the modern hope of Progress grew out of the traditional Hebrew-Christian hope. John Baillie's book, already cited, gives an excellent brief summary of the process whereby the Christian hope, taking on three extra layers around its core like a growing onion, was transformed into the hope of Progress. (Let us only bear in mind that this process involved *decay at the core* as well as growth at the periphery.)

The founders of the modern age, men like Bacon and Descartes, were indebted to Greco-Roman culture in many ways; but in their hopes for the future they were profoundly Hebraic. They considered themselves good Christians, and they *were* Christians, though in their concern for man's future social welfare, here on earth, they stood in sharp contrast to the *contemptus mundi* and the almost exclusive concern for individual destiny after death which characterized medieval Christianity. In its first form, then, the hope of Progress represented only a shift of emphasis within the Christian hope, from its eternal to its temporal and from its individual to its social aspects.

When three successive layers grew around this core, the core was more and more overlaid yet never wholly rotted away.

(1) The Abbé de St. Pierre, in whom the first extra growth culminated, of course regarded himself as a Christian; but he combined two new hopes with the classic Christian hope of a providential guidance of social history, with unprecedented results: his friend Fontenelle's hope for the continued, irreversible progress of *knowledge*, and the hope already suggested by Bacon and Descartes, that every advance in knowledge will bring a concomitant advance in moral and social well-being. (2) German idealistic philosophy, from Lessing to Hegel, made a further and

independent contribution to the hope of Progress: the conviction that human history is indwelt by the divine Reason, whose dialectical *development* has already brought about a steady, inevitable increase of meaning and value from age to age. (3) This idealistic concept of development is to be sharply distinguished from the naturalistic concept of *evolution* (though the same word is often used to cover both) but it is still the Christian values that are believed to increase steadily and inevitably, whether because of divine self-unfolding or because of natural law. Hegel considered that he had provided a secure metaphysical basis for Christian faith and ethics; while Herbert Spencer claimed to be more Christian than the Anglican clergy, most of whom believed a "strong hand" would always be necessary in human society, whereas he believed that when evolution had done its perfect work, men would do good to one another pleasurably without compulsion or obligation, and egoistic competition would be completely replaced by altruistic.[3]

There is in each of the three superadded forms of the doctrine of Progress a highly questionable assumption, disputed by some members of the very school of thought which brought it forth. Rousseau was co-patron of the French Revolution along with the Encyclopedists who picked up St. Pierre's dream of a synchronous advance of knowledge and social well-being; but he saw in the growing complexity of civilization which advancing knowledge brings a bane instead of a blessing. Schopenhauer shared Hegel's idealistic conception of the world, based on Kant's critical philosophy, but he refused to jump from this to Hegel's

---

[3] Cf. his remark at the end of the amazing Chapter XIV in his *Data of Ethics*: "But though men who profess Christianity and practice Paganism can feel no sympathy with such a view, there are some, classed as antagonists to the current creed, who may not think it absurd to believe that a rationalized version of its ethical principles will eventually be acted upon."

optimism about the social process, and reverted to Oriental pessimism. George Santayana viewed the world as naturalistically as Herbert Spencer; but the spectacle of nature and history inspired in him not the faintest glimmer of hope. No ancient sage, no medieval ascetic ever forsook the world more scornfully than Santayana forsook the existent world, to dwell in that world of pure essences wherein alone he found satisfaction. These, however, were protesting voices crying in the wilderness, so long as the steady expansion of Western civilization continued. Questionable inferences seemed reasonable, and even the most wildly Utopian expectations of Herbert Spencer seemed plausible, so long as this encouraging trend of events went on. Since World War I, these optimistic inferences and expectations have lost their plausibility, so that today the hope of steady, automatic improvement which was so common at the turn of the century seems simply incredible.

The frustration of the hope of Progress in its Utopian, turn-of-the-century form has not left the West utterly hopeless. Most Westerners have simply scaled their hopes down to believable proportions. If progress through science is evidently not *automatic*, it may yet be *possible*, through shrewd prevision of dangers implicit in each advance and determined effort to overcome them; if it is not steadily "marching on," the tide of battle may yet be turned by heroic courage and sacrifice. If it is hard to hold the liberal democratic hope of an age of justice and prosperity, entered peacefully by mutual agreement and free trade, perhaps a tough, aggressive Nationalism may establish a "co-prosperity sphere," or violent class war liquidate all obstacles to the "classless society."

In general, this is an age when roseate, idealistic hopes are dying, and only the hardier species of hope can flourish, East or

West. In the West, however, disillusionment has attacked Nationalism, Communism, and other hopes of the "hard-bitten" type, as it has become evident through grim experience that these hopes, too, may lead to the very opposite of what they promise. Therefore, many in the West have abandoned all hope of the future, experimented like Nietzsche with the ancient Oriental idea of "eternal recurrence," and in some instances, finding that two thousand years of Hebrew-Christian tutelage have made it impossible to revert to Stoic or Buddhist indifference toward futuristic hope, have become literally hopeless. The most heroic and typical example of this "hope of the hopeless" is the atheistic "existentialism" of Jean-Paul Sartre and his colleagues, who declare that "each of us is completely alone, surrounded only by meaninglessness, so that if his life is to have any meaning or any value, he must create such meaning and value for himself, not forgetting that death swiftly puts an end to all." [4]

In such a time, Christian hope is required to show that it is the trustworthy answer to this world-wide need of a "hope that maketh not ashamed": not letting men down in disillusionment or pitching them into despair, like many current hopes, but enabling them to face the dangers, disappointments and hardships of this age with unbroken courage, and leading them toward a Promised Land that is no desert mirage, but actually attainable. It is therefore a most significant event when the World Council of Churches dedicates its Second Assembly (Evanston, 1954) to the main theme, "Christ—the Hope of the World," and leads up to the Assembly by stimulating an unprecedented amount of discussion on this theme in its member churches at the local and regional levels, as well as at the world level. Perhaps never before

---

[4] *The Christian Hope and the Task of the Church* (Pre-Evanston volume, Harper, 1954), Concluding Report of Advisory Commission. Section III, B, v.

has such concerted and continuous attention been given to this concluding theme of Christian theology. Let us see what sort of consensus has emerged from this ecumenical conversation, both before and at the Evanston Assembly.

### SECTION 2. GOD'S KINGDOM AS THE UNIVERSAL CHRISTIAN HOPE

It may be well at the the start to set aside certain verbal misunderstandings that may arise from the way the Evanston theme is phrased. To say that the Christian hope is "Christ" is in no way opposed to other familiar ways of expressing the same hope: the hope of "salvation," or "glory," or "life everlasting," or the "Kingdom of God." All these expressions point to a partly accomplished, partly unfinished drama of destiny which began when man was created in God's image, and will not reach its denouement till the curtain is rung down on the last act of human history, but whose crucial turning point came with the coming of Jesus the Christ to establish God's Kingdom on earth—hence the appropriateness of naming it "Christ—the hope of the World."

In spite of the soundness and simplicity of the Evanston phrasing, we shall take as our framework for expressing the Evanston consensus not "Christ" but "God's Kingdom"—partly because this is a more traditional designation for the last topic in Christian theology, and partly because it lends itself more easily to the task of combining the apparently diverse facets of Christian hope in one comprehensive unity. The "Kingdom of God" is in fact, as John Bright has recently shown in his book by that title, the great unifying theme that binds the whole Bible into a connected story, with a beginning, middle and end: a drama of "sal-vation," that leads from creation through sin and grace to the "glory" of "life everlasting"; a divine-human drama whose chief character is the divine-human "Christ." By taking the Kingdom of God as the universal Christian answer to the universal human need of hope, we are thus not by-passing but including the Evanston answer, and other equally authentic answers.

Let us summarize the Biblical witness to the hope of God's Kingdom, before comparing this witness with the Evanston consensus. It begins, as we have noted, with the Creation of the World, in which God manifests his kingly sovereignty over all the universe, but delegates to man a limited "dominion" over nature. Instead of accepting this high honor humbly, and thus at once recognizing God's kingship "on earth as it is in heaven," man grasps at more power and a more complete independence than is given to any creature, and so sets up his sovereignty in opposition to God's.

God does not surrender his rule over man; he brings deterrent punishment to bear upon man's self-will, and offers great promises to those who are willing to enter into Covenant with him to be God's People. These promises are partly fulfilled in the Promised Land of Canaan; but the crisis of the Babylonian Exile, interpreted by the great writing prophets, compels a clean distinction to be made between the Kingdom of David and Solomon and God's Kingdom, or again between the whole People of Israel and that "saving remnant" of them who are God's People in a higher sense. The Old Testament ends, therefore, with a strong sense of unfulfilled yearning for a Kingdom of God yet to come, and a heaven-sent Messiah who is to usher it in. It is true that every Israelite who keeps Torah faithfully thereby "takes the yoke of the Kingdom" upon him, and in a sense enters into it; but the great emphasis is upon a future Day of the Lord which will decisively show forth God's rule in judgment and mercy.

By contrast, the New Testament is pervaded by a sense of hope fulfilled, or as Dodd puts it, "realized eschatology." Jesus announces that the "time is fulfilled," and God's Kingdom on earth is "at hand"; and he invites all who will to enter it by faith and repentance (Mark 1:15). In the healing of diseases and the conversion of sinners, he sees the rival sovereignty of "sin, death, and the devil" beginning to break up, and he sees the usurping Prince of this World, Satan, "as lightning fall from heaven" (Luke 10:18). The powers of darkness strike back at Jesus, and do him to death; but he rises victorious over death, and "sheds forth" the Holy Spirit upon his new community, the Church (Acts 2:33) as a sign that the Messianic Age, the new aeon of God's sovereign kingship among men, has actually begun. Whenever the Spirit falls upon a person, and he is reborn into a new life, "justified" and "sanctified" through penitent faith in God's cleansing and transforming grace, he may be said to enter into salvation and step over into the Kingdom of God, here and now.

Yet though all this "realized eschatology" is in the New Testament, the contrast between the hope of Israel and the hope of Christians is not so absolute as it would seem to be if we stopped at this point. Alongside the sense of hope fulfilled is a powerful sense of burning, forward-looking expectation, on which Albert Schweitzer and others have based an interpretation of the early Christian hope quite opposite to Dodd's. It is now practically beyond controversy that both these strains of thought lie side by side in the New Testament, and neither can be eliminated without doing violence to the text.

Not to prejudge the difficult questions of interpretation to which we must return, we may point out at once that whether we consider the personal, the social or the cosmic aspects of the Kingdom of God in the New Testament, in every case it means something yet to come, as well as something presently realized. (1) The Christian person has "passed from death unto life" and become a son of God (I John 3:2, 14) when he responds to Christ's love with a similar love directed toward his brothers; but his salvation remains incomplete until Christ shall appear at the end of the age to make his redeemed people altogether "like him" (I John 3:2). Even Christian perfectionists, who often seem to place the goal of personal holiness within the present life, finally distinguish between the perfection attainable here by the pilgrim en route, and that which he shall attain when he reaches his heavenly goal, and knows as he is known. (2) Of the Christian Church and the Christian person alike, it may be said that they are *already in God's Kingdom, but still hoping for the Kingdom's coming.* We have seen in Chapter VII that the Church is distinguishable from the Kingdom, though a sign and beginning of its advent. God rules in the Church, and also rules in the world outside the Church, through the admittedly imperfect instrument of Roman law and government (Rom. 13:1–10)—but a new order of divine rule is at hand which shall be to Rome's rule as "day" is to "night" (Rom. 13:11–14). (3) Finally, we may add that Christ's victory over the "power of darkness" that has enslaved God's good creation is an incomplete victory. Though already "delivered" from this power and "translated into the Kingdom of his dear Son" (Col. 1:13), we still live in a creation that "groaneth and travaileth in pain together until now" (Rom. 8:22). According to the book of Revelation (Chaps. 20, 21) it will be only at the end of history, after a thou-

sand-year rule of the saints has been rudely interrupted by a renewed outburst of Satanic rebellion, that death and hell will
finally be put down, and God's eternal reign will be established
over "a new heaven and a new earth" (Rev. 21:1).

The apocalyptic symbolism here is hard to interpret; but Biblical theology is pretty solidly agreed on the main point we are
stressing: that the Kingdom of God in the New Testament is at
once present and future. In the pre-Evanston preparations, Biblical scholars agreed upon this point unanimously [5] while the first
two reports of the Advisory Commission on the Main Theme
were still wavering between an emphasis upon Christ's future
coming and an emphasis upon his abiding presence. What happened in the course of the three long meetings of the Advisory
Commission was that *a balance between these two emphases,*
plainly to be found in the New Testament, *gradually com-
mended itself to the members* (and to their many correspondents
in all parts of the world) *as a tenable and necessary position for
modern Christians to take.*[6] While the first meeting had to ad-
journ with differences still unresolved between those who saw
"the meaning of all human achievement . . . in terms of the
eschatological future" (the "coming Christ") and those who
found its meaning in "the present activity of God in history"
(the "present Christ" [7]), the third and definitive meeting concluded that the extreme consequences of these two opposing
emphases were "temptations" to be firmly resisted by all Christians:

[5] See the *Ecumenical Review,* IV (July, 1952), pp. 419–42, for the report of
the Zetten conference on "The Meaning of Hope in the Bible" (April, 1952).
[6] See Van Dusen's article, "The Issues of Christian Hope" (*Christian Century,* Nov. 25, 1953), for a lively summary of the three meetings of the Commission.
[7] First Report of the Advisory Commission, p. 8, Note.

## D. *Having and Hoping*

16    The fact that our hope is thus anchored in a Kingdom that both has come and is coming gives to the life of every believer a double orientation. He both has eternal life and he hopes for it. He has the first fruits, and therefore he longs for the full harvest. . . .

17    In this situation the believer faces a double temptation. On the one hand he is tempted to despair of this world and to fix his whole attention on that which is to come. . . . In his longing for the heavenly city he may pass by his fellow-man, fallen among thieves, and leave him by the roadside.

18    On the other hand the believer is tempted in the opposite way. . . . He may so confine his attention to the possibilities of this present world as to forget that the whole world lies under judgment. He may confuse man's achievements with God's Kingdom and so lose the only true standard of judgment upon human deeds.[8]

How important and how new is the consensus embodied in these words will perhaps only be realized by those who have followed the Ecumenical Movement for some years past. In the early years of the movement, when there was sharp rivalry between the practical emphasis of Life and Work and the theological emphasis of Faith and Order, there were frequent clashes between "American activists" and "Continental quietists," based upon radically different conceptions of the Kingdom of God. At the Oxford Life and Work Conference (1937), the Americans expressed their derisive rejection of Continental quietism in a parody of W. P. Merrill's well-known hymn, "Rise Up, O Men of God":

---

[8] See the Report, pp. 7–8, as reprinted in *The Christian Hope and the Task of the Church*.

Sit down, O men of God!
 His Kingdom He will bring
 Wherever it may please His will—
 *You* cannot do a thing! [9]

At the Tambaram (Madras) Conference, the following year, a group of Continentals were so profoundly dissatisfied with the American activism which seemed to them to govern the theology of the conference that they drew up a minority report, stressing the impossibility of realizing God's Kingdom by human action within history. While World War II did much to abate the utopian optimism of most Americans, and to deepen the sense of social responsibility in most Continentals, traces of the old antagonism were still noticeable at the Amsterdam Assembly in 1948. An American delegate, after listening to Karl Barth's keynote address, said that if Barth were logical, he would not bait the hook or wet the line when he went fishing; he would expect the Lord to make the fish jump straight into his frying pan without further action on his part! Such clashes are always partly due to misunderstanding of what the other party really means, but it takes time to perceive this, and it is a great achievement when both parties agree to reject as "temptations" the extreme views which at first they attributed to each other.

Can this careful, hard-won balance between "having and hoping," between the Kingdom that is and is to be, between the Christ who is with us and who is yet to come, which runs all through the Report of the Advisory Commission, be fairly described as "the Evanston consensus"? Was there not much dissent from it at the Evanston Assembly? Well, Bishop Newbigin was surely correct in his claim that the report he was introducing

[9] These lines were quoted (by permission) in my *Contemporary Continental Theology*, p. xvi.

for group discussion and general debate already embodied "a consensus of thought much wider than the Commission itself," since "individuals and groups in many churches and in all parts of the world . . . not less than four hundred" [10] in all, had contributed to the third draft by sending in their criticisms of the first and second. A year before Evanston, it was already clear at Geneva that while many parts of the Second Report were attacked, there was a great mass of concurring opinion in favor of Chapter II, where the balance between present and future was stated in terms that foreshadowed the Third Report.

In the second place, much of the dissent at Evanston was based upon misunderstandings which further discussion would have cleared up. In one of the discussion groups, a long debate over "the pilgrim people of God" ended in almost complete agreement among the debaters. Given time, the delegates might have got over their initial impression that the two opening speeches on the Main Theme, by Professors Schlink and Calhoun, were in flat contradiction to each other, and could only be reconciled by dishonest verbal gymnastics. The two protagonists, having had more time to comprehend each other, announced to the press that they differed only in emphasis. Perhaps they might have accepted Dr. Joseph Sittler's statement that they and most of the delegates walked on the same two legs, though some favored one leg more than the other; "but nobody wanted to chop off the leg he had been favoring and hop off on the one he felt safer on." [11] Third, it may be said that where dissent was most definite and deep-seated, it came from opposite and canceling positions, and co-existed even then with a vast amount of agree-

[10] Evanston Papers No. 20A.
[11] See his column in the Chicago *Sun-Times* during the period of the Assembly.

ment. An illustration of this would be the attitude of the Eastern Orthodox delegation, on the one hand, which contended in a public "Declaration" [12] that the Report insufficiently recognized that "the Church of Christ, as the realized Kingdom of God lies beyond Judgment", and the attitude of Reinhold Niebuhr, on the other hand, who declared it to be "heresy" to "exalt the Church as the 'extension of the Incarnation,' as essentially divine, as the mediator of God's judgment, rather than as the locus in human history where the judgments of God can be heard." [13] These really opposite attitudes go back to the real opposition between Catholic and Protestant ideas of the Church, which has already been analyzed in Chapter VII; but a careful reading of the documents would show that Niebuhr and the Orthodox agreed at least 95 per cent from opposite angles, with the Report of the Advisory Commission. Under these circumstances, the "general agreement" with the Report, expressed by the Orthodox delegates in their Declaration, was no meaningless gesture, but an event of high significance.[14]

The Evanston Assembly's "Final Statement on the Report of the Advisory Commission on the Main Theme" was to be sure far from conveying an unqualified recommendation of it to the churches. No item of Assembly business gave rise to such heated debate as this Statement, which had to be drastically amended before adoption. In the final draft, two major criticisms of the Report are mentioned, besides many minor dissatisfactions:

[12] Evanston Paper No. 97A.
[13] Evanston Paper No. 15A.
[14] Much the same comment might be made on the Roman Catholic discussion of the Second Report, printed in *Istina*, where although it is felt that the Church and the divine grace she dispenses are given too small a place in "the economy of Christian hope," there is large agreement with the Report. See the April-June, 1954, number of this periodical, printed in Boulogne-sur-Seine. English offprints are available.

## The Christian Hope

"We find that the note of joyous affirmation and radiant expectancy which should mark a statement of the Christian hope does not sufficiently illuminate the Report. We find certain important omissions: the present work of the Holy Spirit in the Church and the world; specific reference to 'signs of hope'; adequate treatment of the theme of creation and cosmic redemption." In spite of these and other defects, it is said that the Report "exhibits a substantial ecumenical consensus" and "indicates the direction in which we must all move." [15]

Is it consistent to come to this conclusion while offering these criticisms? I think so. With respect to the first criticism I submit that it would be quite unrealistic to expect the Church to exhibit today the kind of joy and radiance that characterized her hopes at the dawn of this century, before these hopes met with such grave disillusionments. The Church today must thread a narrow, rocky path, winding between two quagmires—false hope and hopelessness—and the mood appropriate to her present plight is not one of radiant joy, but one of calm courage, such as sustained her Lord through Gethsemane and Calvary. Thus the Report actually shows the way "we must all move" today and tomorrow. As for the second criticism, it must be admitted that the Report does not attain such perfect balance between all the multiple aspects of the Christian hope as it attains between its "present" and "future" aspects: that the Kingdom of God is at once personal, social and cosmic; that it is at once a divine gift and a human task; that it is at once temporal and eternal. These multiple aspects of the Christian hope are all recognized to some extent in Christian teaching in every age. There is a tacit consensus here parallel to the consensus on the attributes of God, described in Chapter III; but this consensus is frequently

[15] Evanston Paper No. 114AF.

261

disturbed when excessive emphasis on the aspect of hope most relevant to the times obscures some other equally essential aspect.[16] Theology must keep constantly on the alert to maintain the balance of Christian thought in this domain, while responding to new contingencies as they arise. Yet I believe that the Evanston consensus on the Christian Hope has laid a solid and durable foundation, better than we had before, for these necessary future adjustments.

### SECTION 3. UNRESOLVED ISSUES CONCERNING THE CHRISTIAN HOPE

It is normal and not surprising that there should be some issues unresolved among Christians on a matter so profoundly mysterious as the ultimate destiny of all creation. Indeed it may be argued that the man who has no doubts or uncertainties about the date, the manner, the extent and the means of God's final victory over all God-opposing powers proves by his attitude of cocksureness that he is an unfit guide to follow in this high domain. Yes, God has revealed his secret counsels here also; but there is much agreement among present-day theologians that revelation's bearing upon the mystery of the beginning and end of all things is less direct than its bearing upon other themes. At the center of history, God has revealed his nature and his will for us in an actual historical figure, Jesus the Christ. From this center light streams back toward the beginning and on toward the end; faith proclaims that Jesus is both the Incarnate Word

[16] Richard Niebuhr in *The Kingdom of God in America* (Willett, Clark, 1937) has shown how three successive emphases on different aspects of the Kingdom have produced something like three different Gospels in different periods of American history.

whereby the cosmic process was started, and the Coming Judge whereby it will be brought to its appointed end. Yet when we try to imagine in detail how things were in the beginning, or shall be in the end, thought and language break down, and we are forced to think and speak in consciously symbolic terms, or else fall into a literalism which implies that we know more than a human being *can* know. Unresolved issues abound here on every hand; but we select for discussion three, which are urgent in our time: the Second Coming, Eternal Punishment, and the hope of Progress.

## A. *The Second Coming of Christ*

This is one of the issues repeatedly encountered in the preparation for Evanston, but never fully threshed out. A certain ambiguity in the language used continued to confuse the delegates. What precisely did Professor Schlink mean by saying that Christ is "the end of the world with its joy and sorrow," [17] and we must "watch" and "wait" for his coming? What an American Fundamentalist or Adventist would mean? Evidently not, although Adventist visitors took a lively interest in the proceedings, and claimed the regular churches were taking "Bible prophecy" seriously for the first time in many years.[18] Within the Evanston consensus, it was no longer dubious whether belief in the present Kingdom required one to deny the future Kingdom; but the problem remained, how to imagine the coming of the future Kingdom.

The handling of this problem in Professor DeWolf's *Theology of the Living Church* [19] suggests very clearly the nature of

[17] See the *Christian Century*, Aug. 25, 1954; pp. 1002, 1003, where these passages in Schlink's speech are reprinted.
[18] I had conversations with two Seventh-day Adventist visitors at Evanston.
[19] Chap. 36, "How the Kingdom Is to Come."

the issue that was left unresolved at Evanston. With his usual careful handling of Biblical sources, DeWolf observes that there are "two strains of teaching within the Gospels themselves . . . inextricably bound up with a large common body of narrative and teaching." In one of these, which he calls the *apocalyptic* strain, "the Kingdom is expected to be inaugurated by a cataclysmic intervention . . . the Christ, who has departed into heaven, will return in overwhelming, glorious power to establish the divine rule." In the other or *immanental* strain of teaching, the Kingdom is "already present," and "is to grow and spread until it becomes great"; hence the disciples are "not to watch for signs as sinful people do, for the Kingdom is not to come with visible signs." [20] DeWolf feels that it is impossible to attribute both of these views to Jesus without implying that he was "confused," and "taught flatly contrary views." [21] The only other alternative is to "subordinate" one strain of thought to the other. Schweitzer's subordination of the immanental to the apocalyptic is examined and rejected; the conclusion is [22] that the immanental view is Jesus' authentic teaching, and the apocalyptic view is the result of a "bias" in the oral report of the teaching, substituting "the spectacular for the spiritual."

While this "immanental" solution of the problem does not deny that the Kingdom is at once present and future, nor imply that it is "limited to this world," it does reject the whole idea of the Second Coming of Christ—except as the descent of the Spirit was in a sense a Second Coming—and it requires a major operation upon our closely interwoven New Testament sources, almost analogous to the (usually fatal) attempt to separate Siamese twins by surgery. One cannot help asking whether these two strains of teaching in the New Testament are "flatly con-

[20] *Ibid.*, pp. 306, 307.     [21] *Ibid.*, 308.     [22] *Ibid.*, pp. 313–16.

trary" as DeWolf supposes. The answer hinges on the purely literalistic interpretation he gives [23] of the apocalyptic hope: "a unilateral act of sheer power" or "external rule through astronomical displays." Could it be that a less literal interpretation of apocalyptic imagery would lead to a view of Christ's Second Coming less crassly coercive, less flatly opposed to the strategy and method of his First Coming and the promptings of his present Spirit? This is exactly the effect of two books written in preparation for the Evanston Assembly: *The Christian Hope and the Second Coming*, by Paul Minear, and *The Christian Hope: The Presence and the Parousia*, by J. E. Fison. The first is a Biblical study; the second is both Biblical and theological.

On the basis of word studies ranging through the whole Bible, Professor Minear makes clear that Christ's future "coming," "revelation" or "appearance" (*parousia*) is no isolated event, but "the disclosure of a reality that has been secretly at work." The "clouds," the "earthquakes," the warning "trumpets" which announce this coming are not to be interpreted with bald literalism, but are like those which accompany all great "revelations, revolutions, and restorations," all crucial meetings of God and man, throughout Bible history. There were clouds on Mt. Sinai, in the Tent of Meeting, on the Mount of Transfiguration; how else can the eternal God meet mortal man but in clouds that half-veil, half-reveal? Christ's *First Advent* caught men unprepared, "like a thief in the night," and forced them to "flee away naked." The "Keys of Hades" that shall open heaven's gates are the same keys that have already opened the door to new life for all believers. The "dragon" shall finally be slain by that same sword of the Word which mortally wounded him in the battle of Calvary. In short, "the promise of Christ's coming was no

[23] *Ibid.*, pp. 312, 316.

cleverly devised myth of future possibilities; it was the testimony of a community that had witnessed already the majesty and power of God's beloved Son." Detach future from present, read the future with unimaginative literalism, and this hope becomes a matter of controversy—but real New Testament hope is then bisected and destroyed.[24]

What Minear argues on Biblical grounds—that the Second Coming of Christ hangs together with the First—Fison argues on other grounds as well. He cannot believe that Millennial and Adventist sects would have continued to rise up as they constantly do, if their heresy had no truth in it. As he sees it, the "great church" has provoked these sects to rebellion by half-unconsciously altering the original Gospel and suppressing an essential element in it. Instead of the New Testament hope for "a future both on earth and in heaven," it has presented "a future solely in heaven"; instead of the hope for "a present and future Kingdom of God upon earth" it has offered "a present church on earth and a distinctly remote future Kingdom in heaven." [25]

To be sure, there was error on both sides. Even within the New Testament and still more later on, there appeared a tendency which had to be resisted to materialize and mechanize the picture of the parousia and the millennium. The "fire" which is part of the prophetic experience of meeting with God in Daniel's vision of Judgment Day (Dan. 7:9 ff.) becomes a world conflagration in II Peter 3:10–12, and in the medieval *Dies irae*.[26] The "imminence" of Christ's return, which was originally an imminence in "lover's time"—an eager "*Maranatha*" addressed by the Church to the Bridegroom with whom she yearns to be

---

[24] This paragraph is a brief summary of Part II, Chaps. VI–XV, which deals with "The Return of Christ."

[25] Fison, *op. cit.*, p. 40.  [26] *Ibid.*, p. 110.

reunited—is transmuted into "clock time," giving rise to painful disillusionment when Christ fails to return on the calculated date. "It was to deal with this exceedingly dangerous perversion of the eschatological gospel that St. John wrote his corrective, which he couched in the form of a gospel." [27]

Neither in John nor in Paul, however, is the mystical, spiritualizing tendency to rejoice in Christ's presence any full substitute for the hope of his parousia. Mysticism and eschatology belong together; if they get out of balance they pervert the Christian hope. "At the mystical level of love the end can be both expected imminently at any minute and also experienced or realized immanently as having already occurred. The parousia can be the presence too; indeed it must be, or else the future reality is merely phantasy." [28] Since New Testament scholarship has shown the unity of New Testament eschatology, and the key position of parousia in the whole, it is time for the churches to give it an equally central position in their teaching. This might pave the way for reconciliation between the churches and the sects—including that strange Russian sectarianism which welcomed Marx because it was already envisioning a millennium forgotten by the church.[29]

It is interesting to note that both Minear and Fison implicitly grant Professor DeWolf's argument that a conception of Christ's Second Coming flatly opposed to all he taught and was in his First Coming, or out of harmony with the promptings of his present Spirit, is intolerable. Fison further grants that there are some strands in New Testament teaching which are really out of harmony with Christ's Word and Spirit, and must therefore be

[27] *Ibid.*, p. 179.     [28] *Ibid.*, p. 197.
[29] On Marxism and Russian apocalyptic sectarianism, see *ibid.*, pp. 27–28, 229, 256.

'subordinated" as DeWolf proposes. What both men contend, however, is that the Second Coming in its more authentic forms completes the same course of events which began with Jesus and continues under his Spirit's guidance—events which have always been full of surprising, dramatic turns, and will be, to and at the End.

## B. *Eternal Punishment* vs. *Universal Salvation*

Our second issue is closely connected with the first, since the Second Coming of Christ, in all versions of it, is a coming in final Judgment, on which the final destiny of every person and the final outcome of the whole world process depend. On the façade of many medieval cathedrals, one sees Christ sitting in judgment, and on his right and left hand the multitudes of the saved and the damned, the sheep and the goats, led by angels or demons to their eternal reward or punishment. Christian thought has always been distressed and divided over this double outcome of the divine-human drama. The first systematic theologian, Origen, held out the possibility that (if not in this present world-aeon, then in some later one) God's grace might triumph completely over every opposition, and Satan himself might be reconciled to God. St. Augustine contended just as strongly for the opposite view, that the final consummation would consist in the complete separation of those two cities whose intermingling constitutes world history. While the Church has preferred St. Augustine's view to Origen's, she has done so with a troubled mind. Distinguished contemporary theologians, including the father of neo-orthodoxy, Karl Barth, have taken positions leaning to Origen's side, and been attacked for it by their colleagues. The issue remains unresolved.

The problem will clearly appear if we apply the same principle to this doctrine that we have just been applying to the Second Coming: the character of the final Judgment must not be inconsistent with Christ's historical character, nor with his present character as revealed by his Spirit. Both universalism and eternal punishment get into difficulties when this test is tried. The God revealed in Jesus, the God we trust today, is everlastingly a God of judgment, and no outcome of the cosmic drama is acceptable that denies his eternal opposition to evil. On the other hand, he is a God of redemptive love, who delights not in the death of the sinner, and offers reconciliation to all. Moreover, he is the Ruler of the world, and so long as any of his creatures remain in outer darkness, refusing to accept the forgiveness he offers, his rule to that extent is defeated; yet if he uses his omnipotence to *compel* these rebellious children to come in, his Kingdom is no longer a Kingdom of justice and love, but a tyranny against which we ought to rebel. These and other difficulties have been urged with great emotional power by Nicholas Berdyaev in the concluding chapters of his *Destiny of Man*.

The solution offered by Berdyaev—that hell is everlasting but not eternal—is a bold attempt to combine Augustine with Origen, justice with redemptive love, and divine power with human freedom, by means of a somewhat speculative theory concerning two kinds of time, good and bad, real and unreal. Those who find this philosophy of time unconvincing will not be satisfied with the solution. Less speculative, and closer to Christian revelation, is the solution offered by Emil Brunner in his *Eternal Hope*. He finds that there is no way of resolving the antinomy between universal salvation and eternal punishment so long as the two pictures stand side by side in "static symmetry," like the balancing pictures of the saved and lost on a medieval cathedral. Whoever has not felt something wrong in such pictures has not begun to think fruitfully upon this problem. From this static, symmetrical viewpoint there proceed two contrary lines of logic: one leading to double predestination and destroying the universality of God's redemptive purpose; the other leading to universal salvation and destroying all fear of divine judgment. But Biblical revelation is fundamentally dynamic and asymmetrical. It calls us all insistently in one direction, toward reconciliation with God, while warning urgently against disregarding the call.

The meaning is not: these *are* the two realities. Rather it is: come forth from perdition into salvation. . . . What then is our conclusion to be—the word concerning judgment and separation, heaven *and* hell, or the message of universal redemption? . . . Our answer is: both voices are the Word of God. But God's Word . . . is a Word of challenge, not of doctrine. . . . Its implication is not: "There are" . . . a theoretical sentence making me a spectator, an observer of a certain state of affairs. . . .

We must listen to the voice that speaks of world judgment as to the voice of God Himself, in order that we may fear Him; we must listen to the voice which speaks of universal redemption as to the voice of God Himself, in order that we may love Him. . . . Hence the criterion of all genuine theology is this—does it lead to the cry "God be merciful to me a sinner!" and beyond it, to the exclamation: "Thanks be to God, who giveth us the victory through Jesus Christ our Lord." [30]

Practically, this somewhat subtle doctrine of the "asymmetrical" and "dynamic" meaning of the Last Judgment amounts to the same thing as a popular rule of thumb often quoted and used by Christian believers: always think of yourself as capable of falling into alienation from God, no matter how firm you feel in the faith; think of your neighbor as capable of eternal blessed-

[30] Brunner, *Eternal Hope*, pp. 180, 183, 184.

ness, no matter how depraved or indifferent he may seem. This does not dispel the perplexities that enshroud our final destiny, but it assumes an attitude that leads toward clearer light.

## C. *The Truth in the Idea of Progress*

Since the extension of the idea of Progress to the East, and its collapse in the West, are the principal causes of the crisis of hope in our time, a few concluding words about the present status of the idea of Progress may be in order. By the idea of Progress we now mean *the improvement of human relations and social conditions through human forethought, invention, and co-operation.* While the original core of the modern idea of Progress was, as we have seen, the Christian hope of a Kingdom of God marching on through history, the distinguishing mark of the modern idea was its stress upon what man can do to "make a better world." This is not necessarily an unchristian notion; Christianity has always taught that man is called to high responsibility, under God, for the cultivation and improvement of God's good earth, and for the upbuilding of a new divine order upon the foundation laid by Christ and his Apostles. The question now is, *What may Christians reasonably hope to accomplish for human betterment, when the Utopian illusions of the early twentieth century have been duly discounted?*

In the period of sudden and deep-going disillusionment that hit Europe in the wake of World War I, several leading Christian thinkers—Dean Inge in England, Barth and Althaus on the Continent [31]—attacked the idea of Progress in such sweeping terms that they practically abandoned all hope for the future,

---

[31] See Dean Inge, *Outspoken Essays*, Second Series, Barth, *Resurrection of the Dead;* and the first edition of Althaus, *Die letzten Dingen.* I have discussed Inge in *Contemporary English Theology*, Barth and Althaus in *Contemporary Continental Theology*.

here on earth, and set their hopes exclusively on things eternal, things above, as though they were pure Platonists or Oriental mystics. So to speak, the indicator of their hopes suddenly snapped from a horizontal to a vertical position, when they encountered what looked like overwhelming obstacles on the horizontal plane of human history. All three men later modified their views to some extent, under a barrage of criticism which made clear that the whole perspective of the Bible is distorted when eternalism displaces futurism as completely as this. Reinhold Niebuhr, who began to attack the idea of Progress about ten years later than Barth,[32] never rejected the hope of temporal improvement so completely, though he constantly warned that evil grows alongside the good, and will continue to do so while history lasts. The upshot of the whole discussion has been that the idea of the Eternal Kingdom of God is now firmly re-established as the final goal of Christian hope (a position from which the feverish futurism of the turn of the century illegitimately displaced it) but it is no longer denied that temporal improvements through consecrated human endeavor are *part* of the Christian hope.

Why the Eternal Kingdom can never be replaced by any temporal goal, and why the sum of consecrated human endeavors can never add up to a complete realization of the Kingdom on earth, has been well explained by Brunner in his *Eternal Hope*. Historically, he notes that the holy experiments of the Pilgrim Fathers, the Quakers, and many others who have founded Christian commonwealths, do not retain their ideal glow and pristine vigor beyond the first generation. The theological reasons for this well-known historical phenomenon are (1) even deeply

---

[32] *Moral Man and Immoral Society* was the heaviest artillery he fired in this attack.

committed Christians are still struggling with the Old Adam;
(2) there is no assurance "that the children of true Christians
will themselves be Christian"; (3) since there is no prospect that
*all* men will ever become even nominal Christians, Christian
ideals cannot be socially embodied without "a kind of Christian
dictatorship" that corrupts them.[33] Moreover, the parables of the
mustardseed and the leaven are balanced both in Scripture and
in experience, by the parable of the wheat and tares. Evil and
good progress side by side in every age, and no harvest until the
Last Judgment will ever finally gather the sifted good wheat
into the barn. At the end of history, the symbol of the Millennium is still balanced and counteracted by the symbol of the
Antichrist.[34] Hence all realization of God's Kingdom within
history is partial and imperfect.

For a positive statement of the hope of future temporal improvement, we may cite Brunner's remark: "We must not give
up hope that by a strengthening of the truly Christian elements,
both in the cultural and in the political life of humanity, much
could be bettered." [35] This is no careless aside; Brunner has
devoted two volumes of Gifford Lectures to the problem of
*Christianity and Civilisation*, with some very positive results.
Or again, we may cite the conclusion of John Baillie's book on
*The Belief in Progress*: that the one clear hope of progress to
which Christians can confidently cling in our difficult age is the
hope of *missionary* progress. This must not be understood either
as promising continuous missionary advance, or as limiting pro-

[33] *Eternal Hope*, pp. 74–76.
[34] *Ibid.*, Chap. 8, "The Negative Promise: Antichrist." Though we have
stressed mainly this negative point in Brunner's argument, *Eternal Hope* must
be recommended as the best-balanced book produced in preparation for
Evanston. *All* facets of the many-sided Christian Hope are balanced here,
whereas the Report of the Advisory Commission balances mainly two.
[35] *Eternal Hope*, p. 76.

gression to the acquisition of individual converts. Kenneth Scott Latourette's *History of the Expansion of Christianity* shows periods of retrogression alternating with periods of advance; one of the most heroic of missionary churches, the Nestorian Church of the East, has been all but wiped out by repeated bloody massacres. But the history of modern missions also shows heartening instances where a truly living church has remolded its whole cultural environment through wise educational, medical, agricultural projects, and above all through the power of lay Christian witness in daily work and civic affairs. If this social dimension in missions is duly recognized, Brunner and Baillie reinforce each other in support of the hope that the "Decline of the West" may not be a fatal decline, as Spengler supposed, but a testing time which may lead to a revitalization of the Church, and so to a new and more extensive influence of Christianity upon world civilization.[36] Automatic and steady progression— No. Complete elimination of evil—No. But there is every reason to hope that in each generation the Gospel may prove its power to reach and change new areas of life; that God may again and again deliver his People from seemingly hopeless predicaments; that he may help them to overcome hoary evils when they overgrow the whole earth; that he may lead them with their Lord through death and defeat to victory and glory, here and hereafter.

[36] I have expressed my own tempered hope of progress in *Can Christianity Save Civilization?* Harper, 1940. The turbulent years since then have changed my world outlook, but not led me to revoke the main theses of that book.

# REFERENCES AND QUESTIONS

## A. General References

### I. CLASSIC SYSTEMS OF THEOLOGY

1. Origen, *De Principiis* (Ante-Nicene Fathers).
2. Augustine, *Enchiridion* and *City of God* (Nicene and Post-Nicene Fathers).
3. Aquinas, *Summa Theologica*. The most comprehensive of all Christian systems, authoritative for Roman Catholics. May be approached through Father Pegis' *Introduction to St. Thomas Aquinas* in the *Modern Library*.
4. Calvin, *Institutes of the Christian Religion*. The classic Protestant system. Well condensed in H. T. Kerr's *Compend*.
5. Schleiermacher, *The Christian Faith*. The most influential Liberal Protestant system. Mackintosh and Stewart edition.

### II. RECENT AND CONTEMPORARY TEXTBOOKS OF THEOLOGY

1. *Roman Catholic*
   Smith, G. D. (ed.), *The Teaching of the Catholic Church*, London: Burns, Oates & Washbourne, 1948; one-volume ed., 1952. Recent symposium by British Catholics.
   Wilhelm and Scannell, *Manual of Catholic Theology*, Catholic Pub. Soc., 4th ed., 1909. Old but still much used.
   *Initiation Théologique*, Paris: Cerf, 1952 ff. Four-volume survey by French Dominicans.
   Rudloff, L. von, O.S.B., *Everyman's Theology*, Milwaukee: Bruce, 4th printing, 1947. Handbook for Catholic laymen.
2. *Non-Roman Catholic*
   Gavin, Frank, *Some Aspects of Contemporary Greek Orthodox Thought*, Morehouse, 1923. Modern Greek Orthodox theology interpreted by an Anglo-Catholic.

Bulgakov, Sergius, *The Wisdom of God*, Paisley Press, 1937. Russian Orthodox.

——, *The Orthodox Church*, London: Bles, 1935. Russian Orthodox.

Berdyaev, N., *The Destiny of Man*, Scribner, 1937, and many other works. Original restatement of the Eastern Orthodox tradition, with strong mystical trend.

Moss, Claude B., *The Christian Faith*, Morehouse, 1946. Anglo-Catholic.

3. *Conservative Protestant*
   Berkhof, L., *Systematic Theology*, Eerdmans, 1941. Reformed.
   Stump, J., *The Christian Faith*, Muhlenberg, 1942. Lutheran.
   Hodge, A. A., *Outlines of Theology*, Eerdmans, 1928. Presbyterian.
   Miley, J., *Systematic Theology*, Hunt, 1894. Methodist.
   Strong, A. H., *Outlines of Systematic Theology*, Am. Bapt. Pub. Soc., 1908. Baptist.
   The last three are old but still much used.

4. *Liberal Protestant*
   DeWolf, L. Harold, *A Theology of the Living Church*, Harper, 1953. The best recent liberal theology textbook.
   Clarke, W. N., *An Outline of Christian Theology*, Scribner, 1898. Baptist.
   Brown, W. A., *Christian Theology in Outline*, Scribner, 1906. Presbyterian.
   The two most widely used liberal texts in the past generation.
   Knudson, A. C., *The Doctrine of God*, Abingdon, 1930. Methodist.
   ——, *The Doctrine of Redemption*, Abingdon, 1933. Methodist.
   Dickie, J., *The Organism of Christian Truth*, London: Clarke, 1931. Written in New Zealand; "modern-positive" rather than strictly liberal. Another distinction within the liberal school of theology is the new type of liberalism, chastened by neo-orthodox criticism, which has been christened "neo-liberalism." (For the term and its meaning, see my Lyman Lecture on

"Liberalism Old and New," Sweet Briar College, 1953.) De-Wolf's above-mentioned textbook, and my *Realistic Theology*, Harper, 1934, are neo-liberal rather than liberal.

5. *Radical Protestant (Religious Humanism and Naturalism)*
   Reese, Curtis, *Humanism*, Open Court, 1926.
   —— (ed.), *Humanist Sermons*, Open Court, 1927.
   Otto, Max, *Things and Ideals*, Holt, 1924. Humanist.
   Dewey, John, *A Common Faith*, Yale University Press, 1934. Humanist.
   Wieman, H. N., *The Wrestle of Religion with Truth*, Macmillan, 1927. Naturalist.
   ——, *The Source of Human Good*, University of Chicago Press, 1946. Naturalist.
   Neither Wieman's religious naturalism nor any form of humanism lends itself to systematic presentation in textbook form, but these references will help to define these two related points of view.

6. *Neo-Orthodox Protestant*
   Aulén, G., *The Faith of the Christian Church*, Muhlenberg, 1948 (translated from the 4th Swedish ed.). Best systematic presentation of neo-orthodox Protestantism.
   Barth, K., *Credo*, Scribner, 1936. More nearly of textbook dimensions than his mammoth *Church Dogmatics*. But see Otto Weber's fine brief summary, *Karl Barth's Church Dogmatics*, Westminster Press, 1953.
   Brunner, E., *Dogmatics*, Westminster Press, 1950 ff. A three-volume survey of which the first two are available.
   Tillich, P., *Systematic Theology*, Vols. I and II, Univ. of Chicago Press, 1951 ff. A theology "on the boundary" between neo-orthodoxy and liberalism.

7. *Anglican*
   Quick, O. C., *Doctrines of the Creed*, 9th impression, Scribner, 1951. Best recent Anglican theology of textbook size.
   Headlam, A. C., *Christian Theology: the Doctrine of God*, Oxford, Clarendon Press, 1934. Covers Christology as well as Theology.

Temple, William, *Nature, Man and God*, Macmillan, 1934. Greatest work by Anglicans' most influential recent leader.

Selwyn, E. G. (ed.), *Essays Catholic and Critical*, Macmillan, 1926. Liberal Anglo-Catholicism; compare with the conservative Anglo-Catholicism of Moss, under (2) above.

### III. CREEDS AND CATECHISMS

Schaff, P., *Creeds of Christendom*, 4th ed., Harper, 1905. The classic collection of Catholic and Protestant creeds and catechisms.

Denzinger, H. J. D., *Enchiridion Symbolorum*, 21st–23rd ed., Freiburg: Herder, 1937. Official documents of the Roman Catholic faith.

For recent ecumenical statements of faith, see especially the reports of the ecumenical conferences held at Lausanne (1927), Jerusalem (1928), Edinburgh (1937), Tambaram (1938), Amsterdam (1948), Lund (1952), and Evanston (1954).

### IV. SHORT SURVEYS OF THE CHRISTIAN FAITH

Publishers and dates of publication are omitted, since these titles are merely illustrative of this type of book. All are short, and fairly recent. Like the full-length textbooks, these range from Catholicism through conservative, liberal, neo-orthodox Protestantism to Anglicanism. Radical humanism and naturalism are omitted because not well adapted to comprehensive "survey." My short laymen's theology, based on ecumenical statements of faith, is listed at the end, since it attempts to state an ecumenical position above the strife of the schools of thought.

Adam, K., *The Spirit of Catholicism*. Continental (German) Roman Catholicism.

Martindale, C. C., *The Faith of Catholics*. Anglo-Saxon Roman Catholicism.

Berkhof, L., *Manual of Christian Doctrine*. Conservative Protestantism.

Mullins, E. Y., *Christianity at the Cross-Roads*. Conservative Protestantism.

Bennett, John, *Christian Realism*. Liberal Protestantism.

Rall, Harris, *A Faith for Today*. Liberal Protestantism.
Barth, K., *Dogmatics in Outline*. Neo-orthodox Protestantism.
Brunner, E., *Our Faith*. Neo-orthodoxy for laymen.
Niebuhr, R., *Beyond Tragedy*. Neo-orthodoxy "on the boundary line."
Whale, J. S., *Christian Doctrine*. A British Free Churchman's statement.
Vidler, A., *Christian Beliefs*. Anglicanism for the laity.
Horton, W. M., *Our Christian Faith*. For laymen, regardless of denomination.

When this *Christian Theology* is used as a theological textbook, the following procedure (used in my own classes) may be suggested. Each student chooses one other theological text (perhaps one of the "classic systems," perhaps one of the "recent and contemporary textbooks") and studies its views on each of the seven topics treated in Chapters II–VIII. He may very probably wish to study a textbook widely used in his own denomination, whether or not it is mentioned in our brief, highly selective list. At the middle of the term, he chooses a "short survey" and writes a review of it, comparing its distinctive point of view with that of his chosen textbook. At the end of the term, he writes his own theological Credo, beginning with a very short Statement of Faith which may be the Apostles' Creed, or a denominational confession of faith, or his own composition. Building-blocks for this final paper are handed in every fortnight—tentative statements of conclusions on the topics discussed in that fortnight. Each topic begins with a discussion of section 1 (the universal human problem), followed by several days of open class discussion based upon the questions relating to that topic. On the day when the students hand in their conclusions, sections 2 and 3 are discussed in class. The agreements and disagreements in the tentative statements are then analyzed, and compared with the ecumenical agreements and disagreements considered in the chapter just discussed, before we pass to the next chapter and the next topic.

The references which follow the questions on each chapter are designed to enable the student to make a comparison of points of view, such as occurs in an ecumenical conference. The order is not alphabetical but pedagogical. The first one or two references open up the topic, or enable one to survey many points of view at a glance. Then follow Catholic, conservative Protestant, liberal Protestant, radical Protestant, neo-orthodox Protestant, and Anglican references, just as in the above list of "recent and contemporary textbooks." It is desirable to test the student's understanding of these six points of view some time during the term, since they seem to be the livest alternatives for Christian thought in the present generation —at least in America. If the book were used as a textbook in other areas, the prevailing thought currents would be different, and the list of references should be changed accordingly. That is to say, no list can be wholly free from provincialism, even though it be interdenominational, international, and nonpartisan, as this list tries to be. Since every author is an unconscious partisan, I give a few references to my own writings at the end of each list of readings, so that the student may understand what position I represent when I step out of my role as ecumenical interpreter and speak for myself.

## B. Chapter References With Questions

### CHAPTER I. INTRODUCTION

*Questions*

What is the meaning of the word "ecumenical"? How related to "catholic"? Is it possible for a theology to be completely nonecumenical (i.e., purely sectarian, purely provincial or purely partisan) without losing its Christian character? Is it possible for a theology to be completely ecumenical (i.e., literally world wide, superdenominational and nonpartisan) without losing contact with present ecclesiastical realities? Must an ecumenical theology ignore non-Christian faiths and current skeptical questions, and confine itself to defining the agreements and differences among Christians? By your own definition of the term "ecumenical," what recent theological textbooks are most nearly ecumenical in their perspective?

Is religion a required or an optional feature of human life? What seem to you to be the principal enduring needs that religions try to satisfy? Can one argue from the imperativeness of a need to the truth and adequacy of a religion that meets this need? Are all religions equal in their power to convey ultimate truth and satisfy persistent needs, or are there bad and inadequate religions, which ought to be denounced, opposed or corrected?

What are the distinctive characteristics of the Christian faith? In what group of religions does Christianity belong, and what distinguishes it from other religions in that group? What are the chief varieties of Christian life and thought that present live alternatives to contemparary Christians? What major subtypes do you distinguish within the Catholic, Protestant and Anglican divisions of Christendom? What are the principal Christian doctrines that are common to all these divisions? How do these doctrines relate to the needs, problems and questions which all religious men must face?

## References

On this introductory topic, the best plan is to sample the introductory sections of some of the textbooks cited under the General References, comparing their distinctive methods and points of view. On the problem of "essential Christianity," see William Adams Brown's *The Essence of Christianity*, Scribner, 1902, where the principal views are summarized and discussed. Cf. also Harnack's *What Is Christianity?* Putnam, 1901, with George Cross's and C. C. Morrison's more recent books by the same title (1918, 1940).

### CHAPTER II. THE KNOWLEDGE OF GOD

## Questions

What is meant by "knowledge of God"? How related to "knowledge about God"? To "faith in God"? Can God be "known" at all?

Can God be adequately known by rational inference from his works in nature? by direct mystical experience? by special historic revelation? What weight would you give to the following, as authoritative sources of the knowledge of God: the Bible, the life and teachings of Jesus, the opinions of the Church Fathers and the decisions of Church Councils, the witness of your own Christian experience and that of others, the conclusions of modern science and modern philosophy?

What is the relation between the knowledge of God and other human knowledge, more especially scientific knowledge? Is theology a science? Can God be "proved"? Have "natural theology" and "general revelation" any place in Christian thought, or should theology be based exclusively on special revelation?

*References*

Ferré, N., *Pillars of Faith*, Harper, 1948. A good brief summary of the principal views.

Baillie and Martin, *Revelation*, Macmillan, 1937. An ecumenical symposium including many views.

Gibbons, J., *Faith of Our Fathers*, VII-IX [1]. Wilhelm and Scannell, *op. cit.*, Vol. I, Chaps. I-V; Smith, *op. cit.*, I and II. Roman Catholic.

Hodge, *Outline*, III-V; Strong, *Outline*, II; Berkhof, *Manual of Christian Doctrine*, 25–54. Conservative Protestant.

Clark, *Outline*, 10–53; Sabatier, *Religions of Authority and the Religion of the Spirit*, McClure, Phillips, 1904, Introduction and Bk. III; DeWolf, *Theology of the Living Church*, Pts. I and II. Liberal Protestant.

Reese, *Humanism*, Pt. I; *Humanist Sermons*, Preface, 38–48, 79–92; Auer, J.A.C.F., *Humanism States its Case*, Beacon Press, 1933, I, IV. Nontheistic humanism.

Wieman and Meland, *American Philosophies of Religion*, Harper, 1936, III; Wieman, *Religious Experience and Scientific Method*, Macmillan, 1926, I-III. Theistic Naturalism.

Barth, K., *Doctrine of the Word of God*, Edinburgh: Clark, 1936 98–140; Barth and Brunner, *Natural Theology*, Bles, 1946; Tillich, *Systematic Theology*, I, 106–47, 155–59; Aulén, *op. cit.*, 3–22, 79–114. Neo-orthodox.

---

[1] Unless otherwise indicated, Roman numerals refer to chapters and Arabic numerals to pages. Originally published in 1879, this popular exposition of Catholicism by Cardinal Gibbons reached its 67th edition in 1906 (Baltimore, New York. J. Murphy Co.).

# References and Questions

Baillie, J., *Our Knowledge of God*, Oxford University Press, 1939, I, V; Casserley, J.V.L., *The Christian and Philosophy*, Scribner, 1951, 165–85; DeWolf, *The Religious Revolt Against Reason*, Harper, 1949, III–V. Critiques of neo-orthodoxy.

Moss, *op. cit.*, Chaps. 1–3, 34–36; Rawlinson, *Authority and Freedom*, Longmans, Green, 1924, I; Temple, *Nature, Man and God*, Macmillan, 1935, XII, XIII; Richardson, A., *The Gospel and Modern Thought*, Oxford University Press, 1950, I, II. Anglican.

For the author's views, compare my contribution to the above symposium on *Revelation* with my contribution to the symposium on *Religious Realism*, ed. by Macintosh, 1931.

CHAPTER III. THE NATURE OF GOD

## Questions

By what stages has the Christian idea of God developed? What in it is traceable to primitive, pre-Biblical sources? To the Hebrew prophets? To the life and teaching of Jesus? To Greek philosophy?

Classify the attributes of God according to some logical scheme; metaphysical and moral, positive and negative, etc. Is it presumptuous and anthropomorphic to attribute wisdom, love, personality and other human characteristics to God? Have the metaphysical attributes of God (absoluteness, omnipotence, omnipresence, eternity, immensity, infinity, etc.) been unduly stressed in traditional theology at the expense of the moral attributes?

Can God's omnipotence be reconciled with his justice? His justice with his forgiving love? Is it necessary (or possible) to eliminate all inconsistency, all paradox, from our thought of God? What happens (1) when all God's attributes are rationally deduced from one or a few? (2) when paradoxes and irrationalities are deliberately piled up, as in the earlier writings of Karl Barth, or in some of the mystics?

## References

Otto, R., *The Idea of the Holy*, Oxford University Press, 1936, 1–41. The "numinous" as the primitive root of the idea of God.

Brown, *Outline*, VII, "Development of the Christian Idea of God."
Wilhelm and Scannell, Vol. I, Bk. II, Smith, III-V. Catholic.

Hodge, II, VIII, IX; Strong, 18–32, 67–94; Berkhof, 53–74; Stump,
I. Conservative Protestant.

Clarke, Pt. I, I, II, IV; Brown, Pt. II; DeWolf, 89–116; Dickie, 66–
112. Liberal Protestant.

Reese, *Humanist Sermons*, 51–61, 213–18; Dewey, *Common Faith*,
42–55; Otto, M., *Things and Ideals*, XI and XII. Nontheistic humanism.

Wieman, H. N., *The Wrestle of Religion with Truth*, XI-XIII;
*Source of Human Good*, 263–68; Hartshorne, C., *Man's Vision of
God*, Harper, 1941, 1–15. Theistic naturalism.

Brunner, *Dogmatics I, The Christian Doctrine of God*, Pt. I, Sec. I;
Aulén, 120–60; Tillich, 218–52. Neo-orthodox.

Ferré, Nels, *The Christian Understanding of God*, Harper, 1951.
Compare this type of philosophical theology with Tillich's.

Horton, *Theism and the Modern Mood*, Harper, 1930, II-IV, and
book on *God* in the Hazen series, Association Press, 1937.

### CHAPTER IV. GOD AND THE WORLD

*Questions*

Distinguish the Biblical picture of the world from the medieval,
Newtonian, and contemporary world pictures. How much in all
these world pictures is borrowed from secular science, and how
much is an essential part of Christian faith? What theories of God's
relation to the world are really hostile to Christian faith? Between
what limits has Christian thought generally fluctuated, in its view
of God's relation to the world?

How do you believe God created the world? Gradually or suddenly? out of nothing, out of pre-existent stuff, or out of his own
divine substance? Having created it, has he now only to watch it
spinning on its way, or does he sustain it by his power from moment
to moment, and providentially overrule the whole course of events?
Is his providential government regular and invariable, or does he
help those who trust him by special providences and miracles? Are

miracles, angels and demons part of the mythological framework of the Bible, or are they present realities? Can prayer alter the course of events? How does prayer relate to God's providence?

Can the prevalence of evil in the world be reconciled with faith in a divine Creator and Ruler of the world? How can there be a devil, or demons, or bad men, in God's world? What is the most Christian attitude, as you see it, toward natural evils such as disease, earthquakes and floods? toward moral evils such as vice and crime, wars and social disasters? Should evil be faced with resignation, as divinely "sent"? with hope and resolution, as devil's work to be overcome with God's help? or how?

## References

Horton, W. M., *Theism and the Scientific Spirit*, Harper, 1933, synopses. On the successive world pictures Christianity has lived through.

Brown, W. A., *Outline*, XI. Changing and constant elements in the Christian attitude toward the world.

Smith, VI-VIII; Berkhof, 84–120; Stump, III-V. Catholic and conservative Protestant views.

Abbot, L., *Theology of an Evolutionist*, Houghton Mifflin, 1897, I, "Creation by Evolution"; Macintosh, *Reasonableness of Christianity*, Scribner, 1925, VII, "Providence"; Brightman, E., *Philosophy of Religion*, Prentice-Hall, 1940, IX, X; Bertocci, P., *Philosophy of Religion*, Prentice-Hall, 1951, 415 *et seq*; DeWolf, *Theology of the Living Church*, 117-43. Liberal Protestant.

Since both humanism and naturalism reject the reality of a God who transcends the world, they have no doctrine of God and the World. From this point on, with the exception of a few passages (pp. 287, 288) the radical Protestants have no clear theological teachings, so no references can be given.

Aulén, 160–206; Tillich, 252–89; Barth, *Dogmatics in Outline*, Philosophical Library, 1949, 35–64; Lewis, Edwin, *The Creator and the Adversary*, Abingdon Press, 1948, XIV; Heim, *Transformation of the Scientific World-View*, London: S.C.M. Press, 1953. Neo-orthodox in various degrees.

*Christian Theology*

Lewis, C. S., *Miracles*, Macmillan, 1947, II, III, VIII, XII; Quick, 25–66. Anglican.

Horton, W. M., *Realistic Theology*, Harper, 1934, III, *Our Christian Faith*, Pilgrim Press, 1947, II.

## CHAPTER V. GOD AND MAN

*Questions*

What is the actual predicament of man, as you see it, apart from the saving grace of God? From what must he be "saved"? What is the historic meaning of the word "salvation"? Is it outworn?

Is man a child of nature or a child of God? If a child of God, wherein do you discern the "divine image" in him? In his "soul" only or in his whole psychophysical being? in his free will? in his creative mastery of nature? in his quality of "self-transcendence"? Wherein does man's dependence on his natural environment appear, despite all these "divine" qualities of his? Will science ever make him completely independent of nature?

How has man "fallen" from the "state of integrity" in which God meant him to live? By one fatal act of disobedience on the part of "our first fathers," or by many disastrous missteps? By ignorance, or by his own free choice? What is the origin and nature of that "sin" which tends to alienate him from his source and goal? What is the effect of sin upon the sinner and upon those who come after him? Are all men since Adam born in original sin, totally depraved in all their natural impulses, or does God create each new child naturally good until he is corrupted by evil example? Why is it so hard for man to do good? What are the punishments, temporal and eternal, which he must suffer if he goes on sinning? Can he escape from the guilt and power of sin by his own unaided efforts?

*References*

Richards, G. W., *Christian Ways of Salvation*, Macmillan, 1923, III–X; Cross, *Christian Salvation*, University of Chicago Press, 1925, II–VII; Schaff-Herzog Encyclopedia, article "Redemption." Historic views of what we are *saved from*.

# References and Questions

*The Christian Understanding of Man,* Oxford preparatory volume, London: Allen and Unwin, 1937. Various views.

Wilhelm and Scannell, Vol. II, Bks. IV and VI; Smith, IX and X. Catholic. Strong, 124–278, 207–33; Berkhof, 121–71; Stump, VI–VIII. Conservative Protestant.

DeWolf, Pt. IV; Tennant, F. R., *Origin and Propagation of Sin,* Cambridge University Press, 1902, I, III; Rauschenbusch, *Theology for the Social Gospel,* Macmillan, 1919, IV-XI. Liberal Protestant.

Reese,*Humanism,* 15–54; Wieman, *Source of Human Good,* II, IV, V. Radical Protestant.

Niebuhr, *Nature and Destiny of Man,* Scribner, 1941–43, Vol. I, Chaps. VI-IX; Aulén, 259–88. Neo-orthodox.

Temple, *Nature, Man and God,* IX, XV, XX; *Essays Catholic and Critical,* VII. Anglican.

Horton, W. M., *Realistic Theology,* II; *Psychological Approach to Theology,* Harper, 1931, II, III; *Our Christian Faith,* III.


CHAPTER VI. CHRIST THE SAVIOR

*Questions*

What is the place of Christ among the various forces making for man's deliverance from the predicament in which he finds himself? How related to the help that comes from science and technology? from education and social reform? from other moral and religious influences, inside and outside the Hebrew-Christian tradition? Can mankind be delivered from its present disastrous state without returning to Christ? Can Christ *alone* deliver mankind? Does he embody the "whole counsel of God," or does God's saving grace work through other channels as well?

What is the relation between the human and the divine, both in Jesus himself and in those he redeems to a new life of sonship to God? What is the relation between "God the Father Almighty, Maker of heaven and earth" and the redemptive God whose "grace and truth" were "made flesh" in Jesus? What is the relation of the

287

Holy Spirit to God? to the risen and living Christ? to the Church? What is identical, what is distinctive of each "person" in the Trinity? Or do you think the doctrine of the Trinity subverts monotheism, and should be abandoned? If so, what place do you make for God's creative, redemptive and inwardly sanctifying activity in your Unitarian concept of God? Do you think belief in the Virgin Birth is necessary to guarantee authentic Christian faith in the Trinity and the Incarnation?

What, specifically, has Jesus Christ done that helps to deliver modern mankind? How is it possible for him to help us after a lapse of two thousand years? What truth do you see in the "classical," the "Latin," and the "moral" theories of the atoning work of Christ? in the theory of his three "offices" as prophet, priest and king? Is the "sacrificial" theory (Quick) to be considered a fourth main view of Christ's work? State your own view of what Christ can do to save modern mankind.

## References

Athanasius, *Incarnation of the Word of God*, Macmillan, 1946; McGiffert, *History of Christian Thought*, Scribner, 1932–33, Vol. I, Chaps. XII-XIV. Historic views of the person of Christ.

Aulén, *Christus Victor*, Macmillan, 1937, I, VIII; Anselm, *Cur Deus Homo*, Open Court, 1903; Grotius, *Defence of the Catholic Faith Concerning the Satisfaction of Christ*, F. H. Foster's ed., Andover: Draper, 1889, I, II; Bushnell, *Vicarious Sacrifice*, Scribner, 1903, I-III, V. Historic views of the work of Christ.

Smith, XI-XV; Berkhof, 175–219; Stump, II, IX-XIV; Dickie, Division II, "The Lord Jesus Christ: his Person and Work." Catholic, Conservative Protestant, and "Modern-Positive."

Royce, *Problem of Christianity*, Macmillan, 1913, Vol. I, Lecture VI; Rauschenbusch, XIV, XIX; DeWolf, Pt. V. Liberal Protestant.

Wieman, *Source of Human Good*, 39–53, 268–81. Naturalistic.

Barth, *Dogmatics in Outline*, sections 10–20; Brunner, *The Mediator*, Macmillan, 1934, Bk. III, section 2; Aulén, *Faith of the Christian Church*, 207–59; Niebuhr, *Nature and Destiny of Man*, Vol. II, Chaps. I-III; Tillich, Syst. Theol., Vol. II, 78–180. Neo-orthodox.

# References and Questions

Baillie, D. M., *God Was in Christ*, Scribner, 1948, I-III, V, VI. Critique of liberal and neo-orthodox positions.

Quick, XXI; Hodgson, L., *The Doctrine of the Trinity*, Scribner, 1944, IV; Wolf, W. J., *No Cross, No Crown*, Doubleday, 1957. Anglican.

Foster, F. H., *History of the New England Theology*, Chicago University Press, 1907, X, "The Unitarian Controversy."

Martineau, J., *Essays, Reviews and Addresses*, Longmans, Green, 1901, Vol. II, essay on "A Way Out of the Trinitarian Controversy."

Horton, W. M., *Our Eternal Contemporary*, Harper, 1942, II-IV; *Realistic Theology*, IV.

CHAPTER VII. THE CHURCH AND THE MEANS OF GRACE

## Questions

What is meant by calling the Church the "body of Christ"? Are all churches that appeal to Christ's name truly parts of his body? What are the marks that distinguish the true, living Church from a dead church? What are the functions of the true Church, and of her ministers, ordained and unordained? Is the saving grace of Christ transmitted only through the Church, or may men come to Christ without affiliating with organized Christianity?

What are the principal "means of grace" that actually bring Christ's saving power into the lives of modern men? What is the place of the ministry of the Word, the ministry of worship, and the ministry of the Sacraments in the total work of the Church? What special graces are conveyed by the two great Sacraments, Baptism and the Lord's Supper? Can these graces be conveyed in no other way?

Are "good works" altogether opposed to "grace" in the Christian way of salvation, or are good works to be numbered among the means of grace as well as among the fruits of grace? What are the subjective conditions for receiving God's saving grace? ("What must *I* do to be saved?") Must all experience salvation in the same way? Must they be wholly saved before joining the Church?

*References*

*The Nature of the Church*, Lund preparatory volume, Harper, 1952; contains statements by many different churches.

*The Catholicity of Protestantism* (symposium by British Free Churchmen).

Congar, M. J., *Divided Christendom*, London: Bles, 1939; Van de Pol, W. H., *The Christian Dilemma*, Philosophical Library, 1953; Smith, XVI-XXX; Wilhelm and Scannell, Vol. II, Bk. VII. Roman Catholic.

Zander, L. A., *Vision and Action*, London: Gollancz, 1952; Moss, Chaps. 41–45. Non-Roman Catholic.

Berkhof, 279–329; Stump, XXV-XXXII. Conservative Protestant.

Rauschenbusch, XII, XIII, XVII; Knudson, *The Doctrine of Redemption*, VIII, IX. Liberal Protestant.

Niebuhr, *Nature and Destiny of Man*, Vol. II, Chaps. IV, V; Aulén, 329–437. Neo-orthodox.

Williams, D., *God's Grace and Man's Hope*, Harper, 1949, VI, VII. Critique of neo-orthodoxy.

*Essays Catholic and Critical*, X, XIII; Quick, Pt. IV. Anglican.

Waterhouse, E. S., *What Is Salvation?* London: Hodder & Stoughton, 1932. The subjective conditions of salvation.

Horton, W. M., *Realistic Theology*, V; *Our Christian Faith*, VII-XII.

CHAPTER VIII. THE CHRISTIAN HOPE

*Questions*

What is the final goal of Christian hope? How far and under what conditions is salvation in God's kingdom already realized by Christian persons and groups? Can Christian perfection be attained in this life, or is it reserved for a future life? What are the grounds for faith in a future life? What is the meaning of "heaven" and "eternal life"? How should a Christian face death and bereavement? Can we hope for all men to be saved and perfected, here or hereafter, or is "hell" the fate of the persistent sinner? What basis have we for imagining what heaven and hell may be like?

Is it only the individual who has a soul to be saved, or can society and civilization also be saved? By what means? Will social and cosmic evil ever be completely overcome in history? Will a Millennium actually come at some future date, when God's Will shall be done on earth as it is done in heaven? If so, will it come gradually or suddenly, by progress or crisis? If not, how does God finally save the world?

What is the relation of history to eternity? What is the meaning of the Last Judgment and the Second Coming of Christ? What is the meaning of the final victory of Christ, when the last enemy is put under his feet, the last hostile kingdom subdued, and God becomes "all in all"?

## References

Berdyaev, N., *The Destiny of Man*, London: Bles. 1937, Pt. III. Bold and searching exposition of the problem of final destiny.

*The Christian Hope and the Task of the Church*. Evanston preparatory volume, Harper, 1954; contains final report of Advisory Commission on the main theme, "Christ—the Hope of the World."

Minear, Paul, *The Christian Hope and the Second Coming*, Westminister Press, 1954. A study in Biblical eschatology.

Smith, Wilhelm and Scannell, Berkhof, Stump, sections on Eschatology. Catholic and conservative Protestant views.

Brown, *Outline*, XXIII; Rauschenbusch, XVIII; Knudson, X; Baillie, J., *And the Life Everlasting*, Scribner, 1933, I, II, VI-VIII; *The Belief in Progress*, Scribner, 1951. Liberal Protestants veering to neo-liberalism.

Niebuhr, *op. cit.*, Vol. II, Chaps. IX, X; Aulén, 176–80, 437–47; Brunner, *Eternal Hope*, Westminster Press, 1954. Neo-orthodox.

Williams, *op. cit.*, I, IV, V, VIII. Critique of neo-orthodoxy.

Fison, J. E., *The Christian Hope: the Presence and the Parousia*, Longmans, Green, 1954, I-III, V, VII. Anglican.

# APPENDIX

## Christianity and Other Living Faiths[1]

The situation faced by Christian Evangelism and Christian Missions at the present day differs considerably from the situation as reported by the Edinburgh (1910), Jerusalem (1928), and Tambaram (1938) missionary conferences. At Edinburgh, the prospects for a rapid evangelization of the world seemed most promising. As Western civilization then still enjoyed immense prestige in the whole earth, so Christianity, at the close of the "Great Century" of Christian Missions, was regarded with respect and hope, and its incoming welcomed, in most parts of the world. By the time of the Jerusalem conference, World War I had begun the dissolution of Western prestige, and formidable obstacles to the extension of Christianity had appeared. At Jerusalem, the principal obstacle was defined as secularism; and since all world religions found themselves confronted and

[1] This Appendix is based on a paper prepared for the consultation on "Christianity and the Non-Christian Religions," held at Davos, Switzerland, in 1955 under the joint auspices of the International Missionary Council and the World Council of Churches' Department on Evangelism. It makes clear, I think, that the question of relationship between Christianity and other living faiths is itself a major ecumenical issue, which has occupied Christian thought seriously in recent years (especially since Tambaram, 1938) and on which important agreements and differences have emerged. This is, I repeat, an ecumenical discussion among Christians, rather than an interfaith discussion among those whose fundamental faiths are different; but at the end some corollaries are drawn concerning the legitimacy and hopefulness of interfaith discussion. For a comment on the further study of this issue, since Davos, see my article in the *Bulletin of the World Council's Division of Studies*, Vol. II, No. I (March, 1956), pp. 28–31, "How Best Study the Attitudes and Policies Involved in Missionary Confrontation?"

threatened by the same inimical force, it was urged by some missionary leaders that Christians should make common cause with non-Christian religionists in warring against secularism. At Tambaram, it was recognized that the main difficulty was no longer a non-religious secularism, but the rapid rise of new positive faiths, above all Nationalism and Communism, whose religious fervor was unmistakable, but whose implications for Christianity and for all historic faiths were demonically destructive. To say under these circumstances, "let us unite in urging men to be religious," seemed the height of folly; it was necessary to insist that religion might be a delusion and a snare, which must be sharply distinguished from true and saving faith.

Today, Communism has become a far more formidable menace to Christian Missions than it was in 1938. Throughout the vast domain which lies behind the Iron Curtain, religious freedom does not usually extend beyond freedom of worship; and freedom to propagate the gospel—especially through the agency of foreign missionaries—is severely restricted. Missionaries are in fact regarded as spies and agents of Western imperialism, constantly subject to the threat of imprisonment or deportation. With Nationalism, the case is different. As an independent faith, it has suffered a sharp setback. Military defeat has at least overtly destroyed the prestige of Italian Fascism, German Nazism, and Japanese state Shintoism. Yet as a diffused force, masking itself in various disguises, Nationalism is still a powerful factor in world affairs. All the areas recently liberated from Western colonialism are aggressively nationalistic. Perhaps the most characteristic fact of the period since World War II is the mixture of this aggressive nationalism with a revived allegiance to whatever religious faith is indigenous in the region: Islam in the Near and Middle East, Africa, Pakistan and Indonesia; Hinduism in

India; Buddhism in Ceylon, Burma and parts of the Far East.[2]

This revival of the ancient non-Christian faiths, partly inspired by nationalistic self-consciousness, is perhaps the most characteristic problem faced by Christian Evangelism and Missions at the present day. Only Communism vies with it in magnitude; but since Communism tends to exclude and suppress direct missionary activity, while the older religions still tolerate it (at least in the medical, agricultural and educational fields) a strategy to meet this more fluid situation is the most urgent requirement of missionary policy. Conditions of course differ in different areas; but wherever the above-mentioned combination of aggressive nationalism and revived indigenous religion exists, non-Christian governments are imposing new restrictions on Christian missions. Leadership of the Christian movement is more and more restricted to nationals, and overseas missionaries find difficulty in getting visas to some countries. "In the Asiatic countries in particular," according to Dr. Devanandan, "nationalism has stimulated everywhere a general sense that the solidarity of indigenous faiths should be safeguarded against proselytism of any kind."[3] The *right* of conversion is denied more fiercely than ever in Moslem lands (if that be possible!) while in Hindu and Buddhist lands the *need* of conversion is questioned, on the ground that all faiths are essentially one, and seek the same goal. In either case, the ruling religions exert a strong restraining pressure upon Christian evangelism: "On the one hand, they deny the claim of Christianity to be the final—or even the highest—type of religion; on the other hand, they invite the Christians to join them

[2] Cf. the report of Section II, "The Evangelizing Church," at Evanston: "The renascence of non-Christian religions and the spread of new ideologies necessitates a new approach in our evangelizing task. In many countries, these religious revivals . . . are reinforced by nationalism . . ." (V, 33).

[3] *International Review of Missions* (*I.R.M.*), Vol. 41 (1952), p. 183.

in resisting the advance of materialism and scepticism."[4] Christians are sometimes forced to favor a completely secular state, lest a state-sponsored program of religious education be imposed that would violate their Christian convictions.[5] Under all these pressures, Christians are in danger of being driven into a defensive minority complex, quite the reverse of the apostolic boldness which the gospel requires.

In this perplexing and challenging situation, the two chief needs are (1) a sound theological interpretation of the non-Christian faiths, congruous with the main implications of the Christian gospel, and (2) a sound missionary strategy, calculated to overcome groundless hostility, and get the gospel as full, fair and sympathetic a hearing as is possible under the conditions described. Let us consider these needs in turn.

## 1. THEOLOGICAL INTERPRETATION OF THE NON-CHRISTIAN FAITHS

Christians under hostile pressure from non-Christian majorities are tempted to minimize the offense of the Gospel, and to describe the Christian movement as making a loyal, cooperative contribution to the welfare of its cultural environment. This is in the long run as unwise as it is dishonest. It ought never to be denied, and it cannot finally be concealed, that Christians are united in final loyalty to one Lord, who is for them the Savior of the whole world, and whose authority for them takes precedence over every earthly authority whatsoever. (See the Declaration of Unity in the report of the Edinburgh Faith and Order

---

[4] Dewick, *The Christian Attitude to Other Religions* (Cambridge University Press, 1953), p. 14.
[5] See the Rev. Russell Chandran's comments on the Radhakrishnan Report on University Education, *I.R.M.*, Vol. 41, p. 267.

Conference.) For the sake of peace with their non-Christian neighbors, they cannot represent their Lord as merely a prophet like Mohammed, or merely a Hindu avatar or Buddhist bodhi-sattva, nor can they cease to testify to the uniqueness of the revelation of God in him. Canon E. C. Dewick has shown in his Hulsean Lectures on *The Christian Attitude to Other Religions* that agreement concerning the *supremacy of Jesus Christ* under-cuts all theological differences between Christians and cannot be surrendered without betraying the Christian cause: "In him we find the *highest* and *fullest* truth about God and man—a *central* truth, that must determine our judgments on all the major issues of religion, and a *distinctive* truth that is not found with equal clearness elsewhere."[6] Or as the Jerusalem missionary conference classically put the point, "Our message is Jesus Christ. He is the revelation of what God is, and what man through Him may become." This is an offensive and scandalous claim, a stumbling block to intolerant Moslems and a foolishness to toler-ant Hindus and Buddhists; but it is the heart of the Christian faith and must be candidly confessed as such.

What can and should be done, when Christians bear witness to their faith in the presence of a suspicious non-Christian majority, is to make clear that this faith, exclusive as it sounds, does not cut them off from membership in the same common humanity with non-Christians, nor does it commit them to an attitude of general contempt or hostility toward other living faiths. Here we are not so fully on common ground as in our faith in Christ's supremacy. Different attitudes to other faiths, ranging from deep respect to sharp hostility, have been based on divergent theological premises by opposing schools of Christian thought. The Tambaram debate between the advocates of conti-

[6] Dewick, *op. cit.*, p. 137.

nuity and discontinuity in the relationship between Christianity and other religions cannot be said to have led to any generally agreed solution of that difficult problem. Nevertheless, an examination of the positions actually stated by the two parties to that debate, at and after Tambaram, will show that they were not so radically opposed as the logical disjunction between continuity and discontinuity might seem to imply.

Looking first at Dr. Kraemer's defense of discontinuity[7] based upon the dialectical theology of Barth and Brunner, we note that (like all the thinking of that school) it is consciously and deliberately paradoxical in form, and its logic cannot be pressed too strictly without doing violence to its real meaning. It is true that Dr. Kraemer makes an absolute cleavage between the revelation in Christ, which is unique and *sui generis*, and all the religions of mankind, which express man's proud, unbelieving *resistance* to God, rather than a *response* to divine revelation; yet to conclude from this that Christianity is all light and truth, and other religious systems an unmitigated mass of falsehood, would be to miss the author's real meaning. Christianity *as an empirical religion* lies under the judgment of God's revelation in Christ, just as much as—and even more than—other religions; and judged by that standard, it might need to receive correction and enlightenment, quite conceivably through Buddhists or Moslems or even Communists, as God's corrective chastisement came to ancient Israel through "the Assyrian, the rod of mine anger." Non-Christian religions *as systems of thought and culture* are, on the other hand, not to be condemned *en bloc*, and totally displaced by another, allegedly Christian cultural system. No missionary has ever been more respectful than Dr. Kraemer of Eastern (e.g.

---

[7] See the post-Tambaram volume, *The Authority of the Faith*, I.M.C. 1939, chapter by Kraemer on "Continuity or Discontinuity."

Indonesian) patterns of custom, art, material culture, and the like, or less disposed to replace these patterns by Western patterns. How far he might go, consistently with his Barthian theology, toward a friendly appropriation of non-Christian philosophic concepts has perhaps been indicated by Carl Keller's article on "The Vedanta Philosophy and the Message of Christ," which expressly claims Barth's authority for a pretty bold piece of reinterpretation of the Christian message in terms of non-Christian concepts.[8] Standing within the Christian revelation, as both Kraemer and Keller do, how can one avoid *all* such reinterpretation when even the process of *translation* forces one to render Biblical terms like "God" and "Word" into such heavily-loaded vernacular terms as *"Tien"* and *"Tao"*?[9]

We are not, then, to suppose that Kraemer's Barthian doctrine of discontinuity implies an attitude of contempt and disrespect toward non-Christian religious systems. At least in their more secular aspects, these systems contain much that a Christian community rising in their midst should gratefully appropriate— so that Christians can be said to "learn" from them, as well as to "teach" to them. The real unresolved issue between Kraemer and his critics had to do with the specifically *religious* aspect of these systems. If sex, work, race, and state could be regarded by some neo-orthodox theologians as expressions of God's original order of creation—broken and corrupted by sin, but still furnishing a sound basis for God's redemptive renewal of the whole creation—by what strange logic is religion excluded from this

[8] *I.R.M.* Vol. 42, pp. 377–89. Note especially the reference to Barth's *Dogmatik*, I, 2, p. 779, on p. 384.

[9] In his recent article on "Syncretism as a Religious and Missionary Problem" (*I.R.M.* Vol. 43, pp. 253–73) Kraemer says explicitly that syncretism *in the sense of "adaptation"* is "not only unavoidable but . . . necessary and imperative." This article has now been included in Kraemer's important book, *Religion and the Christian Faith*, in which he restates his Tambaram thesis *more biblically* and *more dialectically.*

general judgment on the primary human relationships?[10] Is religion alone pure sin, pure perversity, pure resistance to God, when in other human activities some neo-orthodox theologians see a mixture of divine ordinance with human rebellion, which can be redeemed and reconstructed by Christ's supreme revelation? Does it really compromise faith in Christ's supreme revelation when one interprets the universal phenomenon of religious faith as evidence of the indissoluble bond between man and his Creator, who has so "set eternity" in man's heart that he cannot finally be content with things temporal, however addicted to idolatry and self-worship he may become? *At this point, it is gratifying to note, Kraemer has just restated his position in such a way as largely to remove this objection.*

If discontinuity does not imply sweeping rejection of other religious systems, neither does continuity imply undiscriminating acceptance of them. The word used at Tambaram as a rallying cry for Kraemer's critics was "fulfillment." As Canon Dewick has pointed out, the background of this discussion was the wide prevalence, in the period from Edinburgh, 1910, through Jerusalem, 1928, of a view of the relationship between Christianity and other faiths similar to that expressed in Farquhar's *Crown of Hinduism,* which at this period was even regarded as the "most orthodox" view for missionaries to hold. This view, which has its Biblical prototypes in the Johannine doctrine of the Logos and the Pauline doctrine of the Jewish Law as "a schoolmaster to lead us to Christ" (Gal. 3:24), involves no betrayal of loyalty to the supremacy of the revelation in Christ, and in fact (as

---

[10] This doctrine of the "orders" is best seen in Brunner's *Divine Imperative (Das Gebot und die Ordnungen).* Cf. also the minority report presented by the chairman of the German delegation at Tambaram, reprinted in *The Authority of the Faith,* pp. 169–17. See my review of Kraemer's *Religion and the Christian Faith* in *I.R.M.,* Jan. 1957.

Dewick points out) is regarded by many non-Christians as implying the hope "to destroy, or at least to absorb, all other systems of religion."[11]

Whether this implication be correct or not, the intention of the advocates of "fulfillment" to maintain supreme loyalty to the Christian revelation was made evident by their concessions at Tambaram to the arguments of the other party. Many were willing, like Dr. Hogg, to grant that non-Christian "faiths" (in the plural) are always systematically organized about some ultimate other than Christ, so they cannot be "crowned" or "fulfilled" by Christianity without suffering collapse at their own center. Kraemer's phrase, "subversive fulfillment," was accepted my many of his critics as more accurately descriptive of what happens when the Christian revelation encounters a non-Christian system than any such words as "completion," "addition," or "progression" could possibly suggest. "No man can serve two masters," and no religion can accept a rival ultimate without a struggle—this much was pretty generally agreed at Tambaram, and after.

What the advocates of fulfillment have continued to insist upon, despite all concessions, is the possibility of genuine religious faith (in the singular) among the adherents of non-Christian faiths, of genuine divine activity within religious systems organized about other ultimates than Christ, and hence the possibility of building positively upon some aspects of these systems, as preparations for Christ and not sheer obstacles. Continuity and fulfillment in this sense and in this degree have been upheld by a considerable number of Christian theologians throughout the history of Christian thought, and it would be hard indeed at this late date to get an ecumenical consensus upon a doctrine of

[11] Dewick, *op. cit.*, pp. 48-51.

absolute discontinuity that would flatly deny them. Two recent books seem to open up the prospect of a fuller reconciliation between the two views that opposed each other at Tambaram than was possible at the time. Both of these books emphatically accept the supremacy of the revelation in Christ, for which the discontinuity view has contended; but both believe it to be consistent with the position described above, that there can be genuine faith and genuine divine activity within non-Christian religious systems.

In the first of these books, Canon Dewick's Hulsean Lectures, already cited, on *The Christian Attitude to Other Religions*, a broad definition of religion is adopted (from A. C. Bouquet's *Comparative Religion*) as "a fixed relationship between the human self and some non-human entity."[12]  While the implication is clear that there are religions which must be opposed and resisted by loyal believers in the Christian revelation, Canon Dewick goes on to argue at some length (Chap. V) that loyalty to the supremacy of the revelation in Christ does *not* imply an attitude of hostility or superiority toward all elements in non-Christian religions. The supremacy of the revelation in Jesus Christ on which Christians generally agree does not necessarily mean that this revelation is "complete and exhaustive," since not every kind of excellence, human and divine, could be illustrated within the limited span of the days of His flesh; nor that it is "final and absolute for all time," since even the supreme revelation within history does not "bind the future within the terms of the past, by affirming that no further revelation [say, at the Parousia] ever can be given"; nor does supremacy mean "exclusive" in the sense of absolute discontinuity with all other forms of divine self-disclosure, since this would imply an impossible

[12] Introduction.

view of the Incarnation as "the irruption of a wholly foreign God into a world which otherwise had no contact with Him."[13] When these unnecessary and illogical implications are set aside, it becomes possible for a Christian loyally affirming Christ's supremacy to confer and co-operate with non-Christians on a basis of genuine tolerance and respect, recognizing that his own human understanding of God is in many respects incomplete and provisional, and that God *may* have spoken to his non-Christian friend in ways that can significantly stimulate or correct his own understanding.

A similar conclusion emerges from a very different analysis in Principal Herbert Farmer's Gifford Lectures on *Revelation and Religion*.[14] Farmer does not operate with a broad, generic definition of religion, as Dewick does, but with a *normative* definition, based consciously on the Christian assumption that Reality is supremely revealed in the Incarnation: "the personal encounter of God with man and of man with God."[15] Judged by this definition, political religions and many aspects of the historic religious systems are not religious at all; Christian revelation and faith are not just *a* religion but "the normative concept of religion itself";[16] while the non-Christian faiths are truly religious *in various degrees*. Farmer sees behind the neo-orthodox theologians' refusal to classify the Christian revelation with other religions—illustrated fairly recently in Brunner's *Revelation and Reason*, Eng.tr.1947—a logical fallacy which he takes some pains to expose[17] with the aid of Collingwood's *Essay on Philosophical Method*. In traditional logic, based on the exact sciences, "the various species of a genus are exclusive of one another and exhaust the genus," whereas in "any enquiry into matters of mind

[13] Pp. 150–53.
[14] London, Nisbet, 1954.
[15] P. 35.
[16] P. 41.
[17] Pp. 31–34.

and spirit," classes and species "overlap," and another type of logic is required. Applying this to our problem, we are forced by traditional logic *either* to classify the Christian revelation with other religions and deny its uniqueness, *or* to assert its *sui generis* uniqueness and deny its classifiability with other religions, as Barth, Brunner and Kraemer have done; whereas the logic appropriate to the field of mind and spirit permits us to conceive the Christian revelation as *both* unique *and* comparable, differing from other religions *both* in kind *and* in degree.

The living essence of religion is revealed once and for all, in its sole perfect manifestation, in the Christian revelation and in the relation with God which that revelation makes possible for men, and it is exemplified in other religions in varying degrees of incompleteness, fragmentariness, distortion and perversion [p. 34].

Wherever and whenever, that is to say, God contrives (in spite of all the limiting and perverting conditions of human immaturity and sin) to penetrate to man's spirit and thus to call into existence living Religion—*all* the elements which the analysis of Christian worship has revealed will *tend* to be present together in however obscure, or faint, or fleeting, or germinal, or perverted a form [p. 86].

Until this alternative theological approach has been as carefully explored as Barthian theology's approach was explored at Tambaram, it would be foolish to resign ourselves to the unhappy conclusion that the issue of continuity *vs.* discontinuity is irresolvable, and no agreed theological basis for Christian missions is discoverable. Actually, Kraemer and Farmer are now pretty close to each other.

## 2. THE MISSIONARY APPROACH TO OTHER LIVING FAITHS

Happily, there is wide agreement among Christians in non-Christian environments, whatever their school of theology, as to the practical attitudes they should maintain in dealing with non-Christian faith individually, and non-Christian faiths collectively. They understand, perhaps better than Christians living in "Christendom," that Christian faith is an essentially missionary faith, obliged to testify to its Lord's universal supremacy even where this seems disrespectful to the dominant religious majority; and they understand that it is at the same time a faith that works through love, deeply respectful of all men as God's children and brothers for whom Christ died, deeply desirous of serving and helping them in spite of or even because of their remoteness from the Christian Way. Many of these Christians in non-Christian lands have paid a heavy price to keep their loyalty to Christ uncompromised—disinheritance, separation from their kinsfolk, civil disabilities of many sorts—and yet they cannot be content with a status of Pharisaical purity and apartness, for they love their country and their people, and wish to share the new peace and joy which have been given them through Christ. They know, sometimes with strong inner self-judgment, that neither cowardly compromise nor proud aloofness can possibly express the Christian testimony to which the Spirit moves them. Fearless honesty, combined with genuine humility and tireless good-will—this is the attitude that must underlie the strategy and tactics of Christian Missions in every non-Christian environment.

Under the special conditions that now prevail in many non-Christian countries, a missionary strategy toward the prevailing religion and its adherents is particularly urgent. The first point in such a strategy, agreed to by all schools of thought and never in dispute at Tambaram or any other modern missionary conference, is a careful and accurate *knowledge* of that religion. Without such knowledge, the Christian message cannot possibly speak to the condition of this area; with it, doors may open that seemed closed. (One thinks of the Jesuit missionaries mastering Chinese language and philosophy, or of Frank Laubach breaking down the hostility of the Moros by studying the Koran with them.) It cannot be assumed that fresh converts from a non-Christian faith generally have the requisite knowledge of it; they are often in sharp reaction against a corrupt form of it, which conceals from them its better elements, and makes them unable to understand its strong appeal. Without a degree of empathy that puts the student at least tentatively "inside" the faith he is studying, no real knowledge of an alien faith is attainable. As part of the continuing study of "The Word of God and the Living Faiths of Men," the International Missionary Council and the World Council of Churches are now jointly sponsoring the establishment of study centers in all the principal non-Christian areas, where real knowledge of these faiths and real empathy for them can be developed.

This of course opens the possibility that the Christian may accept and appropriate certain elements in other living faiths which he finds he can honestly approve and which are consistent with Christian faith. While this *may* unconsciously lead to a type of syncretism that really compromises Christian faith, some forms of appropriation or adaptation are necessary and relevant in any strategy of Christian missions, as Dr. Kraemer himself now insists. The very word "indigenous," so constantly used in modern missionary conferences, carries with it D. T. Niles' favorite figure of speech, of a seed sown in a soil, and drawing its development not only from its own resident vitality, but also in part from the soil in which it grows. There must and will be appropriation in this sense from the non-Christian environment, appropriation of elements capable of being reorganized about the Christian center, while at the same time the Christian movement refuses to be absorbed into the surrounding system, and prophetically challenges those elements that are flatly opposed to its Gospel.

Should the Christian movement, in its relations with its non-Christian environment, venture beyond study and selective appropriation? Are *conference* and *co-operation* with non-Christians possible without compromise of Christian loyalty? Canon Dewick devotes a good deal of attention to this question in his Hulsean Lectures, and notes some pretty sharp differences of opinion about it. There are some real grounds for controversy here, because the *basis* upon which Christians and non-Christians confer or co-operate may involve the tacit assumption of the equality of all faiths, or some other assumption which Christians cannot admit. Yet there is much experience to indicate that frank round-table discussion, such as went on between Christians and Buddhists in Dr. Reichelt's Christian monastery near Hong Kong, or co-operation in social service, as in several interfaith social settlements in India, creates an atmosphere of intimate friendship in which Christian witness gets a fairer hearing than elsewhere. It has often been observed that the Y.M.C.A., which is not primarily a missionary organization but a service organization, performs a mighty work of preparatory evangelism in many non-Christian environments, by doing what every true missionary must do at the start of his mission; build a bridge of friendship through self-identification, over which communication can pass.

I believe that the problems connected with conference and co-operation can be clarified, if we note their similarity to the problems encountered in the building of the Ecumenical Movement. The method of Faith and Order is largely a method of conference; the method of Life and Work is largely a method of co-operation. By both methods, men of different religious affiliations are drawn into fellowship, and exert an influence on one another. Roman Catholics have officially held aloof from this movement, because they have feared its assumptions and wished to avoid compromise; but many Eastern Orthodox have found it possible to participate in the movement while frankly witnessing to the exclusive claims of their Church. The analogy here is imperfect, of course; all Christians are bound together in faith and service by common loyalty to one Lord, in the midst of all their differences; but *mutatis mutandis*, there is no reason why the same methods cannot be applied to interfaith relations. In each such relationship, it is necessary to discover a common platform for shared witness and co-operative action, which both parties can honestly stand upon. In the case of Judaism and Islam, Christians can occupy a common platform much broader and stronger than in the case of Hinduism and Buddhism; but in both cases, such a platform is discoverable. Where there is substantial agreement, they can *act* together; where there is serious disagreement, they can *discuss* together, as Christians of different churches do in the Ecumenical Movement. Dishonesty or unworthy compromise is no more necessarily involved in interfaith fellowship than in the Ecumenical Movement. There is much evidence that the Holy Spirit draws men to the truth through honest and open meeting of minds, and through shared response to the call of urgent social needs. By participating in interfaith round tables, and co-operating in interfaith social service, Christians can prove their good-will toward their compatriots of other faiths, and at the same time witness to their own faith in word and deed.

# INDEX

# Index

Experience
  of divine grace, 222
  knowledge of God through, 67, 68
Extreme Unction, 232

Faith, 89, 154, 262
  justification solely by, 23, 238
  metaphysics and, 96, 97
  miracle, 133
  paradox of, 182
  religious knowledge and, 39
  revelation and, 42, 43, 45, 78
  theology and, 5–6
*Faith of the Christian Church, The*
  Aulén), 3, 4, 5, 50, 87
Faith and Order conferences; *see* Edinburgh Faith and Order Conference *and* Lausanne Conference
Faith and Order Movement, xiv, xxi–xxiii, 177–78, 207, 257, 307
Fall; *see* Original Sin, doctrine of
Farmer, Herbert, 303, 304
Farrer, Austin, 151
Feeney, Father Leonard, 227 n.
Fellowship
  Church as institution and, 224–28
  free-church idea of, 239–40
  need for, 204–7, 242
Ferré, Nels, 95, 97–98, 99, 100, 101
Fichte, 117
Fisher, Archbishop, 224
Fison, J. E., 265, 266, 267
Flint, 8
Fontenelle, 248
Forgiveness, 130, 153, 164
Form Criticism, 181, 182
Forsyth, 8
Fosdick, Harry Emerson, 30, 31
Fox, George, 54
Franciscans, 57
Free-church idea of the Church, 239–43
Free will, 150–51, 156
  and divine grace, 157
Freedom
  defense of, by Eastern Orthodoxy, 168
  intellectual, in non-Roman Catholicism, 64

Freedom (*continued*)
  and moral responsibility, 122, 156
  and repentance, 164
Friends, Society of, 217, 218, 223, 241
Fundamentalism, 30, 31, 66–67, 128

Glory, state of, 148, 150 n.
Gnostics, 23
God
  attributes of, 83–84, 86–91, 93, 99, 103–4
  balanced concept of, 101–2
  Christian consensus concerning knowledge of, 45–55
  Christian consensus on man and, 144–54
  Christian consensus on nature of, 85–91
  as Creator and as Judge and Redeemer, 86–87, 118–21, 147–48, 253, 269
  doctrine of man and, 140–41, 144
  of Greek metaphysics and of the Bible, 85, 92–103
  love of, 88, 90, 148, 153, 269 (*see also agapé*)
  man as "image of," 161, 162
  mediation between man and, 169–72
  names given to, 86 n.
  Old and New Testament revelations of, 85
  personality of, 103–10
  philosophical conceptions of, 84, 85
  problem of evil and, 134–39
  problem of knowledge of, 38–45
  relation of, to the world, 111, 114, 118–24
  unity of, 192, 193–94, 196
  unresolved issues concerning knowledge of, 55–78
  unresolved issues concerning man and, 154–68
  unresolved issues concerning nature of, 92–110
  unresolved issues concerning the world and, 125–39
  various ideas of, 80–82

# Index

# Index

# Index

Mediation
  subordinate, 202, 203
  through Christ, 169, 202
  through Mary, 201–2
  universal problem of, 169–73
*Mediator Dei et Hominum* (Pius XII), 233 n.
Merrill, W. P., 257
Messianic Age, 254
Metaphysics, Greek, God of, 92–103
Methodist churches, 241
Minear, Paul, 265, 267
Miracles, 132–34, 197–98
  new faith in, 126
  problem of, 128
*Miracles* (Lewis), 133
Mission of the Church, 215–17
Missions, progress of, 273, 274
*Misunderstanding of the Church, The* (Brunner), 224
Modernism, 29–30, 65, 75
  "humanitarian," 145–46
Monism, 72, 73, 119, 125
Monod, Victor, 115
Monophysitism, 178, 190
Monotheism, 17, 18, 20, 38, 39, 81, 82, 83, 85, 92, 111, 114, 171, 196, 245
Montague, 102
Montaigne, 142, 143
Morgan, Lloyd, 120
Morrison, Charles Clayton, 203 n.
Moslems, 197
"Motive-investigation," 4
Mullins, E. Y., 128
Mussolini, 172
Mystery, 130
  holiness and, 83
  knowledge of God and, 40, 42, 43, 44, 45
*Mystici Corporis Christi* (Pius XII), 227

Nationalism, 247, 250, 251
"Natural" theology, 72
Naturalism, 81–82, 106, 143, 160, 249
  religious, 69–70, 77
"Naturalistic theism," 30
*Nature and Destiny of Man, The* (Niebuhr), 160–64

*Nature, Man and God* (Temple), 77
Nazism, 14, 17, 49
*Nebenordnung*, 72, 77
Needs, human
  love of Christ as answer to, 21
  satisfied by religion, 11–14
Nelson, Robert, 211, 213, 236
Neo-Augustinianism, 160–67
Neo-liberals, 74
Neo-orthodoxy, 31–32, 70–75, 90, 91, 105, 129, 130, 135, 159, 197, 198, 268
Neo-Platonism, 53, 94, 170–71
Neo-Thomism, 57
Nestorian Church, 274
Nestorius, 23
New Israel, 209
Newbigin, Lesslie, 212, 242, 258
Newman, 200
Newton, Sir Isaac, 117
Nicaea, Council of, xxii, 1, 2, 23, 52, 176
Nicene Creed, 3, 20, 35, 52, 208, 244
Nicholls, William, 208
Niebuhr, Reinhold, 31, 71, 73, 74, 205, 260, 272
  neo-Augustinianism of, 159, 160–64, 165, 167
Niebuhr, Richard, 262 n.
Nietzsche, 251
Nihilism, 143, 154
"Non-church movement" in Japan, 226
Nygren, 71, 99

Old Catholicism, 56, 64
Oman, John, 157
*One Church, The* (Craig), 219
*One in Christ* (Skydsgaard), 199
Ontological argument for existence of God, 56, 57, 99
Ontology, 108
*Open Conspiracy, The* (Wells), 205
Oracle, 43
*Organism of Christian Truth, The* (Dickie), 8–9
Origen, 268

316

# Index

# Index

# Index

319

# Index

Thomism, 53
*Thoughts* (Pascal), 142
Tillich, Paul, xviii, xix, 6–7, 10, 13, 29,
    31, 32, 35, 36, 70–71, 73, 74, 78, 88,
    95, 170, 180, 196
  on anxiety, 165
  conception of God of, 138
  on demonism, 133–34
  on God and the World, 124
  on man, 144
  objections of, to personalism, 105,
    108–10
  philosophical theology of, 97–98, 99,
    100, 101
Titanism, 143, 153
"Tome, The," 190
Tournier, 128
Tradition, 49–55, 60–61, 75, 76
Transcendentalism, 195
*Transformation of the Scientific
World View, The* (Heim), 131,
132
Trent, Council of, 61
Trinity, doctrine of, 87, 139, 170, 171,
    177, 183–84, 192, 193–94, 195,
    196
Tritheism, 192, 193
Troeltsch, 67

Ultimacy, 170, 196
Unbelief, 162
*Unfinished Reformation, The* (Morrison), 203 n.
Unitarianism, 177, 179, 197
  Ecumenical Movement and, 9
  view of Christ held by, 191–96
United Church of Canada, Credo of,
123
Universal ministry, 216, 217 n.
Universal salvation, 268–71
Universality implied in "ecumenical,"
1 n.

Van de Pol, Father W. H., 222–23,
227, 231
"Verticalism," 28, 29

Virgin Birth, 130, 196–203
*Vision and Action* (Zander), 92 n.
Visser 't Hooft, W. A., 1 n.
*Vom Geist der Liturgie* (Guardini)
63 n.

Weatherhead, Leslie, 138
Wedel, T. O., 208, 214
Weizsäcker, 128
Wells, H. G., 205
*Weltbild der Zukunft* (Heim), 130
Wesley, John, 54, 202
Westminster Confession, 122, 238
*What Is Christianity?* (Harnack), 19
Whitehead, Alfred North, 106, 117,
120
Wieman, Henry Nelson, 13, 30, 70,
  conception of God of, 90
  objections of, to personalism, 105–8,
  110
Wilson, Archdeacon, 159
Wilson, Woodrow, 172
Word of God
  in the believer's heart, 240
  on judgment and redemption, 270
  meanings of, 236
  relation of Bible to, 235–37
World
  God and, Christian consensus on,
    115–24
  knowledge of, and religion, 112–15
  meaning of term, 111–12
  unresolved issues concerning God
    and, 125–39
World Council of Churches, 9, 10,
    177, 179, 251
"World machine," 117
*Wrestle of Religion with Truth, The*
  (Wieman), 106

*Yezer Hara*, 155
Y.M.C.A., 178, 179, 226
"Younger churches," 8, 127

Zander, L. A., 92 n.
Zwingli, 121, 237

320